HEARING
the VOICE *of*
the LORD

HEARING
the VOICE *of*
the LORD

Principles AND *Patterns* OF
Personal Revelation

GERALD N. LUND

DESERET
BOOK

SALT LAKE CITY, UTAH

Library of Congress Cataloging-in-Publication Data

Lund, Gerald N.
   Hearing the voice of the Lord : principles and patterns of personal revelation / Gerald N. Lund.
     p. cm.
   ISBN 978-1-59038-893-8 (hardcover : alk. paper)
    1. Revelation—Mormon Church.   2. Church of Jesus Christ of Latter-day Saints—Doctrines.   3. Mormon Church—Doctrines.   I. Title.
   BX8643.R4L86 2007
   248.2'9—dc22
                                           2007041345

Printed in the United States of America
Publishers Printing, Salt Lake City, Utah

10   9   8   7   6   5   4   3   2

CONTENTS

CONTENTS

CONTENTS

SECTION I

WHAT IS REVELATION?

The Almighty is with this people. We shall have all the revelations that we shall need if we will do our duty and keep the commandments of God. . . . Remember: If there be eyes to see, there will be visions to inspire. If there be ears to hear, there will be revelations to experience. If there be hearts which can understand, know this: that the exalting truths of Christ's gospel will no longer be hidden and mysterious, and all earnest seekers may know God and his program (Spencer W. Kimball, Conference Report, October 1966, 26).

CHAPTER 1

THE VOICE OF THE LORD

"The voice of the Lord is unto all men" (D&C 1:2).

UNTO ALL MEN

The opening lines of the Doctrine and Covenants begin with a commandment and then a declaration, both of which refer to the voice of the Lord:

> Hearken, O ye people of my church, *saith the voice* of him who dwells on high, . . . listen together. For verily *the voice of the Lord is unto all men* (D&C 1:1–2).

In that one simple yet stunning statement, the Lord sets forth one of the defining characteristics of His relationship with mankind. *God speaks to men!*

It is a theme oft repeated in the Doctrine and Covenants. Here is but a brief sampling:

- "The voice of the Lord is unto the ends of the earth, that all that will hear may hear" (D&C 1:11).

- "Listen to the voice of Jesus Christ, your Lord, your God, and your Redeemer, whose word is quick and powerful" (D&C 27:1).
- "Mine elect hear my voice and harden not their hearts" (D&C 29:7).
- "I [will] gather mine elect from the four quarters of the earth, even as many as will believe in me, and hearken unto my voice" (D&C 33:6).
- "And every one that hearkeneth to the voice of the Spirit cometh unto God, even the Father" (D&C 84:47).
- "And whoso receiveth not my voice is not acquainted with my voice, and is not of me" (D&C 84:52).

THE VOICE OF THE SHEPHERD

During His mortal ministry, the Savior likened Himself unto a shepherd who cared for His sheep. This was more than just a passing metaphor. He explored the imagery in some depth.

> Verily, verily, I say unto you, he that entereth not by the door into the sheepfold, but climbeth up some other way, the same is a thief and a robber.
>
> But he that entereth in by the door is the shepherd of the sheep.
>
> To him the porter openeth; and *the sheep hear his voice:* and he calleth his own sheep by name, and leadeth them out.
>
> And when he putteth forth his own sheep, he goeth before them, and the sheep follow him: *for they know his voice.*
>
> And a stranger will they not follow, but will flee from him: for they know not the voice of strangers. . . . I am the good shepherd, and know my sheep, and am known of mine. . . . *My sheep hear my voice,* and I know them, and they follow me (John 10:1–5, 14, 27).

Even today in the Holy Land, it is a common sight to see a shepherd leading a flock of sheep across a hillside or through a narrow valley.

Unlike in other areas of the world, shepherds in the Middle East do not drive vast flocks of sheep with horses and dogs. The typical flock is small, numbering in the dozens more than the thousands. The shepherd is usually found at their head leading them, rather than behind driving them.

The following description from a Christian minister who spent many years in the Holy Land helps us better appreciate the richness of the Savior's parable of the Good Shepherd:

> [The shepherd] depends upon the sheep to follow, and they in turn expect him never to leave them. They run after him if he appears to be escaping from them, and are terrified when he is out of sight, or any stranger appears instead of him. He calls to them from time to time to let them know that he is at hand. The sheep listen and continue grazing, but if any one else tries to produce the same peculiar cries and guttural sounds, they look around with a startled air and begin to scatter. . . .
>
> As he is always with them, and so deeply interested in them, the shepherd comes to know his sheep very intimately. Many of them have pet names. . . . One day a missionary, meeting a shepherd on one of the wildest parts of Lebanon, asked him various questions about his sheep, and among others if he counted them every night. On answering that he did not, he was asked how he knew if they were all there or not. His reply was, "Master, if you were to put a cloth over my eyes, and bring me any sheep and only let me put my hands on its face, I could tell in a moment if it was mine or not."[1]

SO MANY VOICES

The Apostle Paul, writing to the Corinthians, said, "There are . . . so many kinds of voices in the world, and none of them is without signification" (1 Corinthians 14:10). In modern English, *signification* suggests "significance," "a distinct sound," or "having meaning."

President James E. Faust of the First Presidency explained why we must learn to distinguish the voice of the Lord from all other voices:

> The Spirit's voice is ever present, but it is calm. . . . The adversary tries to smother this voice with a multitude of loud, persistent, persuasive, and appealing voices:
>
> - Murmuring voices that conjure up perceived injustices.
> - Whining voices that abhor challenge and work.
> - Seductive voices offering sensual enticements.
> - Soothing voices that lull us into carnal security.
> - Intellectual voices that profess sophistication and superiority.
> - Proud voices that rely on the arm of flesh.
> - Flattering voices that puff us up with pride.
> - Cynical voices that destroy hope.
> - Entertaining voices that promote pleasure seeking.
> - Commercial voices that tempt us to "spend money for that which is of no worth," and/or "labor for that which cannot satisfy" (2 Nephi 9:51).[2]

So how can we know which voice is the Lord's? How do we come to recognize the voice of the Shepherd? We know that the Lord will never lead us astray or give us untruth, but how can we learn to distinguish His voice from the banging clamor all around us?

SO MANY QUESTIONS

It is abundantly clear that God has promised to speak to His children. He has given the faithful the promise "that they may always have his Spirit to be with them" (D&C 20:77). That seems like such a simple and straightforward concept. And yet even those who have spent a lifetime in the Church sometimes wrestle with questions about personal revelation. Almost always the questions boil down to one issue: *How do I know for sure when it is the Lord speaking to me?*

Clearly it is not enough just to *receive* revelation, we must also learn to *recognize* it, so we can then respond to it.

Here is a sampling of real-life examples that illustrate the uncertainty, and sometimes the downright confusion, that we have about the voice of the Lord.

"I Think I Left the Stove On." Many families have had an experience similar to this. It's vacation time and the family is ready to leave. The children have all been sent to the bathroom one last time; the luggage is stowed in the car; the house is carefully secured. But then, just a few miles from home, someone—often the mother—gets this worried look and says, "I think I left the stove on (or the oven or the iron)." There is a short debate, but the risks are too great and so they return home. Sometimes they find that the stove was indeed left on, and a serious tragedy has been averted. But just as often, when the mother comes back out, she reports that all was well. Then, looking a bit sheepish, she admits that not only was the stove off, but now she remembers checking it a couple of times earlier in the day.

Questions: How can we tell the difference between a premonition from the Spirit and just our own natural tendency to worry? Can Satan give us false revelation? When he seeks to deceive and confuse us about the voice of the Lord, what does it feel like? How can we discern when it is his influence and not the Lord's?

The Most Important Decision of My Life. "I've been dating this wonderful young man," a woman in her mid-twenties reports. "He wants to marry me. I feel like he would make a wonderful husband and father. But I have prayed and prayed. I have fasted several times as well,

> *Who has not heard and felt the enticing of the devil? His voice often sounds so reasonable and his message so easy to justify. It is an appealing, intriguing voice with dulcet tones. It is neither hard nor discordant. No one would listen to Satan's voice if it sounded harsh or mean. If the devil's voice were unpleasant, it would not persuade people to listen to it.*
>
> JAMES E. FAUST,
> *ENSIGN,* JANUARY 2007, 6

but I can't seem to get an answer. For something this important, I need more than just some good feelings. I need a clear, unmistakable answer that this is what Heavenly Father wants me to do.

Questions: Are her expectations too high? Is she looking for something more dramatic when the feelings she is having about this young man are actually the Lord's answer?

I Was So Sure! When I was serving as a bishop some years ago, a colleague and I were talking about giving priesthood blessings and the importance of staying in tune. He then shared an experience he had had when he was a young bishop. He said he had received a call in the middle of the night to go to the hospital. A woman in the ward had collapsed into unconsciousness as she was preparing for bed. Now she lay in a coma. The desperate husband asked the bishop to come and help administer to her. When the bishop arrived, the man was so distraught he asked the bishop to give the blessing. "It was a deeply emotional moment," my friend said. "This couple had five children still in the home. The doctors weren't yet sure what was wrong, but her vital signs were dropping steadily. As I began the blessing, suddenly I had this overwhelming feeling of peace and light come over me. I stopped for a moment and looked into my heart. Was this really from the Lord or just me, I wondered. I had never experienced anything so powerful before, and I decided the feeling was truly from the Lord."

Relieved to have such clear direction, he proceeded with the blessing. "I promised her that she would be healed, that she would be raised from the bed of her afflictions, that she would have the privilege of raising her children to adulthood in this life." The former bishop stopped, searching my face. "It was a wonderful experience. I wept for joy. The husband did as well." Then, in a very soft voice, he concluded. "But I had been home for only a few hours when the husband called to tell me that his wife had passed away without regaining consciousness."

Questions: Did those powerful feelings just come from his own emotions, from his earnest—and righteous—desire to bless a family in crisis? Or was the experience real, but in his eagerness to help, he put his own interpretation on what the feelings meant? Is it possible that we can have true spiritual experiences and yet misinterpret them?

Experiences such as these are commonplace. The questions about personal revelation roll on and on. Here are just a few others:

- *What does it feel like when the Lord is speaking to me?*
- *What is a stupor of thought, and what does it feel like? Can I really just forget something I have been struggling over for months?*
- *What is the burning in the bosom? What does it feel like when it comes?*
- *Am I entitled to get revelation for my adult children after they are married?*
- *Who is entitled to receive revelation for me?*
- *What if I receive a revelation for my family, but my spouse doesn't agree with me?*
- *Why do some people get premonitions that miraculously save them from danger or death, while others who seem equally faithfully are caught in such tragedies?*
- *My boyfriend has received a revelation that we are to marry. I don't feel like he is the best person for me, but if it is a revelation, am I obligated to accept it?*

> *The revelations of the Lord Jesus Christ are sweeter than honey or the honeycomb. We can eat, and continue to eat; drink, and continue to drink. . . . All the pleasure and all the joy that can be bestowed upon a finite being is in the Gospel of salvation, through the Spirit of revelation.*
>
> BRIGHAM YOUNG,
> *DISCOURSES OF BRIGHAM YOUNG*, 6

HOW DO WE LEARN TO RECEIVE, RECOGNIZE, AND THEN RESPOND TO THE VOICE OF THE LORD?

President Boyd K. Packer, speaking to a Church Educational System fireside for young single adults, said that every young Latter-day Saint "has not only the right *but the obligation* to understand what the gift of the Holy Ghost is." He noted that Latter-day Saints typically "use [the gift] so little and so infrequently, but it is ours, and if we prepare ourselves, that voice will speak to us."[3]

Brigham Young also felt that members of the Church did not fully capitalize on this marvelous gift, which is given to all those properly baptized and confirmed in the Church.

> There is no doubt, if a person lives according to the rev-elations given to God's people, he may have the Spirit of the Lord to signify to him his will, and to guide and to direct him in the discharge of his duties, in his temporal as well as his spiritual exercises. I am satisfied, however, that in this respect, we live far beneath our privileges.[4]

President Packer concluded his address with this promise: "Take hold of that supernal gift of the Holy Ghost. Learn to be taught by it. Learn to call upon it. Learn to live by it. And the Spirit of the Lord will attend you."[5]

That is the task that lies before us. The voice of the Lord is unto all men—so has the Lord boldly declared. What can we do to capitalize as fully as possible on that marvelous gift of a member of the Godhead to be our personal Companion, Guide, Teacher, and Protector?

The purpose of this book is not just to define the process we call revelation, or even to state its importance in both our temporal and spiritual lives. What we will attempt to do in these pages is to answer the questions we have about how revelation works, what it feels like, and what we can do to make sure we receive it, as well as to recognize it when we do receive it.

What we want to know is: *How does all of this work for me?* To help us more fully explore that question, the book is divided into sections that will seek to answer the major questions about the voice of the Lord. The hope is that when we have completed this study, we will better know what to do so we are included with those of whom the Savior said: "My sheep know my voice."

CHAPTER 2

WHAT IS REVELATION AND WHY IS IT SO IMPORTANT?

"God shall give unto you knowledge by his Holy Spirit" (D&C 121:26).

WHAT IS REVELATION?*

Though we speak about the concept of revelation frequently as part of the gospel, it may be well for us to quickly review some fundamental concepts concerning it. The English word "revelation" comes from the Latin word *revelatus.* This word is formed from the prefix *re-,* which means "to draw back" or "to remove," and the noun *velum,* which is "a covering" or "a veil." Thus, *reveal* literally means "to uncover," "to remove the veil."[1]** In other words, revelation in its more generic sense means to make something previously hidden visible to the eye or clear to the understanding.

---

* This chapter is a brief review of some doctrinal principles that are generally well understood by most members of the Church. Readers may wish to skim through this chapter quickly or skip it altogether.

** In the New Testament, the Greek word that is translated as revelation is *apocalypsis,* whose meaning is virtually identical to the Latin (see Vincent, *Word Studies in the New Testament,* 1:562–63). Hebrew has an additional richness of meaning because the root is associated with the ear, suggesting an "uncovering of the ear" so that the voice of the Lord can be heard (Wilson, *Old Testament Word Studies,* 354).

In the Church, however, we use the term in a much more specific and limited sense. Simply stated, revelation is defined as *"the making known of divine truth by communication from the heavens."*[2] It is the communication of the mind and will of God to man. This would include a communication of His infinite knowledge and His influence on circumstances and events. This is done through the influence and power of the Holy Spirit. God is the *source* of all revelation. The Holy Ghost is the *medium* of communication.

There is one aspect of this definition that should be obvious to all, but that in practicality is often overlooked or forgotten. Since by definition, revelation is the communication of the mind and will of God to man, then clearly *revelation is always uni-directional.* Revelation always flows vertically from God to man, not the other way around. Man cannot ever reveal anything to God. We may have two-way communication with Him through prayer, but we never reveal anything to Him. The very idea that we could kneel in prayer and share something with God that He doesn't know or that would surprise Him is, of course, ludicrous. He already knows all things, including the thoughts and intents of our hearts (see, for example, Matthew 6:8; Acts 15:18; Alma 18:32; D&C 38:2), so we can never reveal anything to Him. And yet it seems to be the nature of us finite mortals to forget this basic and fundamental truth. Often we act as if God needs our "help" in deciding what we need or how to solve our problems.

> *If God spoke anciently, is it unreasonable to believe that he can speak in our time? What man would think to deny God the right to express himself?*
>
> GORDON B. HINCKLEY,
> *TEACHINGS OF GORDON B. HINCKLEY,* 554

WHY DO WE NEED REVELATION?

There is an infinite gap between the Divine Mind and mortal, human intelligence. How could the finite ever possibly comprehend the

Infinite? Can the temporal conceive of the eternal? How is it possible for a mortal, self-absorbed, imperfect, sinful being to begin to understand Infinite Perfection?

> *The sound of the voice of the Lord is a continuous melody and a thunderous appeal.*
>
> Spencer W. Kimball,
> *Ensign,* May 1977, 78

This is why we need revelation.

As Paul taught, the things of God appear foolish and illogical to the mind that is not touched by the Spirit. He said: "The things of God knoweth no man, but the Spirit of God. . . . The natural man receiveth not the things of the Spirit of God: for they are foolishness unto him: neither can he know them, because they are spiritually discerned" (1 Corinthians 2:11, 14). A moment's reflection can bring us dozens of examples of this principle. For example:

- It is absolutely illogical to think that a person can subsist better on 90 percent of his income than he can on 100 percent, but it's true!
- One could mount a serious argument about why a man would need to become a god in order to save his fellow beings from destruction. But why would a God need to become a man in order to work out the infinite atonement? That is counter to human logic.

It is not possible to explain or understand such things except by revelation. Joseph Smith, whose very life was a constant study of, and an intense tutorial in, divine revelation understood this principle very clearly. Said he:

> "We *never* can comprehend the things of God and of heaven, but by revelation."[3]

> "Salvation cannot come without revelation; it is in vain for anyone to minister without it."[4]

> "The best way to obtain truth and wisdom is not to ask it from books, but to go to God in prayer, and obtain divine teaching."[5]

Elder Bruce R. McConkie summarized it this way: "*God is known only by revelation. God stands revealed or he remains forever unknown.*"⁶ That is a preeminent reason why we need revelation.

A DISPENSATION OF REVELATION

The dispensation of the fulness of times, the last of all the dispensations, was opened with a revelation of stunning magnitude. In response to the simple question of a young, uneducated farm boy, the heavens were opened and in one astonishing moment Joseph Smith saw the Father and the Son and received a remarkable answer to his prayer.

This was no symbolic, mystical experience. In the Sacred Grove that morning, Joseph Smith literally heard with his ears and saw with his eyes. The Father and the Son stood before him, *revealed* in all of their majesty and glory.

But what happened that spring morning was far more than just a one-time appearance of Deity. That day was only the beginning of a constant flow of revelation that has not ceased even today. The heavens were opened. The Father and the Son appeared. Angels descended. Visions burst forth. New scripture was received. Priesthood authority was conferred. Ordinances were restored. The Church was organized. Prophecies were pronounced. The gift of the Holy Ghost was given. The gifts of the Spirit accompanied that gift and still do today.

From the very first moments of the Restoration, revelation has been the driving force of the Church. God declared The Church of Jesus Christ to be "the only true and living church upon the face of the whole

Someone has said that we live in a day in which God, if there be a God, chooses to be silent, but The Church of Jesus Christ of Latter-day Saints proclaims to the world that neither the Father nor the Son is silent. They are vocal and commune as proper and necessary, and constantly express a willingness, indeed an eagerness, to maintain communication with men.

SPENCER W. KIMBALL,
*FAITH PRECEDES
THE MIRACLE,* 65–66

earth" (D&C 1:30). Surely it is revelation that makes the Church both *true* and *living!*

Indeed, it could be said that the dispensation of the fulness of times is *the dispensation of a fulness of revelation.* This does not mean that we have now received all revelation that will ever be given, but as part of this dispensation the Lord has promised to reveal all things to His people (see, for example, D&C 76:7; 101:32–34; 121:28–32). To put it even more forcefully, if it were not for revelation, virtually everything on which our faith is based would crumble. There would be no new scripture, no priesthood, no temples, no inspired Church organization, and on and on. The very things that make our Church unique among all other churches have come directly through revelation.

In Joseph Smith's day, it was a widely held belief even among believing Christians that God had spoken anciently and that was sufficient. Revelation had ceased, so it was said, for we had the word of God in the Holy Bible, and no more was either needed or would be given. The unfolding events of the Restoration shattered that misconception once and for all.

President Spencer W. Kimball put it this way: *"Continuous revelation is . . . the very lifeblood of the gospel of the living Lord and Savior."*[7] Joseph F. Smith, nephew of the Prophet Joseph and sixth prophet of this dispensation, was equally direct:

> We believe also in the principle of direct revelation from God to man. . . . The gospel cannot be administered, nor the Church of God continue to exist, without it. Christ is the head of his Church and not man, and the connection can only be maintained upon the principle of direct and continuous revelation. . . . The moment this principle is cut off, that moment the Church is adrift, being severed from its ever-living head. In this condition it cannot continue, but must cease to be the Church of God.[8]

IN SUMMARY

Perhaps the best way to state how we should view revelation would be to paraphrase Nephi's marvelous declaration concerning Christ:

> We talk of [revelation], we rejoice in [revelation], we preach of [revelation], we prophesy [through revelation], and we write according to our prophecies, that our children may know to what source [Christ, which source we learn about only through revelation] they may look for a remission of their sins (2 Nephi 25:26).

CHAPTER 3

WHAT MAKES REVELATION POSSIBLE?

"Ye shall receive the gift of the Holy Ghost" (Acts 2:38).

THE UNSPEAKABLE GIFT

In November 1839, Joseph Smith went to Washington, D.C., to seek redress for the wrongs committed against the Saints in Missouri. While meeting with President Martin Van Buren, Joseph was asked how the Church differed from the other religions of the day. Joseph told him that we differed in the mode of baptism and in the gift of the Holy Ghost. Then Joseph said: *"All other considerations were contained in the gift of the Holy Ghost."*[1]

Earlier that year, while languishing in despicable conditions in Liberty Jail, the Prophet cried to the Lord, pleading for His intervention in behalf of his people. In the response that followed, Joseph was taught much about himself and the Lord's purposes. As part of that tender and directing instruction, the Lord promised that "God shall give unto you knowledge by his Holy Spirit, yea, by the *unspeakable* gift of the Holy Ghost" (D&C 121:26).

The use of the word "unspeakable" to describe the Holy Ghost may seem a little surprising to the modern reader, for we typically use the word in the sense of something too awful to contemplate. But in this sense it means something that is beyond description, something that words cannot express.

And what mortal tongue can adequately describe the third member of the Godhead? What writer could ever fully capture on paper the nature, personality, character, attributes, and functions of the Holy Spirit? Surely the Spirit's majesty, power, and holiness are indescribable. And the blessings that come to us when we receive that gift are likewise unspeakable—beyond our capacity to fully express.

> *The actual companionship of the Holy Ghost, the divinely-bestowed right to His ministrations, the sanctifying baptism with fire, are given as a permanent and personal possession only to the faithful, repentant, baptized candidate for salvation; and with all such this gift shall abide unless it be forfeited through transgression.*
>
> JAMES E. TALMAGE,
> *ARTICLES OF FAITH,* 149

God's work and glory, His overriding purpose, is "to bring to pass the immortality and eternal life of man" (Moses 1:39). Eternal life is to have life as God. It is not just to be *with* God, but also to become *like* Him.

What role does the Holy Ghost play in bringing about that plan? It is a very simple answer. No mortal person is capable of living in such a way as to become like God through his or her own efforts. No one is that wise. No one is that perfect. No matter how strong our desire, how firm our will, there are simply too many challenges and temptations in this fallen world of ours. Our knowledge, understanding, and wisdom are too finite, too limiting.

To put it in other words, life is far too complicated for us to make our way through it on our own. What rule book could possibly cover the infinite number of situations and challenges and temptations we face in life? Even the scriptures, as wonderful as they are, cannot provide the very specific answers we need as we face the complexity of life. They are a wonderful guide, but in and of themselves they are not sufficient.

A DAILY COMPANION, TEACHER, GUIDE, AND COMFORTER

So how do we make it through this spiritually, and often physically, dangerous journey we call mortality? God does not give us a daily rule book. He gives us a Companion *who is with us daily!* He does not hand us a weekly program, or a binder filled with formulas, or a card box of recipes that tells us exactly what we must do and say and think. He doesn't have to. Instead, He gives us a member of the Godhead to be our companion. He confers that gift upon His children by the laying on of hands of his authorized servants. And if they meet certain conditions, the promise is that "they may *always* have his Spirit to be with them" (D&C 20:77).

One of the things that make a daily book of rules impossible is the fact that every one of us is an individual. Each is unique. Each of us varies in significant ways from all others. We think differently, we act differently, we learn differently.

Take our children, for example, or students in a classroom. Learning styles and abilities vary widely. Some are visual learners; others learn better through audio or sensory input. Some are abstract thinkers; others are more concrete and literal.

The gift of revelation does not belong to one man solely. . . . It is not confined to the presiding authorities of the Church, it belongs to every individual member of the Church; and it is the right and privilege of every man, every woman, and every child who has reached the years of accountability, to enjoy the spirit of revelation, and to be possessed of the spirit of inspiration in the discharge of their duties as members of the Church. It is the privilege of every individual member of the Church to have revelation for his own guidance, for the direction of his life and conduct.

JOSEPH F. SMITH,
GOSPEL DOCTRINE, 34

As an illustration, a husband and wife approaching nearly fifty years of happy marriage are very different in how they accept and process information and in their learning styles. He is very systematic and logical. He tends to concentrate on one task until completion and gets a little frustrated if he has multiple things hanging over him undone.

She is less structured and more spontaneous in her approach. Her approach to life is more random than systematic, more holistic than linear. She may lose interest in a task before completion and is comfortable to go on to other things, returning some other time to finish the first. She handles multi-tasking very well but often gets frustrated because she cannot find things in her more randomized system.

She says his mind works like a "Multi-level Outline"—Point A, one, two, three. Point B, one, two. Point C, and so on. On the other hand, she says her mind works like a game of "Bingo." She has a multitude of thoughts, feelings, ideas, and projects tumbling about in her head, and someone calls out: B-7. O-65. G-52.*

Those who are more like the husband may be tempted to characterize the Bingo mind as willy-nilly, unorganized, unfocused. Those who are more like the wife may say the Outline mind is too precise, too structured, not flexible enough. Both conclusions are dangerous, for we have different learning styles and different approaches to life.

The point is, how is it possible that humanity—with all their infinite shades of differences—can receive instruction and guidance that is perfectly tailored to their individuality? There is only one way. We need someone with an infinite capacity to discern those differences in needs, in wants, in capacity and ability. That someone must also have a limitless ability to adapt his help to each and every situation.

In a word, what we need is a God!

And that is exactly what Heavenly Father has provided for us. With the laying on of hands and four simple words—"Receive the Holy Ghost"—we are offered the daily companionship of the Holy Spirit. This is why, unlike the other members of the Godhead, the Holy Ghost

---

* As a reader, you may have already noted that the organization of this book follows the "Outline" model. Fortunately, for those who are not as comfortable with that style of thinking, each of the chapters are so designed that one can skip around at random, as interest may lead you, and still gain much in the study. There is a logical progression in the order of the chapters, but a "Bingo" approach to this book is not without its own rewards.

does not have a body of flesh and bones. He is a Spirit so that He can "dwell in us" (D&C 130:22). He does not communicate mouth to ear, or eye to eye, or hand to hand. He deals Spirit to spirit, intellect to intellect, feeling to feeling. He is not dependent on language. He needs no visas to cross country borders. He is able to impart light and knowledge completely individualized and tailored to the needs of the receiver regardless of age, culture, race, gender, intellectual capacity, or a host of other givens. This truly is an incomparable, indescribable, unspeakable gift.

If [we] are acquainted with the revelations, there is no question—personal or social or political or occupational—that need go unanswered. Therein is contained the fulness of the everlasting gospel. Therein we find principles of truth that will resolve every confusion and every problem and every dilemma that will face the human family or any individual in it.

BOYD K. PACKER,
CES EVENING WITH A
GENERAL AUTHORITY,
OCTOBER 14, 1977, 5

FOR GOD SO LOVED THE WORLD

The Savior told us that the Father so loved the world that He gave His Only Begotten Son as a gift to mankind (see John 3:16). But that is not the only gift He has given us. We could also appropriately say, "For God so loved the world that He gave the Holy Ghost to all those who are baptized and confirmed in the proper manner."

The Son and His Atonement are compelling proof of God's love. To be given the third member of the Godhead as our personal Guide, Teacher, Companion, Comforter, and Protector is also proof of His great love for us. And just as the infinite Atonement is beyond our ability to fully comprehend in this life, so also is a full understanding of the powers, gifts, privileges, and promises of the Holy Ghost beyond our capacity.

When we think of what the Holy Ghost does for us, we tend to think primarily of the light and knowledge He conveys to us. But His influence goes far beyond that. The Holy Ghost is a God. To have the daily companionship of a member of the Godhead surely has a profound effect upon all aspects of our being, an effect far beyond anything we can imagine.

IN SUMMARY

Parley P. Pratt, one of the first apostles in this dispensation, tried to describe some of the effects of the Holy Ghost:

> An intelligent being, in the image of God, possesses every organ, attribute, sense, sympathy, affection which is possessed by God Himself.
>
> But these are possessed by man, in his rudimental state, in a subordinate sense of the word. Or, in other words, these attributes are in embryo, and are to be gradually developed. . . .
>
> The gift of the Holy Spirit adapts itself to all these organs or attributes. It quickens all the intellectual faculties, increases, enlarges, expands and purifies all the natural passions and affections, and adapts them, by the gift of wisdom, to their lawful use. It inspires, develops, cultivates and matures all the fine toned sympathies, joys, tastes, kindred feelings, and affections of our nature. It inspires virtue, kindness, goodness, tenderness, gentleness and charity. It develops beauty of person, form, and features. It tends to health, vigor, animation and social feeling. It invigorates all the faculties of the physical and intellectual man. It strengthens and gives tone to the nerves. In short, it is, as it were, marrow to the bone, joy to the heart, light to the eyes, music to the ears, and life to the whole being.[2]

That is a gift indeed!

SECTION II

HOW DOES REVELATION COME?

Revelation comes from God to man in various appointed ways, according to the laws ordained by the Almighty. The Lord appears personally to certain spiritually receptive persons; he speaks audibly by his own voice, on occasions, to those whose ears are attuned to the divine wave length; angels are sent from his presence to minister to deserving individuals; dreams and visions come from him to the faithful; he often speaks by the still small voice, the voice of the Spirit, the voice of prophecy and revelation; he reveals truth by means of the Urim and Thummim; and he gives his mind and will to receptive mortals in whatever ways seem appropriate as circumstances require (Bruce R. McConkie, Mormon Doctrine, *643–44).*

CHAPTER 4

HOW DOES REVELATION COME?

"The unspeakable gift of the Holy Ghost" (D&C 121:26).

HOW CAN I KNOW?

We can say with some confidence that probably the number one question people have in their minds about personal revelation is, *How can I know for sure when it is the Lord speaking to me?* Coming out of that are several other related questions. For example:

- What does it feel like when the Lord gives me a revelation?
- How can I recognize if something is coming from the Lord?
- What form does revelation take when it is given?
- Are there other things that are like true revelation that I might mistake for the voice of the Lord?

There is good reason for these kinds of questions. If the Lord does decide to send us a revelation, how tragic it would be if we were to miss it. What good is revelation to us if we don't even recognize it when it comes? Or equally disturbing, what if we have an experience that we mistake for true revelation and are thus led astray?

BEYOND THE TONGUE'S ABILITY

In the previous chapter, we noted some important concepts about the Holy Ghost. We know, for example, that the Holy Ghost does not have a body of flesh and bones as do the Father and the Son. He is a Spirit so that He can "dwell in us" (D&C 130:22). Why is that important?

There are two parts to your nature—your temporal body born of mortal parents, and your immortal spirit within. You are a son or daughter of God. Physically you can see with eyes and hear with ears and touch and feel and learn. Through your intellect, you learn most of what you know about the world in which we live. But if you learn by reason only, you will never understand the Spirit and how it works. . . . Your spirit learns in a different way than does your intellect.

Boyd K. Packer,
Ensign, November 1994, 59

We began our existence as individuals when we were given spirit birth. We became spirit beings in the premortal existence and lived with God there for an undisclosed amount of time. There we learned to see and hear and experience things through our spirit's senses. At birth, however, our spirit was housed in a physical body and we became dual beings. We did not lose the spiritual knowledge and experience we gained there, but a veil was placed over our minds so we cannot remember those things that we learned.

For reasons the Lord has chosen not to fully explain, when He seeks to impart light and knowledge to us—what we call revelation—this is communicated to the spiritual part of us. The communication may also involve the physical senses, but it is the spirit that learns spiritual things. Therefore, the Holy Ghost is a spirit and can "dwell in us." From that truth, we draw two important conclusions:

- The Holy Ghost is the means or the medium through which the Lord speaks to us.
- The Spirit's communication is unlike any other form of communication we experience in this life.

And therein is a problem. How do we define or describe something that is different from all other things we know? How do we recognize it when it comes if it is unlike the everyday experiences we are used to? We may try to liken it to other experiences, but those are inadequate to describe it so clearly and so well that when it comes we will always recognize it for what it is.

Elder Boyd K. Packer pinpointed our dilemma when he said: "The still, small voice [is] difficult to describe to one who has never experienced it and is almost unnecessary to describe to one who has."[1]

FINDING A PHOTO

Spiritual things may be beyond the capacity of the mortal mind and tongue to express. Many years ago, while I was serving as an institute teacher for the Church Educational System (CES) in southern California, Elder Neal A. Maxwell of the Quorum of the Twelve was in the area and spoke to our faculty. Among other things, he spoke of the nature of spiritual things and the difficulty of trying to define and describe them, especially to those who are not familiar with them. Then he used this analogy.

Suppose someone gathered up a million pictures of the faces of different women between the ages of thirty and fifty. Then they put a photograph of our own mother among them. Though it would take a long while to sort through them, and though we might find quite a few pictures that looked somewhat like our mother, none of us would have any trouble picking out our mother from all the others. We could do it instantly, once we saw her.

Now suppose that we have to describe our mother to someone who has never seen her and to do it so accurately that they can pick her picture out from all the rest. That simply is not possible. Our language does not have that specificity. "It simply is beyond the ability of our tongue to tell," Elder Maxwell concluded.

"I HAVE TASTED SALT"

Elder Boyd K. Packer used a different analogy to teach the same point. He said he was seated on an airplane next to a man who claimed to be an atheist. In the course of the flight, the conversation turned to religion. The man ridiculed Elder Packer when he bore testimony that he *knew* that God lived. The atheist responded with, "You don't *know*. Nobody *knows* that. You can't *know* it." When Elder Packer refused to yield, the man demanded, "Tell me *how* you know."

Elder Packer's response illustrates the dilemma we have: "I could not do it. I was helpless to communicate. When I used the words *spirit* and *witness*, the atheist responded, 'I don't know what you are talking about.'" Thinking he had won, the man said, "You see, you don't really know. If you did, you would be able to tell me *how you know*."

> *Tell the people to be humble and faithful, and be sure to keep the spirit of the Lord and it will lead them right. Be careful and not turn away the still small voice; it will teach you what to do and where to go; it will yield the fruits of the Kingdom. Tell the brethren to keep their hearts open to conviction, so that when the Holy Ghost comes to them, their hearts will be ready to receive it.*
>
> JOSEPH SMITH,
> IN *MANUSCRIPT HISTORY OF BRIGHAM YOUNG, 1847–1850*,
> FEBRUARY 23, 1847, 35

What happened next Elder Packer described as a thought, a revelation that came into his mind. He asked the man if he knew what salt tasted like. The man, of course, said that he did, that he knew what salt tasted like as well as he knew anything. Then Elder Packer asked him to assume that he (Elder Packer) had never tasted salt before, and to try to describe to Elder Packer what salt tasted like. The atheist tried in several ways, but he was unable to do so: He could not convey, in words alone, so ordinary an experience as tasting salt. Elder Packer then concluded:

> I bore testimony to him once again and said: "I know there is a God. You ridiculed that testimony and said that if

I *did* know, I would be able to tell you exactly *how* I know. My friend, spiritually speaking, I have tasted salt. I am no more able to convey to you in words alone how this knowledge has come than you are able to tell me what salt tastes like. But I say to you again, there is a God! He lives! And just because you don't know, don't try to tell me that I don't know, for I do!"[2]

That is the challenge we have when we attempt to answer these difficult questions. Our language is not adequate to the task. Acknowledging that, however, let us see if we can attempt, at least to some extent, to describe the indescribable.

CHAPTER 5

WHAT FORM DOES REVELATION TAKE? THE MORE DIRECT FORMS

"And it shall be in his own . . . way" (D&C 88:68).

A BROAD SPECTRUM OF EXPERIENCE

As part of our attempt to answer questions about what the voice of the Lord is like and how we can learn to recognize it, we need to address the specific issue of how revelation comes. Is it always the same experience? Does it take different forms? Exactly what range of experience is included in the definition of revelation?

We need only to open the scriptures to see that God reveals His will and word to man in many different ways, through many different forms, by many varied experiences. In the quotation introducing this section, Elder McConkie noted that revelation comes in various ways (see p. 23). Here are two additional statements from Apostles:

> *Elder Neal A. Maxwell:* There is a spectrum of styles used by the Lord to inspire and guide us. If we seek to make the process too mechanical, we may deprive ourselves of guidance from God that comes in other ways, equally valid.[1]

> *Elder Dallin H. Oaks:* The experience we call *revelation*

can occur through many different forms. Some prophets, like Moses and Joseph Smith, have talked with God face-to-face. Some persons have had face-to-face communication with angels. Other revelations have come, as Elder James E. Talmage described, "through the dreams of sleep or in the waking visions of the mind."

In its most familiar forms, revelation comes by means of words or thoughts or feelings communicated to the mind. . . .

We often refer to these most familiar forms of revelation as *inspiration.* Inspired thoughts or promptings can take the form of enlightenment of the mind (D&C 6:15), positive or negative feelings about proposed courses of action, or even the uplifting emotions that come from inspiring performances, as in the performing arts.[2]

There is a rich and impressive diversity in the means God uses to reveal His mind and will to us or to demonstrate His power, knowledge, and majesty. Revelation is a thread woven so frequently through God's dealing with His people that one could almost call the scriptural and historical record "a tapestry of revelation." But that thread is not of one single color. Rather, it is as rich and varied as life itself.

A CONTINUUM OF REVELATION

There is a useful word used by researchers in the social sciences to describe various social phenomena. The word is *continuum.* A continuum conveys the idea of a continuous grading or ranking within a general category. For example, when we speak of the economic levels of society, it would be a gross oversimplification to categorize people as either rich or poor. Between those two ends, there is a vast range of difference. On the low end are those in extreme poverty; on the upper end we have the "super rich." But in between you have the very poor, the poor, the middle class, the upper middle class, and so on. Thus we have a continuum of economic status.

Revelatory experiences also fit into a kind of gradation or variation, only unlike the rich and the poor there is no suggestion that one end of the continuum is superior to the other. For purposes of our discussion, we will label the two ends of the continuum as *More Direct* and *Less Direct,* as shown below.

Less
Direct

More
Direct

Directness includes such concepts as *powerful, explicit, plain, unmistakable, recognizable, dramatic, intense, unusual, striking, distinct, clear.* On the other hand, *indirect* implies *subtle, indefinable, commonplace, unnoticed, or vague.*

I have drawn a horizontal line between those two ends of the spectrum to suggest what we have already stated, that one end of this continuum is not better or more valuable than the other. At first this may seem counterintuitive—directness certainly sounds better than indirectness. But on further thought, in revelation what matters more than *how* light and truth is given is *what* light and truth is given.

This is a continuum of directness, not importance. We say again for emphasis: ***How*** *revelation comes is less important than* ***what*** *is given in the revelation.*

If we assume that only direct revelations have any real validity, we will overlook other forms of revelation and miss out on much instruction from the Lord. So with that caution, let us now look at the two ends of the spectrum when it comes to revelation.

THE LIGHT OF CHRIST

Perhaps the least direct (but not any less important) form of revelation is what the scriptures call the light of Christ, which is given to all men. The Bible Dictionary contains a concise and clear explanation of the Light of Christ:

The light of Christ is just what the words imply:

enlightenment, knowledge, and an uplifting, ennobling, per-severing influence that comes upon mankind because of Jesus Christ. For instance, Christ is "the true light that lighteth every man that cometh into the world" (D&C 93:2; John 1:9). . . .

The light of Christ is related to man's conscience and tells him right from wrong (cf. Moro. 7:12–19). The light of Christ should not be confused with the personage of the Holy Ghost, for the light of Christ is not a personage at all. *Its influence is preliminary to and preparatory* to one's receiving the Holy Ghost. The light of Christ will lead the honest soul who "hearkeneth to the voice" to find the true gospel and the true Church and thereby receive the Holy Ghost (see D&C 84:46–48).[3]

The interesting thing about the Light of Christ is that while it is the least direct form of revelation—the vast majority of the world has no conception of its existence—it is at the same time the most pervasive form of revelation. It is given to everyone; it permeates everything; it strives with every person to help him or her do good and live better lives.

One of its functions is to enlighten the minds of men in the arts, sciences, exploration, invention, and many other fields of endeavor. Brigham Young said that the Light of Christ "is the Fountain of truth that feeds, clothes, and gives light and intelligence to the inhabitants of the earth, no matter whether they are saints or sinners."[4] And President

Everyone is blessed at birth with the Light of Christ. . . . That means that every soul who walks the earth, wherever he lives, in whatever nation he may have been born, no matter whether he be in riches or in poverty, had at birth an endowment of that first light which is called the Light of Christ, the Spirit of Truth, or the Spirit of God—that universal light of intelligence with which every soul is blessed.

HAROLD B. LEE,
*TEACHINGS OF
HAROLD B. LEE,* 99

33

Joseph Fielding Smith tied the Light of Christ directly to human progress:

> Do you think that these discoveries and inventions by Marconi [telegraph], by Edison [electric light], by Bell [telephone], by Stephenson [steam-powered locomotives] and by the other inventors and discoverers without naming them, have come just because these men have been sitting down and concentrating their minds upon these matters and have discovered them through their thought or accidentally? Not in the least, but *the Spirit of the Lord, the Light of Christ, has been back of it, and has been impelling them to do these very things.*[5]

THE MORE DIRECT FORMS OF REVELATION

Let us move now to the opposite end of the revelation continuum and discuss the more direct forms of revelation. We will do this only briefly because, while they are very dramatic and direct, these are rarely the kinds of experiences most members of the Church have with revelation. A whole host of more commonly experienced forms of revelation can be found closer to the left side of the line—that is, they are less direct and spectacular—but we will save them for a fuller discussion in the next chapters.

Visitations

On the right side of the continuum, perhaps the most direct and dramatic form of revelation involves heavenly beings coming personally to visit individuals on the earth. Obviously this is a very direct form of revelation. All of the synonyms we used above to describe directness apply here. Visitations and visions are powerful, explicit, plain, and unmistakable and are clearly recognized experiences. They are also dramatic, intense, unusual, and very distinct. In almost all cases the experience involves the physical senses—seeing, hearing and, in some cases, touching.

Even within this very specific category, we have two variations—the first would be to have a visitation from a member of the Godhead; the second would be to have a visitation from other heavenly beings.

It seems safe to say that the most direct and dramatic revelatory experience any mortal being could ever have would be to receive an actual visitation from one or more members of the Godhead.* While these experiences are very rare compared to other forms of revelation, there are nevertheless a number of cases where such experiences are recorded. For example:

How does God reveal himself? Though the ways may be infinite, the perfect and crowning way is by direct revelation, by visions, by personal visitations.

BRUCE R. MCCONKIE,
*DOCTRINAL NEW TESTAMENT
COMMENTARY,* 3:137

- Ten of the early apostles were gathered together when the resurrected Savior not only appeared in their midst but partook of food with them and invited them to touch his resurrected body (Luke 24:36–43).
- The Nephites not only were privileged to see, hear, and touch the resurrected Christ, but they had Him with them for several days, teaching and ministering to them (3 Nephi 11–27).
- Joseph Smith received a personal visitation from both the Father and the Son as the opening revelation of the Restoration (JS–H 1:14–20).

Closely related to these visitations from one of the Godhead would be visitations from other heavenly beings, who are commonly called angels.** There are 543 references to angels in the four standard works,

---

* The technical name for such experiences is *theophany,* from *theos,* God, and the Greek word meaning to be made manifest or to be seen.

** Joseph Smith taught that there are two classes of beings in heaven: Angels, who are resurrected personages with physical bodies, and spirits who have not yet been resurrected (see D&C 129).

and more than a hundred more in Joseph Smith's *History of the Church*. Clearly, this kind of experience, while still very unusual, has occurred with much greater frequency than the appearances of God. Just a small sampling would include:

- An angel announced the coming birth of John the Baptist to Zacharias and of Jesus to Mary and Joseph (Matthew 1; Luke 1). An angel then appeared to the shepherds at Bethlehem when Jesus was born (Luke 2:9–10).
- The angel Moroni came to Joseph and told him about the Book of Mormon (JS–H 1:27–54).
- John the Baptist, Peter, James, John, Moses, Elias, and Elijah restored the priesthood and priesthood keys (D&C 13; 110:11–16; 128:20).

It could be said that while Joseph's vision of the Father and the Son *opened* the Restoration, it was angelic ministration that *sustained* it.

> *I have had the administration of angels in my day and time, though I never prayed for an angel. I have had, in several instances, the administration of holy messengers.*
>
> WILFORD WOODRUFF,
> *DISCOURSES OF WILFORD WOODRUFF*, 286

But angelic ministration was not just limited to the initial events of the Restoration. Over the ensuing years angels have come to give instruction, comfort, or direction. One instance of this happened when Wilford Woodruff and others were attacked by the powers of darkness while they were in London. They were saved when "three holy messengers [came] into the room and filled the room with light. They were dressed in temple clothing. They laid their hands upon our heads and we were delivered."[6]

We should note that in many cases, the ministering of angels may occur without them ever being seen or heard. As Elder Oaks has taught, "The ministering of angels can also be unseen. Angelic messages can be delivered by a voice or merely by thoughts or feelings communicated to the mind. . . . Most angelic communications are felt or heard rather than seen."[7] Moroni noted that if the time comes when angels cease to minister unto men, it is because of unbelief and lack of faith, and "awful is the state of man" (Moroni 7:37–38).

Visions

Visions typically refer to an experience where the person is in a waking state and sees grand and glorious things by the power of God.* The very word, which means "to see," suggests that these kinds of experiences are also a very direct form of revelation. Like visitations, they involve the physical senses—individuals both see and hear and personally experience things. Generally these visions are grand in scope and vast in what is revealed. Often they involve a revelation of future events. Examples:

- Moses and Enoch were shown the earth and all the inhabitants thereof (Moses 1:1, 27–41; 7:21–67).
- Lehi had a vision of the Tree of Life and the journey through mortality (1 Nephi 8).**
- John the Revelator was shown the events associated with the Second Coming of Christ (Revelation 4–22).
- Joseph Smith and Sidney Rigdon saw the three degrees of glory in vision (D&C 76:19–119).

Audible Voice

When the scriptures record the idea of "hearing" the voice of the Lord, at least three different shades of meaning may be implied.

---

* We should note that sometimes the word "vision" is used to describe a personal visitation, because of the glorious nature of the experience. The clearest example is the First Vision, which is the name we give to Joseph's experience in the Sacred Grove. In other cases, a person may see members of the Godhead or other heavenly beings in vision but they are not physically present.

** Some visions are called dreams because they occurred—or at least they began—at night while the individual was sleeping. Lehi's experience started when he was sleeping, but he may have been quite awake during the experience. Nephi called Lehi's experience a "dream or vision" (1 Nephi 8:36). Those experiences that occur while the person is asleep are treated later in this chapter.

1. In some cases the individual hears a literal, audible voice.
2. Sometimes the voice is not outwardly audible, but it is described as "a voice in the mind."
3. Many times when the scriptures say that God spoke to someone, the record most likely refers to the kinds of experiences that we typically call inspiration or personal revelation.

More will be said of the second and third kinds of experiences in the next chapter. Here we will look only at a few instances where individuals heard an audible voice, which is a more direct, definable experience than the whisperings of the Spirit. Again, this is not a common experience, but there are numerous examples of it.

- At the baptism of Jesus, those present heard a voice from heaven saying, "This is my beloved Son, in whom I am well pleased" (Matthew 3:17).
- A still small voice was heard by the Nephites before Jesus appeared to them (3 Nephi 11:1–7).

Two modern examples are shared by apostles of this dispensation:

President Harold B. Lee: I think maybe I was around ten or eleven years of age. I was with my father out on a farm away from our home, trying to spend the day busying myself until my father was ready to go home. Over the fence from our place were some tumbledown sheds that would attract a curious boy, and I was adventurous. I started to climb through the fence, and I heard a voice as clearly as you are hearing mine, calling me by name and saying, "Don't go over there!" I turned to look at my father to see if he were talking to me, but he was way up at the other end of the field. There was no person in sight. I realized then, as a child, that there were persons beyond my sight, for I had definitely heard a voice.[8]

Elder Dallin H. Oaks: As a young girl, my grandmother, Chasty Olsen, . . . was tending some children who were playing in a dry riverbed near their home in Castle Dale, Utah. Suddenly she heard a voice that called her by name and directed her to get the children out of the riverbed and up on the bank. It was a clear day, and there was no sign of rain. She saw no reason to heed the voice and continued to play. The voice spoke to her again, urgently. This time she heeded the warning. Quickly gathering the children, she made a run for the bank. Just as they reached it, an enormous wall of water, originating with a cloudburst in the mountains many miles away, swept down the canyon and roared across where the children had played. Except for this impelling revelation, she and the children would have been lost.[9]

Dreams

Dreams form a category of revelation that is a little more difficult to fit neatly into a slot. We can find numerous examples of revelation in the form of dreams; but sometimes dreams more closely represent a vision that occurs during the night hours after the person has retired. Another difficulty is that some dreams are of a more grand and sweeping nature, while others are given to individuals as another form of personal revelation.[*]

Here we will note some examples of the grander version, which fits under the heading of more direct kinds of revelation. A few examples of revelatory dreams from scripture and Church history include:

- Joseph, son of Jacob, had dreams in which he symbolically saw his family bowing down to him in submission. In Egypt he interpreted the dreams of others, including Pharaoh (see Genesis 37, 40, 41).

---

[*] Not all dreams are revelatory in nature, of course. The subconscious mind continues to function while we sleep, sometimes in very normal expressions of our thoughts and feelings, but often in weird, bizarre and even frightening ways. It would be safe to say that the vast majority of our dreams do not constitute revelation from the Lord, and it would be a concern if we looked for spiritual meaning in every dream of the night.

• King Nebuchadnezzar had a dream—interpreted by Daniel—in which he symbolically saw the various kingdoms of the world, including the kingdom of God set up in the last days (Daniel 2).

• The wise men were warned in a dream not to report back to Herod as had been requested (Matthew 2:12). About that same time, Joseph was warned in a dream to take Mary and Jesus into Egypt to escape Herod (Matthew 2:13).

Patriarchal Blessings

Sometimes the Spirit gives us revelation through priesthood blessings. Father's blessings, blessings given as part of ordinations, confirmations, or administrations to the sick—all these provide opportunities for the Spirit to give direction to an individual. These will be treated in more detail as we look at the less direct forms of revelation.

However, patriarchal blessings could be considered a more direct form of revelation, since they come in a structured experience where an individual receives personal revelation through an ordained patriarch. These are recorded so that a copy can be given to the individual for personal use throughout his or her life. (It is also the only individual priesthood blessing where a copy is kept in the archives of the Church.) Thousands of individuals can testify of

> *A patriarchal blessing is a revelation to the recipient, even a white line down the middle of the road, to protect, inspire, and motivate activity and righteousness. A patriarchal blessing literally contains chapters from the recipient's book of eternal possibilities. . . .*
>
> *Your blessing is not to be folded neatly and tucked away. It is not to be framed or published. Rather, it is to be read. It is to be loved. It is to be followed.*
>
> *Your patriarchal blessing will see you through the darkest night. It will guide you through life's dangers. . . . Your patriarchal blessing is to you a personal Liahona to chart your course and guide your way.*
>
> Thomas S. Monson,
> *Live the Good Life,* 38–39

promises, declarations, or warnings given in patriarchal blessings—often by a patriarch who did not personally know them—which were fulfilled later in their lives, sometimes in very remarkable ways.

IN SUMMARY

Let us now return to our discussion on the continuum of revelation that we introduced at the beginning of this chapter. We could add those various forms to our diagram so that it looks like this:*

Now that we have explored the nature of the Lord's voice, we are ready to discuss the less direct forms of revelation.

We have briefly noted some of these more direct forms of revelation. We have not spent much time discussing them because this book is about the principles and patterns of *personal* revelation.

For us as members of the Church, these more direct and dramatic forms of revelation come very rarely or not at all. I am not hesitant to say that I have never seen an angel, heard an audible voice speak to me, seen any kind of vision, or had any kind of remarkable dream. Nor have most of the people I know. The Lord has chosen to speak to me through quieter, more subtle, forms of revelation, and my life has been continually blessed by that. Early in my life I envied those who had such direct experiences with the Lord. However, I long ago realized that the abundance of revelation I have received in quieter, more subtle ways provides me with more than sufficient proof of God's reality, of His mercies, and of His intimate knowledge of me and my needs.

---

* The placement of specific forms of revelation in an ascending or descending order is somewhat arbitrary, since there is some variation within individual forms of revelation as well as between them.

CHAPTER 6

HOW DOES THE LORD SPEAK TO US?
I. THE STILL SMALL VOICE

"The still small voice, which whispereth" (D&C 85:6).

A VOICE THAT WHISPERS

Now that we have examined the more direct forms of revelation, let us turn to the other end of the spectrum, those forms of revelation that are best described in words like indirect, subtle, indefinable, commonplace, unnoticed, or vague. However, before we do so, we first need to understand two basic concepts about the very nature of the Lord's voice. Simply stated they are:

- The voice of the Lord is a still small voice.
- The Lord speaks to the mind and the heart.

We will examine these concepts separately at first, then combine them together to continue our study of the less direct end of the revelation spectrum.

Amid other instructions given to the Prophet Joseph Smith in November 1832, the Lord inserted the following illuminating statement about the voice of the Lord: "Yea, thus saith the still small voice, which whispereth through and pierceth all things, and often times it maketh my bones to quake while it maketh manifest" (D&C 85:6).

This passage gives us four pieces of information about the voice of the Lord:

The voice of the Lord is *still.*
The voice of the Lord is *small.*
The voice of the Lord *whispers.*
The voice of the Lord can have a *powerful impact* upon the heart.

Those first three descriptions help explain why there are so many questions, so much uncertainty, and frequent confusion about the voice of the Lord. It would be so much easier to know when the Lord was speaking to us if He would use a microphone and eighty-megawatt speakers whenever He did so. There would be far fewer questions if each time the Spirit communicated with us our room shook or a light appeared or our whole body began to tingle. But just the opposite is true. Speaking of the still small voice, Elder Boyd K. Packer said:

Man is apt to look too high or expect too great things so that they often times mistake the Spirit of God and the inspiration of the Almighty. It is not in the thunder or whirlwind that we should look for the Spirit of God but in the still small voice.

WILFORD WOODRUFF,
DISCOURSES OF WILFORD WOODRUFF, 45

The Spirit does not get our attention by shouting or shaking us with a heavy hand. Rather it whispers. It caresses so gently that if we are preoccupied we may not feel it at all. . . .

Occasionally it will press just firmly enough for us to pay heed. But most of the time, if we do not heed the gentle feeling, the Spirit will withdraw and wait until we come seeking and listening.[1]

There is a challenge. Who has not ever been preoccupied? Or more to the point, who is not *almost always* preoccupied with one thing or another? Our lives are full and complicated, filled with the press of work, the demands of family, the diversions of recreation, the concerns of personal problems, our interactions with friends, relatives, and associates. It is sobering to think that in such times, we may receive promptings and not even be aware of them. And even if we do take note, is it any wonder that sometimes we say to ourselves, "Was that the Lord speaking to me just now? Is that what His voice feels like?"

THE LANGUAGE OF THE SPIRIT

In a previous chapter, we noted how difficult it is to describe in human language things of the Spirit. Our tongue simply does not have the capability to adequately describe the language of the Holy Ghost. In our attempt to liken this communication to things we understand, we find ourselves using phrases like "seeing with our spiritual eyes" or "hearing with our spiritual ears." The scriptures are filled with similar language. (For example, see Matthew 13:15; D&C 110:1.)

Are not these expressions an attempt to describe in terms we *can* understand a part of us that we *do not* understand?

With that idea in mind, let us consider these descriptors about the Lord's voice being still and small and whispering. What do they mean?

> *There is one unerring voice that is ever true. It can always be relied upon. It should be listened to, although at times this voice too may speak unwelcome warning messages. I speak of the still, small, inner voice which comes from the divine source. . . . You can know by the whisperings of the Holy Spirit if you righteously and earnestly seek to know. Your own inspiration will be an unerring vibration through the companionship of the Holy Ghost.*
>
> James E. Faust,
> In the Strength of the Lord, 333–34, 401

How can a voice be *still?* That sounds like a contradiction of terms. Does *small* mean limited in volume, or is there more to it than that? *Whisper* seems clear enough, but that carries some interesting implications. When a person whispers, it is not only more difficult to hear them because the volume is softer, but it is also more of a challenge to understand them because the quality of the voice changes when we whisper. How does that apply to the voice of the Lord?

Perhaps we can better understand what it means to call it a still small voice if we examine how others who are familiar with the voice have tried to describe it. As noted above, Elder Packer said that it is very difficult to describe the still small voice to those who haven't experienced it, but almost unnecessary to those who have.

That provides some hope for us. If this is a language of the Spirit, we can improve our understanding of it by carefully studying the words of those who have "learned" that language for themselves.

> *I learned . . . that the description of the Holy Ghost as a still, small voice is real. It is poetic, but it is not poetry. Only when my heart has been still and quiet, in submission like a little child, has the Spirit been clearly audible to my heart and mind.*
>
> HENRY B. EYRING,
> *ENSIGN,* MAY 2006, 16

So let us study the language used by people who know what the still small voice is like to see if that helps us better understand our own experiences with that voice. We will start with four scriptural accounts of people experiencing the still small voice; then, later, we will sample what those whom we sustain as modern prophets, seers, and revelators have to say about it as well.

THE PROPHET ELIJAH

After Elijah's contest with the priests of Baal (see 1 Kings 18), the prophet Elijah had to flee for his life to escape the fury of Jezebel. He ended up in the wilderness on Mount Horeb living in a cave.

One day the Lord came to speak to Elijah. At first, a "great and strong wind" raged so violently that it actually shattered the rocks into pieces. "But the Lord was not in the wind." After the wind came an earthquake, which in turn was followed by fire. But again, the author

We could come away from our study of Elijah with no more important lesson than to recognize how the Lord communicates with his children here upon the earth: through the still, small voice. . . . That sweet, quiet voice of inspiration that comes more as a feeling than it does as a sound. That process through which pure intelligence can be spoken into the mind and we can know and understand and have witness of spiritual things. The process is not reserved for the prophets alone, but every righteous seeking soul who will qualify and make himself worthy can have that manner of communication, even as a gift.

BOYD K. PACKER,
HOLY TEMPLE, 107

of Kings noted, "But the Lord was not in the earthquake: . . . the Lord was not in the fire" (1 Kings 19:11–12).

Finally, in sharp contrast to these impressive and very dramatic demonstrations of God's power, there came "a still small voice" (v. 12). The impact of this last experience upon Elijah is made clear with these words: "And it was so, when Elijah heard it, that he wrapped his face in his mantle [probably as a sign of reverence, submission, and humility], and *went out,* and stood in the entering in of the cave" (v. 13). There the Lord proceeded to give him specific instruction and counsel. Evidently during the wind, the earthquake, and the fire, Elijah stayed inside the cave, likely because he feared for his safety, but the still small voice held no such threat and he was drawn out to converse with the Lord.

NEPHI, LAMAN, AND LEMUEL

We find another insight about the still small voice from Nephi's experience with his two older brothers. Again and again they had seen evidence of the Lord's over-watching care. Yet none of these had done much for Laman and Lemuel. When Nephi was told to build a ship so they could sail to the promised land, the two brothers not only mocked and ridiculed his efforts, but they also openly opposed him.

Finally, Nephi could take no more. After berating them for refusing to see the hand of the Lord in their progress thus far, he said:

Ye have seen an angel [a very dramatic form of revelation], and he spake unto you; yea, ye have heard his voice from time to time; and he hath spoken unto you in a still small voice, *but ye were past feeling, that ye could not feel his words;* wherefore, he has spoken unto you like unto the voice of thunder, which did cause the earth to shake as if it were to divide asunder (1 Nephi 17:45).

Note what Nephi teaches us about the still small voice. He tells us that that voice is *felt.* He doesn't say the brothers couldn't *hear* the voice, but rather that they could not *feel* it. Of this experience, Elder Packer said:

If we stop and feel during prayer, we sometimes hear a still small voice, which enters quietly into our mind and heart. It is so simple and so precise that we often pass it by, thinking that it is just our own idea or a passing thought, not revelation. However, as we reconcile these whisperings to what we know to be true, we soon learn to recognize them; and by recognizing them, we become more able to listen carefully.

Joseph B. Wirthlin, *Finding Peace in Our Lives,* 174

The Holy Ghost speaks with a voice that you *feel* more than you *hear.* It is described as a "still small voice." And while we speak of "listening" to the whisperings of the Spirit, most often one describes a spiritual prompting by saying, "I had a *feeling.*"

Revelation comes as words we *feel* more than *hear.*[2]

So what does it mean to *feel* a voice? Here is another example of the tongue's inability to fully describe something. We are not talking about a series of sounds that ping upon the eardrums, or even a string of verbalized thoughts that run sequentially through the mind. The Spirit speaks to us and suddenly we have a feeling. There is no other way to describe it. Later we may try to formulate what that feeling was like and put it into words, but when it first comes, it does not come as words; it comes as a feeling.

Upon reflection, this may be the answer to our previous question. We said the very idea of a *still* voice seems like a contradiction of terms. How can a voice be still? Once we better understand the nature of the voice, the supposed contradiction goes away. The voice of the Spirit is generally not audible. It does not create vibrations of sound in the air. It is a *silent* voice. It speaks to us through a different medium than sound waves. Thus, it is literally a still voice.

NEPHI AND LEHI AMONG THE LAMANITES

From another scriptural experience with the still small voice, we get additional insights into the nature of the voice itself. Nephi and Lehi (the sons of Helaman) went to the Land of Nephi to preach to the Lamanites. They were seized and thrown into prison. After many days without food, their captors came into the prison to take them out for execution. Before they could do so, however, the two prophets were encircled by a ring of fire. The Lamanites were struck dumb with astonishment. Then the two brothers began to preach to them. As they did so, the earth shook exceedingly and those within the prison were enveloped in a cloud of darkness (see Helaman 5:16–28).

Fire, earthquake, and darkness. It sounds very similar to Elijah's experience, doesn't it? The Lamanites experienced three very dramatic, outward signs of God's power, but this did not convert them. It only filled them with terror. Then came the voice. Note Mormon's description of that voice:

> It was not a voice of thunder, neither was it a voice of a great tumultuous noise, but behold, it was a *still voice of perfect mildness*, as if it had been *a whisper*, and it did pierce them even to the very soul (Helaman 5:30).

The voice spoke to them three times in all. As it did so, their terror gave way to wonder and desire. As they began to pray to the source of the voice, they were filled with joy and were then converted (see Helaman 5:32–45).

Once that change of heart had taken place, the voice then spoke to them a fourth time. Mormon gives us more information about the nature of the voice.

> And it came to pass that there came a voice unto them, yea, a *pleasant voice, as if it were a whisper*, saying: Peace, peace be unto you (Helaman 5:46–47).

Note that the voice was a voice of *mildness*. Could that be part of what is meant by it being called a *small* voice? The voice of the Lord is not only quiet—low in volume—but also it is not strident in any way. Sometimes even a soft voice can be filled with anger, malice, or threat. But this voice was mild and it was *pleasant*. There was no fear here. It brought peace and joy and true conversion.

There are spiritual influences that are just as deep and meaningful as anything that is tangible to the natural senses; yet they cannot be described or explained. They come through the still small voice of the Spirit. They are penetrating but cannot be described any more than the feelings of love, sympathy, friendship, can be defined and fathomed.

JOSEPH FIELDING SMITH,
*MAN, HIS ORIGIN AND
DESTINY*, 16–17

IN THE LAND BOUNTIFUL

Perhaps the most dramatic scriptural example of the still small voice is the account of the Savior's visit to about 2,500 people in the land Bountiful (3 Nephi 11). In this case, the voice was audible from the beginning, but they could not understand it at first. It spoke a second time, and still they could not understand it. We have to assume that this wasn't a language problem.

What is recorded in one verse is very instructive. When the voice spoke a third time, this time they *"did open their ears to hear it"* (v. 5), and "the third time they did understand the voice which they heard" (v. 6). This is clearly speaking of their spiritual ears and not their physical ones. Something happened after the second time that caused them to seek a different level of perception and finally they "heard."

It is in this chapter that we find the most detailed description of the voice itself. Mormon not only tells us what the voice was like, but he also tells us what the voice was *not* like.

> *We must be in tune to hear the Lord's word. All too often when God speaks in this still, small voice, as He did to Elijah in the cave, it may not be audible to our physical hearing because, like a faulty radio, we may be out of tune with the infinite.*
>
> HAROLD B. LEE,
> *TEACHINGS OF HAROLD B. LEE*, 423

It was *not a harsh voice, neither was it a loud voice;* nevertheless, and notwithstanding it being a *small voice* it did pierce them that did hear to the center, insomuch that there was no part of their frame that it did not cause to quake; yea, it did pierce them to the very soul, and did cause their hearts to burn (3 Nephi 11:3).

The quiet gentleness of the voice is underscored by the declaration that it was neither harsh nor loud. However, the effect once again is more dramatic and more profound than seeing an angel, watching fire come down from heaven, being immersed in darkness, or feeling the earth shaking beneath one's feet. There's something about our spiritual sensors that are deeply affected by the voice of the Lord. Note the description of its effect on the Nephites: It pierced them to the center, to their very souls.[*] It caused them to physically tremble. It caused their hearts to burn.

IN SUMMARY

In this section we have been trying to answer the question *What is the voice of the Lord like?* An important part of that answer is what the

---

[*] We should remember that "the spirit *and* the body are the soul of man" (D&C 88:15).

Lord has chosen to tell us about the nature of His voice, which is that it is a still small voice that whispers. It is mild and pleasant, not harsh or loud. It is felt more than heard.

We promised to look at what modern prophets, seers, and revelators have said about this voice. Before doing that, however, we need to explore another unusual characteristic of the voice of the Lord.

CHAPTER 7

HOW DOES THE LORD SPEAK TO US?
II. TO THE MIND AND HEART

"I will tell you in your mind and in your heart" (D&C 8:2).

THE MIND AND THE HEART

Earlier we said that the Lord has given us two different statements on what His voice is like. The first is that it is still and small and whispers. The second statement was given through the Prophet Joseph to Oliver Cowdery before the Church was organized.

Oliver Cowdery arrived in Harmony, Pennsylvania, in April 1829. He had traveled from Palmyra to investigate for himself whether the reports he had heard about Joseph and the gold plates were true. The Lord gave him the confirmation he sought (see D&C 6), and then told him that he was immediately to begin assisting Joseph in the translation of the Book of Mormon, serving as his scribe.

A few days later, Oliver expressed a desire to also have the gift of translation. In response, the Lord gave through Joseph what is now Doctrine and Covenants 8. That revelation included a simple and yet remarkable statement on the nature of revelation.

Yea, behold, I will tell you *in your mind and in your*

heart, by the Holy Ghost, which shall come upon you and which shall dwell in your heart.

Now, behold, this is the spirit of revelation; behold, this is the spirit by which Moses brought the children of Israel through the Red Sea on dry ground (D&C 8:2–3).

In the mind and in the heart. That is a key concept that requires further exploration.

THOUGHTS AND FEELINGS

If the Lord wanted to speak to our minds, what word would we use to describe how his message comes? Probably we would say those revelations would come to us as *thoughts.* And if He wanted to speak to our hearts, we would say that in those cases, His voice would come to us as *feelings.* And therein lies an important insight about how the voice of the Lord communicates to us.

We noted earlier that the fact that the voice of the Lord is still and small and whispers is part of the challenge we have in recognizing personal revelation. How can we be sure we've heard those almost imperceptible whisperings? So it is with this aspect of the Lord's voice as well. If He speaks to us through thoughts and feelings, how are we to distinguish between His thoughts and feelings and our own?

Someone has compared human consciousness to a great stream of thoughts and feelings. Every waking moment of our lives (and often in sleep as well), our minds are filled

Now, someone asks, "Why do the revelations come in that manner? Why don't they come preceded by 'thus saith the Lord'?" They haven't always come that way, even in the days of old. . . .

For many it seems difficult to accept as revelation those numerous messages . . . which come to prophets as deep, unassailable impressions settling down on the prophet's mind and heart as dew from heaven or as the dawn displaces the darkness of night.

SPENCER W. KIMBALL,
TEACHINGS OF SPENCER W. KIMBALL, 457

53

with thoughts and we are experiencing feelings. It is like a mighty Mississippi River of thinking and feeling.

Our emotions cover a vast range of different feelings—boredom, attentiveness, frustration, excitement, anger, happiness, sadness, fulfillment, disappointment, pleasure, hurt, humiliation. Trying to list every emotion we feel is as impossible as trying to list every thought we think.

In its most familiar forms, revelation comes by means of words or thoughts or feelings communicated to the mind. . . . This is the experience . . . Nephi described when he reminded his wayward brothers that the Lord had spoken to them in a still small voice, but they "were past feeling" and "could not feel his words." (1 Ne. 17:45.)

DALLIN H. OAKS,
LORD'S WAY, 23

So when we receive a thought or a feeling through the Holy Ghost, how do we recognize it as being different from our own? How do we distinguish it from this never-ending flow of our own thoughts and feelings? To use the river analogy, it is as though from time to time there is a soft plop as one of the Lord's "pebbles" is dropped into this mighty Mississippi of our consciousness. Should we be surprised, then, that many times when the Lord speaks to us in this way we miss it entirely?

SO HOW DOES IT WORK?

One of the most challenging (and intimidating) things that General Authorities and Area Seventies are asked to do is to choose a new stake presidency during the creation of a stake or the reorganization of an existing stake presidency. It involves visiting a stake where typically the authority doesn't know any of the leadership personally. Even more challenging, the General Authority is often assigned to go to a country where he does not speak the language and has to do everything through translators. Yet in a period that lasts no more than about twelve hours, a decision must be made that is harmony with the Lord's will.

Fortunately, through many years of experience a process has been tried and proven viable that makes this quiet miracle work week after week all over the world. Since this process is a wonderful illustration of how the voice of the Lord works in a very practical and real-life situation, a brief description of the process may be of value, along with some actual examples of how it works.

First of all, there are always two authorities assigned to such conferences so that they can confer together and confirm what the Lord is prompting them to do. This also fulfills the law of witnesses (see D&C 6:28). In most cases they arrive in the stake on Friday evening or early Saturday morning to begin a series of interviews. The priesthood leadership of the stake (normally the stake presidency, patriarch, bishops and branch presidents, and high councilors) are asked to come in for brief, private meetings with the two presiding authorities. In the individual interviews, each priesthood leader briefly shares a little information about himself and then is asked for names of brethren he would recommend for consideration as the new stake president. He is also asked to briefly explain why he feels as he does.

I am going into a stake tomorrow, and to my knowledge I don't know anyone in that stake. And yet, by one o'clock tomorrow afternoon I will know who the new stake president should be.

You may ask, "Brother Ballard, will you hear voices? Will angels appear? How will you know?" I will know by the prompting of the Spirit, which is the way this work is accomplished. And I will know as assuredly as I know that I am standing before you tonight whom the Lord has been preparing to preside over that stake.

M. Russell Ballard,
CES Evening with a General
Authority, January 8, 1988, 5

This process is based on an example found in the Old Testament. When Samuel was told by the Lord to choose a replacement for King Saul (1 Samuel 16:1), the phrases used to describe what happened in that process are instructive: "Jesse called Abinadab, and made him *pass before* Samuel" (v. 8). "Jesse made Shammah to *pass by*" (v. 9). "Jesse made seven of his sons to *pass before* Samuel" (v. 10). Not until Samuel saw David did he finally *feel* who was to be the next king. When that finally happened, the account says simply: "And the Lord said, Arise, anoint him: *for this is he*" (v. 12).

The series of interviews with the priesthood leadership of the stake allows the potential candidates to "pass before" the presiding authorities. As they do so, thoughts and feelings begin to come to them. Sometimes they come quickly. Other times they come only after the interviews are completed. Rarely are these thoughts and feelings dramatic or remarkable. They are almost always very gentle and very subtle, *almost like a whisper.* Sometimes they come when the person first enters the room. A very quiet feeling comes that he could be the one. Other times it is something the person says that triggers a feeling of rightness. Often thoughts come into the minds of the interviewers, and they are prompted to ask a question that helps reveal the heart of the person being interviewed.

Occasionally, feelings may come from simply hearing the name of a person the authorities have not yet met. It is no more than a fleeting feeling that this name could be significant. Later, when that person comes in, they have a feeling of peace about him.

It is not always a positive confirmation. Sometimes a man comes highly recommended by others, but during the interview there is no confirming witness, and the authority knows that this is not the man the Lord has chosen at this time.

When the interviews have been completed, the two authorities close the door and spend time together reviewing their experience. They go over the list of names again. They share thoughts and feelings they may have had during the process. They discuss impressions that have come. This fits another scriptural model on how to receive revelation. Oliver Cowdery was told that it was not enough to simply ask the Lord for an answer. He was to study it out in his mind, and then ask the Lord if his decision was right. Then would come a confirmation, either as a stupor of thought or a burning in the bosom (see D&C 9:8–9).*

In some cases, this discussion may last only a few minutes because both authorities have a clear conviction about who the person is to be. In other instances, there may be no such feelings with either of them, and a more prolonged discussion is required to let the feelings and impressions come. Though it doesn't happen often, there are times when they receive no confirmation about any of the men they have met. In such cases other names are sought and further interviews are conducted. But whatever particular route the process may take, the two brethren who have the assignment constantly search their mind and heart. They look inward, reviewing feelings they have had or thoughts that have come to them.

During this private consultation process (or studying it out in their minds), eventually the two brethren come to a consensus. They reach a joint decision. At that point, they kneel together in prayer and put their decision before the Lord. Typically, each prays individually, placing the chosen name before the Lord and asking the Lord "if it be right" (D&C 9:8). When the prayers are finished, they briefly sit, quietly looking inward, searching their heart and listening for that still small voice of confirmation. When it is clear they are in complete harmony on the matter, they invite the chosen person back and extend the call.

Again, I wish to emphasize how "normal" this process seems on the surface, even though it is quite remarkable. Time after time the process works, but it has never been—at least for me—something that people would think of as dramatic or miraculous. To an observer, the process would seem perfectly normal. But it works. Over and over, week in and week out in countries all across the globe. It works!

ANOTHER WITNESS

It has been a little surprising to me how often, once the decision is made and the call extended, the Lord sends what I call a "confirmation"

---

* This model will be discussed in much greater detail in future chapters, so more will not be said of it here.

or a "second witness." It is a second witness because the first comes during the selection process. Again, these are not great or dramatic experiences, but just quiet ways the Lord lets us know, once more, that His will was achieved. It may come when the wife says something that indicates that she had received some feelings about what was coming. Or the candidate may make a comment that causes the two visiting authorities to look at each other and smile, because it fits perfectly with something they had talked about earlier. It may come in the setting-apart blessing or in a host of other ways.

The Lord gives to many of us the still, small voice of revelation. It comes as vividly and strongly as though it were with a great sound.

HEBER J. GRANT,
GOSPEL STANDARDS, 30

There was one challenging case where an Area Seventy and I were assigned to reorganize the stake presidency in a stake that had some peculiar and rather pressing needs, and we felt particularly concerned that it be done right. This was in a country where I didn't speak the language, and so I had to have the Area Seventy translate for me throughout the proceedings. That complicated it for me, adding to my concern that it be done right. During the interviews, we both felt good about one of the bishops, and upon receiving the quiet assurance that this was right, we called him to be the stake president. But even as he accepted and his wife expressed her support for him, I can remember thinking to myself, "O Lord, this feels right, but this is so important. I hope we read Thy inspiration correctly."

Then at the end of our interview, as he stood up to leave, he said to us, "Well, now I understand the dream I had the other night." At the questioning look on our faces, he explained. He said that in his dream he saw himself in the stake president's office sitting across the desk from the current president. This was not unusual for him because he was a bishop and was often with the stake president. "But," he went on, "as we finished our meeting and I stood up to go, the president also stood up, removed his suit coat, and came around the desk and placed it around my shoulders."

As he said that, I immediately thought of the prophet Elijah placing his mantle on Elisha to signal that Elisha was chosen by the Lord to carry on the work after Elijah was taken. I instantly offered a silent prayer of thanks for that "second witness." The man we had called was indeed the man the Lord had chosen before we even arrived. In one way it was a remarkable experience because of what it signified, but in another way the experience itself was quite ordinary. The bishop received a quiet impression to share his dream with us. He spoke in a calm tone, much as if he were telling us something about his family. For something so remarkable, it was remarkably unremarkable.

> *Many men seem to have no ear for spiritual messages nor comprehension of them when they come in common dress. . . . Expecting the spectacular, one may not be fully alerted to the constant flow of revealed communication.*
>
> Spencer W. Kimball,
> *Teachings of Spencer W. Kimball,* 457

On that day I gained a deeper appreciation for why the Lord says the still small voice can pierce the heart and cause it to burn. My heart was deeply touched that day, and I was filled with gratitude for that additional witness from the Lord. That witness indicated not only that we had understood His will regarding the new stake president, but it also told us that He was there, that He was watching over this stake, that He is indeed at the head of the Church and actively leading and directing the work of His Heavenly Father.

That is just one example of how this whole wonderful process of revelation works.

HOW DO PROPHETS, SEERS, AND REVELATORS DESCRIBE THE VOICE OF THE LORD?

In chapter 5, we examined how scriptural writers have tried to describe what the voice of the Lord is like. We will now hear from some who have experienced it and have tried to help us better understand what it is like.

While the words the Brethren use as they describe their experiences with revelation may not always perfectly clarify our understanding, they do relate to our own feelings and experiences. As we read their words we find ourselves nodding and saying, "Yes, I understand what he means there. I have experienced that myself."

Throughout this chapter and the previous one on the still small voice, we have included numerous quotes of those who have been sustained as prophets, seers, and revelators. Some of these have come in the body of the text. Others were displayed as separate quotes. From these we will extract a few descriptive phrases these brethren use as they talk about the still small voice and the voice that comes into our minds and hearts. We will not try to further define what these phrases mean but will let their words stand on their own. In all cases, "it" refers to the voice of the Lord.

Joseph Smith:

It yields the fruits of the kingdom.
If our hearts are open it brings conviction.
It whispers consolation to the soul.

Boyd K. Packer:

It caresses gently.
It is a sweet, quiet voice of inspiration.
It comes more as a feeling than as a sound.
Pure intelligence can be spoken into the mind.

Joseph Fielding Smith:

It can be as deep and meaningful as anything tangible.
It is penetrating.

Spencer W. Kimball:

It comes as deep, unassailable impressions that settle on the mind as dew from heaven.

They are deep feelings.

It is an impressive consciousness of direction from above.

Dallin H. Oaks:

It can take the form of enlightenment of the mind.

It can come as positive or negative feelings about how to act.

It can uplift our emotions.

Harold B. Lee:

It is not audible to our physical hearing.

Joseph B. Wirthlin:

It enters quietly into our mind and heart.

It is so simple and precise we assume it is our own idea or a passing thought.

As we reconcile these whisperings to what we know to be true, we learn to recognize them.

IN SUMMARY

So there it is:

• The voice of the Lord is still, small, and whispers.
• The Holy Ghost speaks to us in our minds and in our hearts.

But are these statements really two different descriptions of the Lord's voice? *Or are they merely two different ways of expressing the same idea?* The fact that the voice of the Lord comes most frequently through thoughts and feelings, which are easily missed or mistaken for something of our own, is just another way of saying that the voice is still and small and whispers.

Why is it a *still* voice? Perhaps precisely because it speaks to us through thoughts and feelings rather than audible words.

Why is it a *small* voice? Could that be because it comes as such a mild, gentle feeling, it seems small and insignificant compared to our other emotions? And these feelings or thoughts are so subtle, so indirect, so like our everyday experiences, it is as though the Lord were *whispering* them to us in the midst of a tumult of other sounds.

CHAPTER 8

How Does Revelation Typically Come?
I. As Thoughts

"I will tell you in your mind" (D&C 8:2).

THE LESS DIRECT FORMS OF REVELATION

Our purpose in this chapter is to explore the more common, but less direct and dramatic, forms of revelation. These are the experiences that fall to the left half of the spectrum of revelation.

Before doing so, however, several observations and cautions should be noted.

- We need to say at the outset that it is not possible to list and describe all the various ways in which revelation comes. Revelation is so intensely personal that it changes in some degree for each individual.
- Even though revelation is so varied, we will try to group it into some general categories of experience.
- All of the examples used in this and other chapters are actual experiences. A few come from the scriptures and a few from General Authorities, but the large majority are from what some might call "the common, everyday member" of the Church.

- With few exceptions, we will not give the identity of individuals, so the focus can be on the experience, not the person. Published accounts would be an exception to that, of course.
- Many of these experiences are quite commonplace. In some cases, the revelation seems to come almost at random, unrelated to any particular spiritual quest.

With these preliminary observations in mind then, here are the five groupings of revelatory experiences. Each category will be treated in a separate chapter. The five categories are these:

- Revelation that comes to the mind as thoughts
- Revelation that comes to the mind as enlightenment and understanding
- Revelation that comes as feelings
- Revelation that gives warning and protection
- Revelation that comes through the influencing of events and circumstances (as divine intervention)

While there is some overlap in these categories—especially the first three—there is still some value in treating them separately as we seek to better understand what it feels like when revelation comes to us.

REVELATION THAT COMES TO
THE MIND AS THOUGHTS

We spent considerable time in the last chapter explaining what it means to have thoughts given to us through the Spirit. The Lord said that the Holy Ghost often speaks to our mind (see D&C 8:2). Thoughts from the Lord usually come without any distinct markers or emphasis. Typically they come in nonverbal form, as ideas more than sentences. However, there are times when actual words and sentences are given. The challenge is learning to recognize them for what they are when they do come.

From the following examples, we see that even in this particular category there are various kinds of experiences, such as having thoughts come into our minds, having things brought to our remembrance, "hearing" a voice in our mind, and so forth. Many of these examples are written in the first person because this is how they were shared with me.

Take the Friend. The following was shared by an auxiliary leader:

> One Sunday while I was serving as Primary president, as I was just leaving the house I had a quick thought to bring my *Friend* magazine with me. I didn't usually bring it, unless I was teaching in Sharing Time, which I wasn't this day. I didn't recognize it as a prompting, but I did put the magazine with my things for church. When I got to Primary, I learned that my counselor, who was teaching Sharing Time, had forgotten hers and needed it for her lesson. To be perfectly honest, it would not have ruined her lesson if she didn't have the magazine, but it did make it easier for her. I just assumed afterwards that it was the Spirit that prompted me to bring the magazine, since there was a need for it later.

What is revelation? It is the inspiration of the Holy Ghost to man. Joseph Smith said to Brother John Taylor in his day: "Brother Taylor, you watch the impression of the Spirit of God; you watch the whisperings of the Spirit to you; you carry them out in your life, and [this] will become a principle of revelation in you, and you will know and understand this spirit and power." This is the key, the foundation stone of all revelation. . . . In my own experience I have endeavored to get acquainted with that Spirit, and to learn its operations.

WILFORD WOODRUFF,
DISCOURSES OF WILFORD WOODRUFF, 45–46

This is an example of something relatively minor. Nevertheless, by responding to that thought, she added something to what the children were taught that day. Does the Spirit really help us with such small matters? It certainly seems so.

Heavenly Father Knew What I Needed. From a woman with a unique need, which could be described as a trivial matter:

> My husband was in graduate school full time and, with me being a stay-at-home mom, our finances were pretty tight. The washing machine had gone out and we didn't have money to call a repairman. I had asked my husband to fix it, but he was under a tight deadline to complete a project and said I would have to wait until the weekend—four more days! As my laundry stacked up, I felt more and more frustration and despair. Finally one morning I folded my arms on top of my washing machine, bowed my head, and said a simple prayer. "Heavenly Father, I am overwhelmed by laundry. I can't afford to hire a repairman and my husband is unavailable. If it is Thy will, couldst Thou help *me* to know how to fix my washer?"
>
> I lifted my head and felt prompted to open the washing machine. I then lifted off the top. (I hadn't even known it came off.) I looked down at all those parts, and my eyes focused on one particular part. I felt this was the part with the problem. I lifted it out and took it to a parts store. I placed it on the counter and said to the man, "I don't know what it's called. I don't even know what it does. But I need a new one of these." He brought me the part, which cost about $4. I returned home, put it in place, and my washer worked great. You wouldn't think a broken washer would be that important to the Lord, but He knew it was important to me, and so He blessed me with the inspiration to know how to fix it.

Note her language here. "I felt *prompted.*" "He blessed me with *inspiration.*" But how did that inspiration actually come to her? It came as thoughts. Later she told me that she had reservations during this experience. Was it even right to ask for His help in such matters? But when she returned and found that it was the right part and that the washing machine worked, she had her answer to those questions.

Virtually every faithful Latter-day Saint can share experiences where a thought comes into their mind, quietly, without fanfare, barely noticed if one is preoccupied with other things. And it is frequently accompanied by that very question. "Lord, is this really from Thee?"

- A bishop sitting on the stand in sacrament meeting looks out on his congregation. As he notices one member the thought comes, "You need to talk with him or her."
- Our minds are fully engaged in an engrossing task of one kind or another. We are totally concentrating and focused. Then, as if it were thrown through the window of our mind, a thought completely unrelated to anything we were doing comes. It may be instruction; it may be an answer; it may contain direction.

President Thomas S. Monson shares an experience like that which had significant consequences for a friend:

> Stan, a dear friend of mine, was stricken by cancer. He had been robust in health, athletic in build, and active in many pursuits. Now he was unable to walk or to stand. His wheelchair was his home. The finest of physicians had cared for him, and the prayers of family and friends had been offered in a spirit of hope and trust. Yet Stan continued to lie in the confinement of his bed at University Hospital.
>
> Late one afternoon I was swimming at Deseret Gym, gazing at the ceiling while backstroking width after width. Silently, but ever so clearly, *there came to my mind the thought:* "Here you swim almost effortlessly, while your friend Stan is unable to move." I felt the prompting: "Get to the hospital and give him a blessing."
>
> I ceased my swimming, dressed, and hurried to Stan's room at the hospital. His bed was empty. A nurse said he was in his wheelchair at the swimming pool, preparing for

therapy. I hurried to the area, and there was Stan, all alone, at the edge of the deeper portion of the pool. We greeted each other and returned to his room, where a priesthood blessing was provided. Slowly but surely, strength and movement returned to Stan's legs. First he could stand on faltering feet. Then he learned once again to walk, step by step. Today one would not know that Stan had lain so close to death and with no hope of recovery. . . .

That day Stan learned literally that we do not walk alone. I too learned a lesson that day: never, never, never postpone a prompting.[1]

How Did You Know? Another way thoughts come into our mind and provide revelation is through the giving of blessings. One leader described an experience he had while filling an assignment from his stake president.

> We were setting apart a committee that had been called to plan the annual YSA convention. The stake president had asked me to assist him in setting apart each member of the committee. One young woman sat down on the chair before me. I had never met her before and knew nothing about her. I laid my hands on her head and proceeded with the setting apart and blessing. In the midst of the blessing, a couple of times I found myself saying things that surprised me a little. They weren't anything dramatic, but they just came into my mind, and so I expressed them. When I finished, the young woman stood up and turned around to face me. To my surprise, tears were trickling down her cheeks. "How did you know?" she whispered. "I have been deeply troubled about a question and have been fasting and praying about it for some time. And tonight in your blessing, you gave me exactly the answer I needed. How did you know?" I didn't know, I told her, and I assured her that it wasn't me that gave

her the answer. It came from the Lord. It was His way of letting her know that He knew her, and loved her, and was answering her prayers.

BRINGING THINGS TO OUR REMEMBRANCE

While speaking to the Twelve in the Upper Room, the Savior promised them that the Holy Ghost would "bring all things to your remembrance" (John 14:26). Having things brought to our remembrance usually occurs by having the Lord suddenly place thoughts into our minds. These are not new thoughts, as in our previous examples, but rather a remembering of something known before but temporarily forgotten. Here is an example of how this can happen.

The Holy Ghost brings back memories of what God has taught us. And one of the ways God teaches us is with his blessings; and so, if we choose to exercise faith, the Holy Ghost will bring God's kindnesses to our remembrance.

HENRY B. EYRING,
ENSIGN, NOVEMBER 1989, 11

I Forgot to Call Your Sister. A woman, whom we will call Mary, had long-term problems having children. After a long search, she finally found a doctor, whom we'll call Dr. Johnson, who was able to successfully diagnose the cause and prescribe a treatment that brought the couple the wonderful blessing of having four additional children. Mary had a younger sister named Barbara, who lived in another state. Barbara was able to have children, but with each successive pregnancy, it became more difficult and eventually she had trouble carrying a child to full term, losing them at four or four-and-a-half months. After Barbara had suffered several miscarriages, Mary one day wondered if Dr. Johnson might be of help to Barbara. While the family was together in Utah for the Christmas holidays, the two sisters talked about this possibility. Though the apparent cause of their problems seemed quite different on the surface, they decided it was worth at least an inquiry. They agreed that Mary would contact Dr. Johnson, explain the situation, and see if there was anything he might do. Since it was the holidays, it was not possible to contact him until after Barbara had returned home again, but Mary did so the first day the doctor was back in the office.

After hearing Barbara's symptoms, Dr. Johnson said he wasn't sure if he could help, but he took Barbara's number and promised to call and talk to Barbara personally. Months went by and nothing happened. In the busyness of life, neither sister got around to following up, and Barbara decided the doctor had determined he couldn't help her and that was why there had been no call.

About five months later, Barbara and her family were back in Utah for a wedding. At a family gathering on Sunday evening, Barbara let it be known that she was newly pregnant once again. She expressed concerns about whether her doctors would be able to help prevent another miscarriage. That of course reminded Mary that Dr. Johnson had never called Barbara. Mary determined she would call him the next morning while Barbara was still in town. However, the next morning, before Mary could follow through on that promise, her phone rang. It was Dr. Johnson. "I am so embarrassed," he began, "but I was sitting here at my desk working on some things this morning, and suddenly, out of the blue, I had this thought flash into my mind. 'You never called Mary's sister as you promised you would.' I feel awful," he said. "I completely forgot, but if you'll give me her number again, I'll call her." But Mary knew why he had suddenly remembered. She told him that Barbara was in town at that very moment. Dr. Johnson called Barbara and two days later, Barbara was in his office for a consultation.*

---

* This event happened at the time this book was being written, and there has not been sufficient time yet to report whether Barbara was able to carry the baby to full term. But one thing has occurred since the paragraphs above were written. In their consultation, Dr. Johnson told Barbara to have her local doctor check the levels of a certain hormone in her body. She made the request, but the doctor said he had previously checked them and they were fine. Barbara called Dr. Johnson back to report, but he was absolutely insistent. "Get those levels checked, and do it now." When they did so, they found that they were at a dangerously low level. An injection was given and the baby was stabilized. As this book goes to press, Barbara is into the sixth month of pregnancy and is still carrying the baby.

A VOICE IN THE MIND

What we find in some accounts is more than just a thought or an impression that comes into the mind. Some people have revelation that they describe as being like someone is speaking in their mind. These experiences seem to come as actual sentences, as clearly defined direction, or answers to a question. Enos described it thus: *"The voice of the Lord came into my mind"* (Enos 1:10).

"It Was As Though Something Were Saying to Me . . ." President Harold B. Lee, some years before he became a General Authority, was asked by the First Presidency to create a program that would help care for the Saints in the midst of the Great Depression. He later reported:

This [experience of Enos] is a very common means of revelation. It comes into one's mind in words and sentences. With this medium of revelation I am personally well acquainted.

MARION G. ROMNEY,
CONFERENCE REPORT,
APRIL 1964, 124

> There I was, just a young man in my thirties. My experience had been limited. I was born in a little country town in Idaho. . . . And now to put me in a position where I was to reach out to the entire membership of the Church, worldwide, was one of the most staggering contemplations that I could imagine. How could I do it with my limited understanding?
>
> As I knelt down, my petition was, "What kind of an organization should be set up in order to accomplish what the Presidency has assigned?" And there came to me on that glorious morning one of the most heavenly realizations of the power of the priesthood of God. It was as though something were saying to me, "There is no new organization necessary to take care of the needs of this people. All that is necessary is to put the priesthood of God to work. There is nothing else that you need as a substitute."

With that understanding, then, and with the simple application of the power of the priesthood, the welfare program has gone forward now by leaps and bounds, overcoming obstacles that seemed impossible, until now it stands as a monument to the power of the priesthood.[2]

Psalm 100. Elder B. H. Roberts of the First Council of the Seventy was serving as a reserve chaplain in the Utah National Guard when his unit was called to active duty in World War I. Thus he became the first full-time LDS chaplain to serve in the military. While serving in France, he had an unusual experience in hearing the voice of the Lord.

On Thanksgiving Day 1918 a worship service was arranged by representative chaplains from the major denominations. Roberts was assigned a seat at the rear of the review stand and had not been asked to participate on the program. During the service the conducting officer abruptly announced, "Elder Roberts, the Mormon chaplain from Utah, will now step up and lead the Thanksgiving Psalm." Dazed, Roberts arose and walked forward; he was familiar with the Psalms but not with that title. The *impression then came* that he should read "The One Hundredth Psalm." Opening his Bible he read aloud the lines:

We do not realize the implications of what we ask. We ask amiss and then wonder why such petitions are not granted precisely as submitted. . . . Those who are meek experience, on occasion, not knowing what to "pray for as [they] ought." Instead they let the Spirit itself make intercession. (Romans 8:26.) . . . "And they did not multiply many words, for it was given unto them what they should pray, and they were filled with desire." (3 Nephi 19:24.) "He that asketh in the Spirit asketh according to the will of God; wherefore it is done even as he asketh." (D&C 46:30.)

NEAL A. MAXWELL,
MEEK AND LOWLY, 10

"Make a joyful noise unto the Lord, all ye lands. Serve the Lord with gladness: come before his presence with singing. Know ye that the Lord he is God: it is he that hath made us, and not we ourselves; we are his people, and the sheep of his pasture.

"Enter into his gates with thanksgiving, and into his courts with praise; be thankful unto him, and bless his name. For the Lord is good; his mercy is everlasting; and his truth endureth to all generations."

Returning to his seat, Roberts noticed that his fellow chaplains were looking not at him but at the floor. He concluded that this public invitation had been an attempt to embarrass him and the Church. Back at his tent he knelt in prayer, thanking the Lord for coming to his aid in this moment of need.[3]

"Pray for a Miracle." Here is a more dramatic example of a voice in the mind. However, it is dramatic more because of the results than in the way the revelation came to the woman telling the experience.

We had struggled to grow our family. Having babies didn't come as easily to us as to others. But after undergoing an in vitro procedure, I was finally pregnant for only the second time in ten years. We were overjoyed. At 17 weeks, I did a routine AFP testing, which screens for birth defects. A few days later, I received a call from my doctor. "Sheri," he said, his voice grave. "I've just received the results from your AFP test. The marker that indicates the presence of neural tube defects such as encephalitis, hydrocephalus, or spina bifida, is quite high. I am greatly concerned. I have never seen a reading this high in my 30 years as an OB. I want you to come in Monday for an ultrasound." Then he said, "Sheri, this is not a matter of *if* there is a problem, but only how

73

extensive the problem will be. Your baby may die at birth or she may spend her life in a wheelchair."

I hung up the phone and started to cry. I fell to my knees and prayed for what must have been an hour. I poured out my heart to the Lord. Gradually, my prayers began to change. I prayed for strength to accept the Lord's will. I prayed for strength to deal with whatever challenges this was going to bring into our lives. But as I was saying this, *I felt Heavenly Father say to me, "Pray for a miracle."* I was so surprised by that. It had never occurred to me to pray for a miracle. But that night I began to pray for a miracle.

On Monday morning, my husband and I arrived at the office. The doctor had procured the finest ultrasound technician he could find. The technician spent an hour. She examined the brain, every vertebra in the back, all of the organs. She searched again and again. She couldn't find a single thing that was abnormal. When we came out of the ultrasound room, there were three grim-faced doctors waiting to hear the dire results. When the technician reported what she had *not* found, my doctor, with tears in his eyes, said, "Go home and testify that you have witnessed a miracle, for there is no mistake, no coincidence. This is nothing short of a miracle." Five months later I gave birth to a beautiful baby girl who was normal in every way. Even now, some eight years later, we still call her our miracle baby.

DREAMS

Here we use the word "dream" in the same sense that it is used in the world—it is an experience of the mind that occurs while we are sleeping but is still remembered after awakening. Not all dreams are revelatory in nature, of course.

On the other hand, there is no question but what from time to time the Lord does use dreams as a means of communicating with us.

Through dreams we may receive direction, be warned of some danger or threat, or see something that helps us prepare for some future happening in our lives. President Harold B. Lee said of dreams:

> There's one more way by which revelations may come, and that is by dreams. Oh, I'm not going to tell you that every dream you have is a direct revelation from the Lord—it may be fried liver and onions that have been responsible for an upset or disorder. But I fear that in this age of sophistication there are those of us who are prone to rule out all dreams as of no purpose, and of no moment. . . . We too may have a dream that may direct us as a revelation.[4]

Dreams differ from the other examples of revelation in that in dreams we receive information through the visual images we experience in our minds. We "see" things in the dream that become revelatory to us when we awaken. Since dreams occur much less frequently than the forms of revelation discussed above, we will note only a few examples.

The Mission to England. When Heber C. Kimball arrived in Preston, England in 1837, he found that some of the people there had seen him and his fellow missionaries in dreams and recognized them immediately upon meeting them for the first time.[5]

Something Important to Your Family. Ten years before being baptized, a woman from Iceland had a dream in which her deceased father appeared and said to her, "Mya, you will later do something in a foreign country that will be very important for your family." She had no idea what he meant until twenty-nine years later, when she went to the London Temple and did the temple work for her deceased ancestors.[6]

A Copy of the Liahona. When she was fifteen years old, a young Brazilian woman had a dream in which she saw Jesus sitting on a large rock and teaching a group of people. Sixteen years later a copy of the *Liahona* was put into her hands, and she was astonished to see on the cover a picture of Jesus that was exactly the same scene she had seen in her dream.[7]

CONFIRMATION

There is a common element in most of these examples we have shared. Even though some of the individuals wondered if their experience was really from the Spirit, in almost every case they had at least some kind of confirmation that this was more than just their own thinking. Sometimes the confirming experience wasn't particularly dramatic, but it was still there. In some cases the confirmation doesn't follow immediately, but eventually it comes.

The Lord allows things to work out so that, if we are sensitive, if we are paying attention, we have an experience that serves to witness to us that the Spirit truly was working with us. B. H. Roberts was directed to a perfect "Psalm of Thanksgiving"; the woman from Iceland did the temple work for her ancestors and remembered the dream of her father; the doctor remembered that he was supposed to call Barbara at the very time she was back in town. And so it is again and again.

Sometimes a witness comes to show that something we thought was revelation really wasn't. But this "negative confirmation," if we may call it that, is another way we learn. I think with some ruefulness of one example from my own life that was a gentle lesson in not letting one's own feelings get in the way of revelation. Our third daughter had submitted her mission papers and was waiting for her call. At that time my wife and I were in Hong Kong training teachers for the Church Educational System. The area director for CES had invited Elder Monte J. Brough, who was then serving as Area President for Asia, to speak to the group. In his talk, he told of how Mongolia had been opened for the Church. It was a remarkable and inspiring story. He concluded by saying, "And we have just learned this week that the first full-time missionaries from America have been called to come to Mongolia." I felt a thrill of exultation. I looked at my wife and said, "That's where Lori's going. She's going to Mongolia." It felt so right—the timing of her call, us being in Asia to hear Elder Brough's account. As soon as we got back to our hotel, we called home to Lori. "Did you get your call?" I asked excitedly. "Yes." I held my breath. "Where to?" There was a pause, and then, "I'm going to Raleigh, North Carolina."

So much for my feeling of exultation. So much for feeling it was so right. Clearly I had let my emotions get the best of me, but within a short time I knew that I was wrong. What I had felt was not from the Lord. It was pure me. I received a "negative confirmation."

IN SUMMARY

We have shown that in the great majority of these cases, the Lord also helps us identify those experiences that are from Him (or not). The experiences shared in this chapter are generally quite subtle and indirect when compared to a vision or a visitation. But they are of great importance, for they show that the Spirit directs, protects, warns, guides, and blesses us in simple, everyday ways.

President Harold B. Lee summarized very well the breadth of ways the Lord blesses us. He said:

> The Lord will guide us if we live right. The thing that all of us should strive for is to so live, keeping the commandments of the Lord, that He can answer our prayers, the prayers of our loved ones, the prayers of the General Authorities, for us. . . . If we will live worthy, then the Lord will guide us—by a personal appearance, or by His actual voice, or by His voice coming into our mind, or by impressions upon our heart and our soul. And oh, how grateful we ought to be if the Lord sends us a dream in which are revealed to us the beauties of the eternity or a warning and direction for our special comfort. Yes, if we so live, the Lord will guide us for our salvation and for our benefit.[8]

CHAPTER 9

How Does Revelation Typically Come?
II. As Enlightenment

"I will impart unto you of my Spirit, which shall enlighten your mind" (D&C 11:13).

LIGHT, ENLIGHTENMENT, AND ILLUMINATION

In one of the early sections of the Doctrine and Covenants, we are told of another function of the Spirit.

> I am the *light* which shineth in darkness. . . .
>
> Verily, verily, I say unto you, I will impart unto you of my Spirit, *which shall enlighten your mind,* which shall fill your soul with joy;
>
> And then shall ye *know,* or by this [the Spirit] shall you know, all things whatsoever you desire of me (D&C 11:11, 13–14).

There is an interesting play on words here. Both in mortality and after the Resurrection, Christ declared Himself to be the light of the world (see John 8:12; 3 Nephi 11:11).[1] Here He tells us that one of the functions of the Holy Ghost is to en*light*en our minds. *Light* and *enlightenment*—they are closely related concepts.

When we consider what revelation is by definition—the

communication of light and truth from the mind of God to the mind of man—we begin to see some interesting links, which better help us understand this process we call revelation.

The concept of enlightenment is found throughout the scriptures in phrases like, "*enlightened by the Spirit* of God" (Alma 24:30); "by my Spirit *will I enlighten* them" (D&C 76:10); or "the commandment of the Lord is pure, *enlightening the eyes*" (Psalm 19:8).

Frequently the idea of enlightenment is found in tandem with the concept of *understanding.* For example: "The word is good, for it beginneth to enlarge my soul; yea, it *beginneth to enlighten my understanding*" (Alma 32:28); "*Your understanding doth begin to be enlightened,* and your mind doth begin to expand" (Alma 32:34; see also Ephesians 1:18).

And as if that isn't enough for us to contemplate, two additional concepts are also closely linked with enlightenment, and those are *knowledge* and *wisdom.* After telling us that the Holy Ghost will enlighten our minds, the Lord then says: "Then shall ye *know*" (D&C 11:14). Listed with the gifts of the Spirit are both knowledge and wisdom so "that all may be taught *to be wise and to have knowledge*" (D&C 46:17–18).

Those various words—*revelation, enlightenment, understanding, knowledge, wisdom*—taken together define yet another way in which the Lord speaks to us through the Spirit. But this form of revelation differs significantly from having thoughts come to us or even having sentences spoken in our minds. Enlightenment and understanding are more complex, more comprehensive, more profound and have much greater influence than mere thoughts.

> *The Spirit of God speaking to the spirit of man has power to impart truth with greater effect and understanding than the truth can be imparted by personal contact even with heavenly beings. Through the Holy Ghost the truth is woven into the very fibre and sinews of the body so that it cannot be forgotten.*
>
> JOSEPH FIELDING SMITH,
> *DOCTRINES OF SALVATION,* 1:47–48

Perhaps this analogy will help us better see the difference between the two. When we are reading a book, information and knowledge are conveyed from the writer to our intellect in a linear fashion; that is, the knowledge comes one word and concept at a time and in a sequential order. This happens very swiftly, of course, and our mind processes these linear "bits" into comprehensive, complex thinking patterns. As an example, consider what a writer does when he or she describes a specific place or setting for us. Word by word he begins to build a mental image of that place. As we process those individual words, our mind is able to envision to some degree what is being described.

However, when that same book is transformed into a movie and the scene that was so carefully described on the page is now shown on the screen, the information is conveyed to us holistically, all at once. We see color, shape, relationship, and movement as a whole, rather than in a linear fashion.

In a similar way, when we receive revelation through enlightenment and understanding it differs from thoughts coming into our mind in a fundamentally and significantly different way. When the Spirit puts a thought into our minds, it comes as a small piece or bit of information that we then integrate into other things we know or are thinking. But when the Spirit enlightens our mind, it is like putting a picture on the screen. We suddenly "see" the whole scene, the whole complexity at the same moment, and our mind processes it in a very different way than individual thoughts.

Years ago, in a religion class at Brigham Young University, a professor also used the metaphor of light to try to help us better understand how the Holy Spirit works and our part in making the most of those times when He is functioning with us. He likened our minds to a room into which we enter and turn on the light. The light provides illumination that then allows us to see whatever is in the room. If the room is bare, without

> *The greatest of all testimonies is the illumination of the soul by the gift and power of the Holy Ghost.*
>
> ORSON F. WHITNEY,
> CONFERENCE REPORT,
> APRIL 1930, 135

furniture, carpet, pictures on the wall, and so forth, we will see the room clearly, but we will only see a sparse, bare room. However, if the room is richly furnished, by that same illumination, we are enabled to see so much more than we could in the first instance.

Another synonym for light or enlightenment is *illumination.* Thus, if the Holy Ghost enlightens us, it could be said that the Holy Ghost is an Illuminator, and even though we can't define how He does it, we know that He does illuminate (that is, bring light) to our minds.

With that introduction, let us now look at various ways the Lord enlightens our minds and expands our understanding.

STROKES OF IDEAS

The Prophet Joseph Smith taught:

> A person may profit by noticing the first intimation of the spirit of revelation; for instance, when you feel *pure intelligence* flowing into you, it may give you *sudden strokes of ideas,* so that by noticing it, you may find it fulfilled the same day or soon; (i.e.) those things that were presented unto your minds by the Spirit of God, will come to pass.[2]

These strokes of intelligence or bursts of light and truth can come to us in many ways, and many members of the Church experience this form of revelation regularly. Here are just a few examples:

- A teacher is preparing his lesson, pondering the meaning of a particularly difficult passage, when sudden light and understanding flood into his mind, and he understands that specific passage in a new way.
- In ward council, a difficult issue is being discussed. One person makes a simple comment, and that is like turning on a light in the room.
- Illumination may come from the words of someone else, such as a speaker in sacrament meeting or a teacher in a class. He or she

makes a simple statement, but it is as though the Lord puts a spotlight on those words in our minds. They come with great impact, and our minds expand with understanding.

AHA! EXPERIENCES

Some years ago psychologists coined a phrase to describe a unique learning experience—they called them "Aha! experiences." This seems to be another way of saying what Joseph said when he talked about sudden strokes of ideas. These experiences come when the mind is wrestling with some kind of challenge or problem. It might be trying to understand a complex formula, see the relationship of mechanical functions, write a brilliant piece of music, or know what to say to a teenager who's making things difficult at the moment. Then in a moment, something clicks—some people say it's like your mind makes "half a turn"—and understanding comes, the solution is there, the music is conceived. These moments are so remarkable, and so satisfying for us, that we may actually give a soft cry of "Ah!" or "Aha!" Thus the name, "Aha! experiences."

This Is Really True! Here is an experience shared by a Gospel Doctrine teacher:

> We were talking about the principle of faith. The discussion had been going well, with good participation from the class. Then one of the brethren raised his hand and asked me a question about how faith would be applied in a certain situation he was facing. It was a very thought-provoking question, and one I had never thought of before. For a moment, I was stumped. But then an idea came. I picked up the chalk and turned to the board. I then began to sketch out this simple flow chart on the board, putting in statements about each step in the process as we went. About halfway into it, it suddenly came to me, even as I was drawing it on the board and talking: "Hey! This is good! *This is really true!*"

That's when I knew that this wasn't coming from me. Both the class and I were being taught by the Spirit.

That Can't Be Right! After I shared the concept of "Aha! experiences" with a group of teachers, one of them shared this experience with me. This had occurred during his own personal scripture study some years before:

> I was studying the Doctrine and Covenants and was reading along in Doctrine and Covenants 10. Then I came to verse 55, which reads: "Therefore, whosoever belongeth to my church need not fear, for such shall inherit the kingdom of heaven." I stopped dead and read it again, then a third time. I found myself shaking my head in puzzlement. "That can't be right," I thought. "All one has to do is be a member of the Church and they will inherit the kingdom of heaven? How can that be?" I thought about it for another minute or two but finally gave up. It was the Lord speaking, so it had to be true, but it didn't make sense.
>
> I pushed the thought away and went on with my reading. A few moments later, I came to verse 67 and read: "Behold, this is my doctrine—whosoever repenteth and cometh unto me, *the same is my church.*" I almost jumped, it hit me so forcefully. The problem wasn't with the Lord, it was with me. I was putting my definition

> *The Lord will increase our knowledge, wisdom, and capacity to obey when we obey His fundamental laws. This is what the Prophet Joseph Smith meant when he said we could have "sudden strokes of ideas" which come into our minds as "pure intelligence." . . . This is revelation. We must learn to rely on the Holy Ghost so we can use it to guide our lives and the lives of those for whom we have responsibility.*
>
> EZRA TAFT BENSON,
> *TEACHINGS OF EZRA TAFT BENSON,* 114

on the word "church," thinking that it was defined by having a membership record. The Lord's definition was much more profound. Now it made perfect sense. Membership is not what counts with the Lord but faith and repentance and discipleship.

THE GIFT OF DISCERNMENT

One of the gifts of the Spirit mentioned in the scriptures is that of discernment (see D&C 46:23, 27; 63:41). The Lord told Oliver Cowdery that only God knows the thoughts and intents of our hearts (D&C 6:16). This ability to discern what is in the mind or heart of another is a remarkable manifestation of the Holy Spirit. Stephen L Richards, a member of the First Presidency, explained what this gift is:

> This gift, . . . when highly developed arises largely out of an acute sensitivity to impressions—spiritual impressions, if you will—to read under the surface as it were, to detect hidden evil, and more importantly to find the good that may be concealed. The highest type of discernment is that which perceives in others and uncovers for them their better natures, the good inherent within them.[3]

This is another example of how the Spirit speaks to our mind. However, again this kind of experience is different from just having a thought come into our heads. Discernment implies knowledge, understanding, and enlightenment. While examples of this gift are found throughout the scriptures, there are two wonderful examples of this in the Book of Mormon.

Alma, Amulek, and Zeezrom. Alma and Amulek were preaching to the hard-hearted people of Ammonihah. As Amulek was speaking, the lawyers, described as "learned in all the arts and cunning of the people" tried to cross him, to trip him up, to make him "contradict the words which he should speak." But, as Mormon records, "Now they knew not that Amulek could *know of their designs.* But it came to pass as they began to question him, *he perceived their thoughts"* (Alma 10:15–17).

Ammon and King Lamoni. After Ammon, barely three days into his mission with the Lamanites, had that miraculous experience in protecting the flocks of King Lamoni, he returned to the presence of the king. Lamoni was so awestruck that he could not speak. Even when Ammon asked what the king wanted of him, Lamoni did not answer. "And it came to pass that Ammon, *being filled with the Spirit of God, therefore he perceived the thoughts of the king"* (Alma 18:16) and began to teach Lamoni.

I Knew What Was Troubling Her. An institute teacher reported his own experience with discernment:

> I was teaching a lesson on temple marriage. I was talking about the importance of remembering the "this-world" blessings of a temple marriage, and not just the "next-world" blessings. Suddenly I noticed a girl near the back of the class jerk her head away in disgust. She was frowning deeply and looked angry and sullen. She had always been a pleasant person and a model student and this sudden change came as a great surprise.
>
> In one burst of understanding I had my answer. I

didn't know anything about this girl's family situation, but in that moment I knew just as surely as I knew my own family, that her parents, who had been married in the temple

Satan has had great success with this gullible generation. As a consequence, literally hosts of people have been victimized by him and his angels. There is, however, an ample shield against the power of Lucifer and his hosts. This protection lies in the spirit of discernment through the gift of the Holy Ghost. This gift comes undeviatingly by personal revelation to those who strive to obey the commandments of the Lord and to follow the counsel of the living prophets.

James E. Faust,
Ensign, November 1987, 33

were either divorced or were moving in that direction very quickly. I immediately changed both my tone and the point I was trying to make.

I began to talk about the covenants we make in temple marriage and how these are what bring the blessings, both in this world and the next. I then testified that if we are faithful, then our marriage can truly become a celestial, eternal marriage, whether we come from a home where the parents have been sealed or from parents who are not members. As I talked, I saw her countenance begin to soften. Then I saw her nod slowly at what was being said and soon the anger was gone and she was fully participating again.

I gave silent thanks to the Spirit for letting me see into her heart that day and to know what to say to help heal it.

TESTIMONY

One of the most common forms of enlightenment and understanding is found in the simple concept of testimony. A testimony implies more than just having information about something or knowing about it. In a courtroom, a witness offers testimony of what he or she knows to be true. The same is true in a gospel sense. To have a testimony means that we believe what we know to be true and of value for us.

In its deepest expression, a testimony includes the idea of conversion. It involves (1) having a deep and comprehensive understanding of a doctrine or principle; (2) believing that principle is true and of value to us personally; and (3) incorporating that doctrine and principle into our lives.

Elder Dallin H. Oaks in a conference talk used the word "becoming" to describe the difference between a testimony and true conversion:

> It is not . . . enough for us to be *convinced* by the gospel; *we must act and think so that we are converted by it.* In contrast to the institutions of the world, which teach us to *know*

something, the gospel of Jesus Christ challenges us to *become* something. . . . The final judgment is not just an evaluation of a sum total of good and evil acts—what we have *done*. It is an acknowledgment of the final effect of our acts and *thoughts—what we have become*. It is not enough for anyone just to go through the motions. The commandments, ordinances, and covenants of the gospel are not a list of deposits required to be made in some heavenly account. *The gospel of Jesus Christ is a plan that shows us how to become what our Heavenly Father desires us to become.*[4]

Someone else once said that a true testimony begins in the head, moves to the hands, and then is transferred to the heart. In other words, first we *know*, then we *do*, and then we *become*. In the Sermon on the Mount, the Savior likened this process to building a house upon the rock.

> Whosoever heareth these sayings of mine, *and doeth them*, I will liken him unto a wise man, which built his house upon a rock: And the rain descended, and the floods came, and the winds blew, and beat upon that house; and it fell not: for it was founded upon a rock (Matthew 7:24–25).

We are discussing testimony under the umbrella of enlightenment and understanding because one of the primary functions of the Holy Spirit is to bear witness—or to testify—of the reality of the Father and the Son (see 3 Nephi 11:36).[5] This involves both intellectual and emotional processes. In other words, we get this witness both through thoughts and feelings. The Spirit conveys truth and light to our intellect, but He also quickens our understanding, softens our hearts, and helps facilitate those changes in our lives that are evidence of real conversion. These things do not happen naturally to the natural mind.

A GROWING ASSURANCE

I remember an experience we had with our youngest son. They had discussed Alma 32 in Primary one day, and each child came out of class with a Styrofoam cup in which a bean had been planted. He was excited. We had to water it carefully and place it where it would get plenty of light. The next morning, the first thing he did was head for the room where he had put the cup. Suspecting what was coming, I hurried to the door to listen. After a moment came a very disgusted, "Dumb ole seed!" We were able to talk him out of throwing it out. In a few days he was thrilled to see the first shoot of green. Then we transferred it to the garden, and eventually we ate the beans from a plant taller than he was.

The thing that gives Alma's analogy of the seed such power is that it so perfectly describes how most of us gain our testimony. For the vast majority of individuals, gaining faith is a process of slow growth and change within us. Elder Neal A. Maxwell likened trying to discern a change in our hearts to watching grass grow.[6] This is not a very dramatic form of revelation, but it is a reality and a very typical way the Spirit works with us.

Because of this very gradual and imperceptible increase in our testimony and conversion, some conclude they don't have a testimony. In many cases, it is because they are expecting something more dramatic, more discernible, more "real."

Here is an example of how these kind of feelings may cause us to be misled.

I've Never Felt Anything in Here. The second example is another experience I had with one of my own children. I came home from work one day to find my wife waiting for me at the door. "You need to talk to Julie," she said. When I asked what was wrong, she just repeated that I needed to go speak with her. Julie is our second daughter and was, I think, a junior in high school at that time. I went into the kitchen and found her crying quietly. At first she wouldn't say why, but eventually she said she was upset because she didn't have a testimony.

I was dumbfounded. From the time she was small, she had always exhibited faith and testimony. "Why do you feel like you don't have a testimony?" I asked.

She tapped her fingertips to her chest, "Because I've never felt anything in here."

"What do you mean?" I pursued. "What kind of feeling are you looking for?"

She hesitated for a moment, then said, "I'm not sure. Something like Alma the Younger, I guess."

By pressing her a little, I found out that all of this had been triggered by a lesson in seminary that day. It had been on testimony. The four examples the teacher used to teach about testimony were the Apostle Paul, Enos, Alma the Younger, and King Lamoni! No wonder she was discouraged! Those are all wonderful, powerful stories of conversion and testimony, *but they are not typical.*

"Let me ask you a question," I said. "You read your scriptures every night. We don't make you do that. So why do you?"

Receiving a big answer quickly and all at once is possible and, in fact, does occur in some exceptional circumstances. Perhaps we give overmuch emphasis to the miraculous experiences of Joseph in the Sacred Grove, of Paul on the road to Damascus, and of Alma the Younger. If our personal experiences fall short of these well-known and spiritually dramatic examples, then perhaps we believe something is wrong with or lacking in us. I am suggesting that the particular spiritual process evidenced in these three examples . . . is more rare than it is routine, more the exception than the rule.

DAVID A. BEDNAR,
RICKS COLLEGE DEVOTIONAL,
SEPTEMBER 11, 2001, 3

She looked at me like I was daft. "Because I love to read the scriptures."

"And how many days are you consecutive now?" (In her seminary, they had a reading program where if you read the scriptures every day, you were "consecutive.")

Her answer was something like "Three hundred and twenty-one."

"Your Young Women's advisor told me the other day she can always count on you to stay after an activity and help with cleanup. Why do you do that?"

Again she seemed a little vexed by my question. "Well, someone has to do it, don't they?"

Then, near tears myself, I said to this sweet young woman, "Julie, did it ever occur to you that the way you are living is evidence that you do have a testimony?"

She just shook her head. She had not thought of it in those terms at all. And then at last she saw it. After a moment she smiled and said softly, "Thanks, Dad."

Julie, now long married with teens of her own, and I were recently speaking of this problem. Many youth seem to go through a period of wondering if they have a "real" testimony. Often, their uncertainty comes because they compare themselves to others who have had more dramatic and defined confirmations. She used a wonderful analogy that ties directly to our idea of illumination and enlightenment.

When the Holy Ghost brings light and knowledge to the mind, it is like He floods a room with bright sunlight. Children who grow up in active, faithful homes grow up in that sunlit room. Light and truth is all around them every day. So when the Holy Spirit begins to bring light and knowledge to their own minds, it doesn't seem that remarkable. In some cases, it is so much like the light they have known all their lives that they barely even notice the light now found within themselves.

Compare that to a person who has been living in the darkness of the world, such as Paul, Alma the Younger, King Lamoni, new investigators, a child who has grown up in a less-active home, and so on. When the Holy Ghost fills their mind with light and truth, it is such a dramatic contrast to what they've known before that it becomes a very unusual and remarkable experience for them. It isn't that their testimony is any more real than the testimony of those already in the sunlight, but it may be much more vivid and discernible to them when it comes.

90

IN SUMMARY

In addition to giving us light and knowledge in the more common form of thoughts coming into our minds, the Lord speaks to our minds in another way. The scriptures call this process "enlightenment," which suggests that light and knowledge is conveyed to our minds and hearts. The Spirit actually illuminates our minds in a way we cannot fully describe, but with that illumination comes light, knowledge, comprehension, testimony, and conversion.

CHAPTER 10

How Does Revelation Typically Come?

III. As Feelings

"I will tell you . . . in your heart" (D&C 8:2).

FEELINGS AND EMOTIONS

As noted earlier, the Lord defined the spirit of revelation as occurring when the Holy Ghost speaks to our minds and hearts (D&C 8:2–3). We have discussed how revelation can come to our minds. We will now look at the other half of the equation: how the Lord speaks to our *hearts.*

We have already cited several scriptures or statements by the Brethren that say that the Holy Ghost speaks in a voice that is more felt than heard. We saw how Laman and Lemuel had reached the point where they could not *feel* His words (1 Nephi 17:45). There is something about this Spirit-to-spirit communication that is intricately involved with the seat of our own emotions. Elder Packer has said that "in your emotions, the spirit and the body come closest to being one."[1] On another occasion he wrote: "The spiritual part of us and the emotional part of us are so closely linked that it is possible to mistake an emotional impulse for something spiritual."[2]

Clearly delineating between our own emotions and those feelings that come from the Lord is as challenging as distinguishing between our own thoughts and the thoughts that come through the Spirit. However, this does not mean it is impossible to do so. As in the previous chapter, we will do this largely by using examples from real life and letting people try to describe in their own words how revelation *feels*.

In some ways, the process of understanding feelings is more intuitive than rational, more sensed than defined. Ironically, one of the ways we come to know when a feeling is from the Lord is that *we learn what such feelings **feel** like.* Even though that seems like circular reasoning, it is nevertheless true. As noted before, this is why the voice of the Lord is likened to a whisper.

This may be frustrating for those who are still learning what those feelings are like. It doesn't necessarily help them when they hear people say things like: "I can't explain it, but you just know when it's from the Lord." Or, "You have to learn how to tell the difference." Or, "You have to learn how to listen inside yourself." But frustrating or not, that is reality. This is part of the undefinable language of revelation.

From the following illustrations, we can see that feelings given to us through the Spirit are quite varied, ranging from peace and light to

We hear the words of the Lord most often by a feeling. If we are humble and sensitive, the Lord will prompt us through our feelings. That is why spiritual promptings move us on occasion to great joy, sometimes to tears. Many times my emotions have been made tender and my feelings very sensitive when touched by the Spirit.

The Holy Ghost causes our feelings to be more tender. We feel more charitable and compassionate. We are calmer. We have a greater capacity to love. People want to be around us because our very countenances radiate the influence of the Spirit. We are more godly in character. As a result, we are more sensitive to the promptings of the Holy Ghost and thus able to comprehend spiritual things.

EZRA TAFT BENSON,
COME UNTO CHRIST, 20

darkness and anxiety. We also have the same challenge we had with revelation where the Lord speaks to our minds. It is easy to mistake our own emotions for revelation.

PEACE TO THE SOUL

When Oliver Cowdery went to Palmyra, New York, to teach school, one of the families that provided him board and room was Joseph Smith Sr. and his wife, Lucy Mack Smith. By then Palmyra was buzzing about Joseph Smith and the "gold plates." Hearing these stories, Oliver became curious. By now Joseph was in Harmony, Pennsylvania, working on the translation of the Book of Mormon, so Oliver could not talk to him directly. Joseph's family was reluctant to talk about Joseph much because they had endured so much ridicule and persecution. But eventually, Oliver gained the trust of the Smiths, and Joseph's father told him about the plates. Oliver began to pray and meditate on what he had heard and told Joseph Smith Sr. that he felt "impressed . . . that he should yet have the privilege of writing for Joseph."[3]

He went to Harmony to meet Joseph, arriving on Sunday, April 5, 1829. Two days later he was serving as scribe. About that time, Joseph received a revelation for Oliver, in which the Lord told Oliver that He had answered his prayers in a special way.

> If you desire a further witness, cast your mind upon the night that you cried unto me in your heart, that you might know concerning the truth of these things.
>
> Did I not speak *peace to your mind* concerning the matter? What greater witness can you have than from God? (D&C 6:22–23).

Feelings of peace are a common way the Spirit speaks to us. Whether we are struggling with a challenge, seeking strength to endure adversity, or searching for the answer to a vexing question, suddenly the turmoil and the uncertainty and the anxiety are replaced with a deep feeling of peace. Words cannot adequately describe this feeling. But it permeates the soul and brings rest to the troubled heart.

For example, a parent tells of a wayward daughter who had given the family great heartache. As this girl reached her mid-teens, she changed friends and started moving away from the Church and the Lord. As the parents watched with heavy hearts, the behavioral problems deepened. Her choices led her ever downward. Months would go by without them even knowing where she was. Years of earnest, pleading prayers were sent heavenward in her behalf. One day when the mother heard particularly disastrous news, she was overcome with despair. The situation looked absolutely hopeless. She went to her bedroom and poured out her heart to the Lord. Then something unexpected happened. "I was weeping a great deal, my heart broken for this girl that I had held as a baby and rocked so many times. Then, like a great wave washing over me, a profound sense of peace replaced my grief. I didn't hear anything or see anything, but in that moment, I knew that the Lord had not forgotten me, nor had He forgotten my daughter. There was no sense that something magical or miraculous was going to happen. I knew that any change would come slowly, step by step. But I knew the Lord was there. I felt His influence as surely as if He were in the room. My tears of grief and sorrow turned to tears of joy and gratitude. The Lord had not forgotten our child."

> *Though persecutions arise, though reverses come, in prayer we can find reassurance, for God will speak peace to the soul. That peace, that spirit of serenity, is life's greatest blessing.*
>
> EZRA TAFT BENSON,
> *ENSIGN,* FEBRUARY 1990, 5

"YOU SHALL FEEL THAT IT IS RIGHT"

In yet another revelation to Oliver Cowdery, the Lord gave two insights about what it is like to feel His words. Oliver had tried to translate and failed. The Lord chided him somewhat for thinking that all that was required was for him to ask. The Lord told Oliver that he was to study the matter out in his mind and make a decision. Then he was to ask the Lord if the decision was right. "And if it is right," the Lord went on, "I will cause that your bosom shall burn within you; therefore, you shall *feel* that is right. But if it be not right you shall have *no such feelings,* but you shall have a stupor of thought that shall cause you to forget the thing which is wrong" (D&C 9:8–9).

This is an oft-quoted scripture but it does raise some additional questions. Exactly what is meant by the burning of the bosom? And what is a stupor of thought? The questions stem from putting our own interpretation on the Lord's words. When He says burning, we tend to take it literally. But note what the Lord said immediately after referring to the "burning of the bosom." "You shall *feel* that it is right." Rather than some actual physical experience, this suggests more of a strong feeling of conviction or assurance that the decision we have made is right. The words of two Apostles concerning this scripture confirm this:

> *Elder Boyd K. Packer:* This burning in the bosom is not purely a physical sensation. It is more like a warm light shining within your being.[4]

> *Elder Dallin H. Oaks:* This may be one of the most important and misunderstood teachings in all the Doctrine and Covenants. The teachings of the Spirit often come as feelings. That fact is of the utmost importance, yet some misunderstand what it means. I have met persons who told me they have never had a witness from the Holy Ghost because they have never felt their bosom "burn within" them.
>
> What does a "burning in the bosom" mean? Does it need to be a feeling of caloric heat, like the burning produced by combustion? If that is the meaning, I have never had a burning in the bosom. Surely, the word "burning" in this scripture signifies a feeling of comfort and serenity. That

is the witness many receive. That is the way revelation works.[5]

A STUPOR OF THOUGHT

In a similar fashion, perhaps the confusion about what the stupor of thought means comes from putting a literal interpretation on the phrase "shall cause you to forget." When I was much younger, I used to ask myself that very question about the stupor of thought. How could I wake up some morning and say to myself, "Now, what was that problem I have been struggling with for the past six months?" That didn't make sense to me.

The primary meaning for the word *forget* is "to cease to remember." We almost always use the word in that way, and if that is how the word is being used in this passage, it does seem puzzling. But the dictionary shows a less common usage. To forget can also mean "to neglect willfully, disregard, or slight," or "to cease or omit to think of something."[6]

It helps if we remember that the stupor of thought is the opposite from the burning in the bosom, and that the burning was not meant in the sense of actual heat. It implied a strong feeling of rightness or conviction. If that is the case, then couldn't the "forgetting" just mean that we lose the conviction we had before? That we disregard what before we regarded quite seriously? My wife and I had two different experiences that have helped me to better understand the stupor of thought.

We must study our problems and prayerfully make a decision, then take that decision and say to the Father, in simple, honest supplication, "Father, I want to make the right decision. I want to do the right thing. This is what I think I should do; let me know if it is the right course." Doing this, we can get the burning in our bosom, if our decision is right. If we do not get the burning, then we must change our decision and submit a new one. When we learn to walk by the Spirit, we never need to make a mistake.

Marion G. Romney,
*Learning for the
Eternities*, 165–66

I had completed a master's degree in sociology at BYU and had determined to pursue a doctorate with the hope of becoming a university professor. We spent a lot of time "studying it out" in our minds. We did research on the various graduate schools, finally settling on five. We weren't questioning whether getting a doctorate was the right thing to do. We had already decided that. We were only trying to decide what school would be the best one for us. We took a trip east to visit each of the schools on our list. But something remarkable happened. By the time we finished, we both knew that getting a doctorate in sociology was not what we were supposed to do. There was no mental anguish over this, no sense of loss or regret. It just didn't feel right anymore, and so I "forgot" that course of action.

After giving up the idea of a doctorate in sociology, I decided to pursue advanced studies in some aspect of religion. This time I turned my eyes westward to California. I began looking for programs in Bible studies. I found a very prestigious graduate school that was considered to have the finest program in theology west of the Mississippi River. I applied, and to my surprise, the acceptance came a few weeks later. The Church Educational System, for whom I worked, was kind enough to transfer us to Southern California to teach in the institute of religion program there so that I could continue to support my family while I worked on my degree.

We were very pleased with how all of this had turned out and it felt right. That summer we moved down to California and got settled. A few weeks later I went to the school to get registered. I was actually standing in line to pay my tuition when something happened. As I waited there in the California sunshine, I began to have second thoughts. This school was very academic, but their focus was primarily on the history, culture, linguistics, and so forth, of the Bible rather than on faith, discipleship, or doctrine.

I was just three people away from the cashier's window when there came this sudden, overwhelming feeling. "What are you doing here? This is *not* what you want!" At first I could hardly believe it. After all that we had done—given up the degree in sociology, found a new program, moved our family to California, and so forth—and suddenly I was having second thoughts? Wasn't it just a little late for that? But I couldn't shake the feeling. I moved up one place in line, but that feeling wouldn't go away. It only intensified. "This is not for you." So then and there, I turned and walked away, tearing up my tuition check, and never looking back.

It was only much later, as I looked back on those two experiences, that I realized that in both cases I had experienced what the Lord told Oliver Cowdery was a stupor of thought. Twice I had made a major decision that felt good. And in both cases they were good decisions, arrived at only after a lot of careful study and thought. There was nothing wrong with either course I had set for myself. They were honorable choices. But suddenly those decisions were "forgotten." What intellectually and even emotionally had made a lot of sense, spiritually didn't feel right. Now, nearly forty years later, I look back on those two decisions and see how profoundly different my life would have been if I had pursued either of those other courses of action.

HOW DO FEELINGS FROM THE LORD COME TO US?

A Signboard in a Blizzard. There is an illustration from Church history that shows how a thought or feeling can come with such power that it compels us to action. As the rescue party for the Martin and Willie Handcart Companies were headed east, their wagons filled with desperately needed supplies, they ran into a major winter snowstorm at South Pass, Wyoming. Quickly the blowing, drifting snow made travel very difficult. The captain of the company decided to pull off the trail and move down into the willows along Rock Creek, which provided better shelter, and let the storm blow itself out. A man by the name of Harvey Cluff recorded what happened.

> For protection of ourselves and animals, the company moved down the river to where the willows were dense enough to make a good protection against the raging storm from the north. The express team had been dispatched ahead

as rapidly as possible to reach and give encouragement to the faltering emigrants, by letting them know that help was near at hand. Quietly resting in the seclusion of the willow copse, three miles from the road I volunteered to take a sign board and place it at a conspicuous place at the main road. This was designed to direct the express party who were expected to return about this time. So they would not miss us. In facing the northern blast up hill [and in deepening snow] I found it quite difficult to keep from freezing.[7]

The express party referred to here was a small group of riders sent ahead of the wagons to try to locate the handcart companies. What Cluff didn't know was that the express party had found the Willie Company, then gone on to find the Martin Company. They stopped at Devil's Gate to wait for the wagons to catch up with them. So they were not going back along the trail at this time.

Even more important was something else the rescue party down in the willows didn't know. The Willie Company was stopped at the sixth crossing of the Sweetwater, about twenty to twenty-five miles from where the rescue party had holed up. They were out of food and totally exhausted, unable to advance farther. They knew the wagons were coming because the express party had told them so before riding on to find the Martin Company. Leaving his people in camp at the sixth crossing, Captain James Willie decided to see if he could find those oncoming wagons and encourage them to come forward with all haste. He took a second rider, Brother Joseph Elder, with him.

Anyone who has been in a full-scale Wyoming blizzard finds it almost inconceivable that two men would set out in such a storm, but so desperate was the condition of the handcart Saints that they had no choice. What they had no way of knowing, of course, was that the rescue wagons were not on the trail, but down below in the willows waiting out the storm.

I have learned that strong, impressive spiritual experiences do not come to us very frequently.

BOYD K. PACKER,
THAT ALL MAY BE EDIFIED, 337

But the Lord knew the full situation and what needed to be done. When Brother Cluff first had the feeling to take the signboard back up to the trail, he could have thought of a hundred reasons for not going. This was not only going to be a very difficult task, but venturing out alone into that blizzard was also downright dangerous. Yet the feeling that he should place the board was so strong that he felt he had to act. I would guess that by the time he returned to camp he was probably wondering if it had really been worth it.

In this case, the confirmation that those feelings were from the Lord was not long in coming. Cluff records in his account: "*I had only been back to camp a short time* when two men [Willie and Elder] rode up from Willie's handcart company. The signboard had done the work of salvation."[8]

> *Most of the revelation that comes to leaders and members of the Church comes by the still, small voice or by a feeling rather than by a vision or a voice that speaks specific words we can hear. I testify to the reality of that kind of revelation, which I have come to know as a familiar, even daily, experience to guide me in the work of the Lord.*
>
> DALLIN H. OAKS,
> *ENSIGN,* MARCH 1997, 14

If Willie and Elder arrived in the camp just "a short time" after Cluff had returned, they must have been within minutes of reaching that point in the trail where the signboard was placed. Had Cluff not felt compelled to act, if he had hesitated or rationalized that no one would be out on the trail on that night, or if he had waited a little to get warm by the fire, Willie and Elder would have passed on by and been lost. In addition to the almost certain deaths of those two faithful brethren, how many more of the Willie Handcart Company would have died as a result of further delays had it not been for a man who had a strong feeling to put up a signboard in a blizzard?*

---

* Brother Cluff ended his account with these words: "I have always regarded this *act of mine* as the means of their salvation. And why not? An act of that importance is worthy of record and hence I give a place here."

THE NOT-SO-POSITIVE FEELINGS

Sometimes the feelings we get from the Spirit are not positive and uplifting. The Lord doesn't always send peace and joy or give us a strong positive conviction of the rightness of our actions. Sometimes He may send feelings that could be described as negative emotions. Take the case where the Spirit may warn of some danger to us or loved ones. This may come as a feeling of uneasiness or apprehension. He may leave us feeling confused or unsure of ourselves when we start down a path that could weaken us spiritually. A bishop may feel an oppressive spirit when something is wrong in his ward that needs correcting. These are all possible negative feelings that can come from the Lord.

But there is a second problem. Often our own emotions are negative, on the down side. We feel sad, depressed, anxious, fearful, worried, sick at heart, and so on. These are part of our everyday living experience. We must be careful that we don't assume such feelings, especially when they are strong feelings, come from the Lord. (Of course, we also need to avoid the opposite error—automatically assuming such feelings do *not* come from the Lord.) Sometimes we get depressed just because life takes a steep downturn for a while. Let's not automatically assume our depression is a sign that the Lord is punishing us somehow. Some people, who are natural worriers, may think they are getting premonitions from the Spirit when there is nothing wrong. Or here is another possibility. We may undertake a course of action or a project and find it so challenging that we grow discouraged. It is tempting to say that this is the Lord's way of telling us that what we are doing is wrong.

And as if all of that didn't complicate matters enough, there is yet a third possible source of negative emotions. We may actually receive false spiritual messages or whisperings from the Evil One that can leave us feeling dark or gloomy. We won't say much about those in this chapter since counterfeit revelation will be discussed in chapter 21.

"God Loves Me." Here is an interesting instance where both positive and negative emotions worked together to give an individual a clear answer from the Lord.

There was a period of several years in my life when I did not believe that God loved me. I believed He existed, but due to some difficult circumstances in my life, I could not believe that a God who loved me would allow me to suffer in such agonizing and pervasive ways. For two years, I fervently ended every prayer with the question "Do you love me?" Because I did not receive a resounding answer, "YES!" I eventually came to the conclusion that indeed, God did not love me.

Shortly thereafter, while driving between my two jobs, I decided to stop and get some dinner. I had a particular craving and decided to go to a particular restaurant. As I did so, however, there came to me a thought, accompanied by strong feelings, that I should not eat at this particular establishment. I brushed it off as just me being silly and paranoid after a long and stressful day. As I reached the restaurant, the strength of that uneasy feeling only increased and it occurred to me that this might be God's way of telling me something. But the rebellious and skeptical part of me kicked in, and I decided that a God concerned with the entire world would not take the time to tell me where to eat or not to eat, especially since that same God did not love me.

I smugly ate a delicious meal and left the restaurant somewhat gloating to myself that "lightning had not struck" me after all. However, by the next day, I was grossly ill with food poisoning. Only several hours into my misery did I see the irony of the fact that being sick was the answer to the question that I had been asking for two years. Somehow, lying in that spinning, dark room, there came an immense feeling of comfort and peace because I now knew that God did know and love me. He did not want me to suffer. I felt such astonishment that I could only repeat over and over in my mind, "God loves me. God *loves* me. God loves *me!*"

Since that day, I have never felt the need to ask that question again.

DIRECTIVE FEELINGS

Another way that feelings can provide revelation is when impressions come that direct us to do something. (Often these feelings are closely linked with thoughts too.) People say things like, "I had this feeling I needed to call." "I suddenly felt like I should turn down the next street." "I had a strong feeling to stop the car."

Teach Suzy to Ride a Bike. Here in the testimony of a mother we find another case where there came direction in a quiet way on an issue that was not some large pressing question:

> In general conference, President Monson was the concluding speaker in one of the Sunday sessions. As he spoke, I had the sudden feeling that I needed to teach my daughter, Suzy, to ride a bike. It seemed a little odd because President Monson hadn't talked about bicycles, and my thought didn't seem that spiritual. But I've learned to write down impressions while listening to conference, so I did. We had family coming for dinner later than afternoon and I was preparing things. Just as I began preparing dinner, Suzy came in. "Mom, will you teach me to ride my bike?" Normally I would have told her it had to be another time, but because of the prompting, I left everything and spent a half an hour with her outside. I have no idea why this was so important for that to happen right then, but it must have been important to her, and my Heavenly Father is also her Heavenly Father and knew the tender desires of his young daughter.

In this example a mother was left wondering why those feelings came when they did. In that case, she was not seeking help from the Lord, nor was she asking a question. The impression just came to her, so she at first wondered if it really was an impression from the Spirit. But she received the confirmation that the feeling was from the Lord when her daughter appeared just a few minutes later.

His Answer Didn't Come through Us. In our next example, we have parents who were deeply concerned about the course their daughter was taking and pled with the Lord for His help. However, the answer didn't come through them, but through another avenue completely.

> When she was a senior, Elizabeth, our oldest daughter, who had always been so obedient and compliant, started dating Edward, a missionary who had recently returned to our ward. He was a worthy young man and so there was no concern at first. But quickly things turned sour. In contrast to her nature, this young man was quite sober, almost a cheerless young man. He also began to totally monopolize her, becoming quite possessive and demanding. He didn't like her spending time with her friends or family.
>
> This was her first serious relationship and so she found it all quite exciting. When we became somewhat concerned and tried to "cool" the relationship, she became very resistant. We learned later that he was privately telling her that we were the ones being possessive, that we were treating her like a child. Our relationship with her became more and more strained. When she went to BYU, he drove down four or five times a week to see her, and to make it clear to all the boys in her ward that she was "taken." Soon he was not only talking marriage, but starting to press her pretty vigorously to accept his proposal.
>
> We saw a change in her that became alarming. She became withdrawn, more like he was, and her naturally cheerful disposition seemed to have disappeared. He was pressuring her hard to get married, and she was starting to

weaken. Greatly alarmed, we as her parents added regular fasting to our fervent prayers.

Then one day, she came home and announced that she had broken it off with him. We were elated, of course, but she wouldn't give any details as to what had brought this on. Only some time later did we learn from our stake president that he had received a strong impression that he needed to talk with Elizabeth. He asked her to come in the next time she was home. Without saying anything about the feeling he'd had, he asked her how she was doing. When she told him that she was dating Edward very seriously, he said, "I knew in that instant that this was why I felt what I did." Edward was in our stake and the president had been counseling with him for some time, not for unworthiness, but because of his troubled emotions. The stake president looked our daughter in the eye and said, "Now I know why I was supposed to talk to you, Elizabeth. As your stake president, I am counseling you now, as firmly as I know how, stop dating Edward. He is not the one for you."

The parents concluded their story with this. "Our daughter is now married to a fine and wonderful man and has a very happy marriage. One can only imagine the joy we felt to have our prayers answered, and it mattered not at all that the Lord chose to answer them by giving direction to someone other than ourselves."

CHAPTER 11

HOW DOES REVELATION TYPICALLY COME?

IV. AS WARNINGS

"He that keepeth Israel shall neither slumber nor sleep" (Psalm 121:4).

THE HOLY GHOST AS A PROTECTOR

In this chapter, we will look at another manifestation of how the Lord gives us revelation by having the Spirit speak to us through our minds and hearts: He gives us warnings of danger and other problems. This is quite straightforward and is experienced by many people in one form or another. In some cases, those warnings may come as thoughts to our mind. In other cases, they will come as feelings. Many times both thoughts and feelings are involved.

Before looking at those examples, however, one point needs to be made. It is a common thing for us to say that we received a premonition from the Spirit, or that we were warned by the Holy Ghost not to do something. And this is not incorrect. However, technically it would be more correct to say that we were warned by God *through* the Spirit. The Spirit always operates under the direction of the Father and Jesus Christ. So it is the Father and the Son, in their perfect love and perfect knowledge, who actually watch over us and protect us. The role of the

Spirit should not be minimized, but let us not forget that it is our Heavenly Father and His Beloved Son who are watching over us.

SCRIPTURAL AND HISTORICAL EXAMPLES OF WARNING

There are numerous examples of this warning function of the Spirit. Here is just a sampling:

- The Apostle Paul said that he "perceived" that if they sailed on to Rome when the season was so late, there would be great danger. They refused to heed his warning and were shipwrecked and nearly killed (see Acts 27:10–11).
- Joseph was warned in a dream that Herod would seek to kill the baby Jesus and was told to flee into Egypt for a time (see Matthew 2:13).
- Lehi was warned in a dream that the people of Jerusalem were going to kill him, and that he needed to take his family and go into the wilderness (1 Nephi 2:1–2).
- Wilford Woodruff also had several experiences where he was warned of danger. One of those occurred when he was sent to Boston by President Brigham Young to gather some of the Saints. He was traveling in a carriage with his wife and children. At a member's home he parked the carriage beneath a large oak tree. "I had not been there but a few minutes," he said, "when the spirit said to me, 'Get up and move that carriage.' I told my wife I had to get up and move the carriage.

  "She said, 'What for?'

  "I said, 'I don't know.' . . .

  "In thirty minutes a whirlwind came up and broke that oak tree off within two feet from the ground. It . . . fell . . . right where mine had stood. . . . That was the still, small voice to me—no earthquake, no thunder, no lightning—but the still, small voice of the Spirit of God. It saved my life. It was the spirit of revelation to me."[1]

MODERN EXAMPLES OF BEING WARNED OF GOD

A Quiet, Peaceful Prompting. A soldier received a last-minute Christmas leave to return home to Idaho from California. It was too late by then to find transportation, so he began to hitchhike. In Nevada, he was picked up by three young men. But once he and his duffel bag were in the backseat and they started off again, he realized that the men were drunk and still drinking. Fearful for his life, he asked them to stop the car and let him out. They refused. Praying for help, he reported that "then had come a very quiet, very peaceful prompting telling me to get down on the floor and put my duffel bag over me." He did so, wedging himself in and pulling the heavy bag on top of him. A few minutes later, the vehicle hit another car head on. The three young men and a couple in the other car were killed, but the soldier survived without serious injury.[2]

This is a case where both thoughts and feelings were involved. He described it as a "quiet, peaceful prompting." But for all of that quietness and peacefulness, he received very specific instructions on what to do.

A Very Depressing, Dark Feeling. Here is another case where someone was warned through feelings, but in this instance they were neither peaceful nor quiet. This is another example of how sometimes the feelings we get through the Spirit are negative. Elder Milton R. Hunter, a member of the First Council of the Seventy, was on assignment in Southern Mexico. Finished with their business in one location, they boarded a small, one-engine plane to fly several hundred miles to Tuxtla, in the state of Chiapas. Their route took them over several mountain

> *On occasion, the Lord will give you an answer before you ask. This can occur when you are unaware of a danger or may be doing the wrong thing, mistakenly trusting that it is correct.*
>
> RICHARD G. SCOTT,
> *ENSIGN,* MAY 2007, 9

ranges and one of the densest jungles in the world. The weather was stormy so the pilot took the plane above the clouds. Elder Hunter recorded what then happened.

We had traveled a few hours when darkness came on with the immediacy it does in the tropics. Suddenly, the Holy Spirit told me that . . . if we did not change our course quickly we would all get killed.

I immediately told Bill [the pilot] that we were going the wrong direction. . . .

A very depressing, dark feeling came over me. It was a feeling of gloom and despair. [The pilot] asked, "President Hunter, which direction do you think we ought to go?"

I quickly replied, "Turn immediately to the right and go north."

Bill turned the plane to the right. A sweet, peaceful feeling came into my heart, and the Holy Spirit let me know that all would be well.

On a beautiful, clear spring morning, Joseph retired to the woods. He paused when he arrived at a quiet, secluded spot. He looked around to make sure he was alone. Then he knelt and began to pray. No sooner had he done so than an overwhelming feeling of darkness swept over him, as if some evil power was trying to dissuade him. Rather than surrender, Joseph intensified his pleas to God—and God Himself responded.

M. Russell Ballard,
Ensign, November 1994, 65

They landed safely a short time later. To their surprise, a large group of people were waiting at the small airport. When they asked why so many were there, they were told that another plane with three Mexicans was missing and feared lost. Some time later they learned that the other plane had slammed into a mountain, killing all aboard.[3]

A Strong Impression. Elder Dallin H. Oaks reports an impression that once saved his life. He was hiking alone in the mountains. He was moving down the mountain toward the road where he had left his car. It was pitch dark and he was feeling his way slowly through the brush and deadfall.

I was relieved when the gully flattened out to a sandy bottom beneath my feet. I picked up my pace for about 10 steps and suddenly had a strong impression to stop. I did. Reaching down, I took a rock and tossed it out into the darkness ahead of me. I heard no sound for a few seconds, and then there was a clatter on the rocks a long distance away. I knew immediately that I was standing on the lip of a sheer drop-off.

[He retraced his steps and eventually got off the mountain.]

The next day I revisited the spot in the daylight and saw my tracks, which stopped just two or three feet from a drop-off of at least 50 feet. I was glad I had heard and heeded a warning. Where did that lead? It saved my life.[4]

IN SUMMARY

In a process that involves both thoughts and feelings, one common form that revelation takes is a warning or a premonition that something is wrong, that we are in danger, or that we should take a certain course of action, which then helps us avoid that danger.

One other thing should be noted. As we have seen in previous chapters, in almost every one of these cases, a confirmation followed the giving of the revelation. Sometimes it was immediate. Sometimes it came hours or days later. These confirmations came in many different ways, but they did confirm that the warnings had come through the Spirit.

CHAPTER 12

HOW DOES REVELATION
TYPICALLY COME?
V. AS DIVINE INTERVENTION

"I have covered thee in the shadow of mine hand" (Isaiah 51:16).

A DIVINE INFLUENCE

This chapter contains the final portion of our answer to the question: *How do the less direct forms of revelation come to us?* We have already examined how they come to our minds as thoughts and impressions and how they come to our hearts as feelings. We also looked at how the Spirit brings general enlightenment and understanding. We have stressed all along that while these are less direct forms of revelation, they occur far more often than the more direct means the Lord uses to communicate with us.

We will now look at another common way the Lord reveals Himself to us. Many members of the Church can cite examples of these particular kinds of experiences from their own lives. Though perhaps a little more direct than thoughts or feelings, this form, which we will call the Lord's *intervention,* would still fall on the less direct end of the continuum of revelation.

By divine intervention, we mean those times when the Lord chooses to influence events and circumstances in an unusual or unexpected way.

Things fall into place or unrelated things come together or circumstances change sufficiently that the outcome is changed. Things turn out differently than we would have otherwise expected.

Some may not think of these kinds of experiences as a form of revelation because they don't involve the communication of light and truth in the same way as when the Spirit speaks to us through thoughts and feelings. And yet when we have such experiences, it is another witness that God lives. It is another way He uses to reveal His character and attributes. By definition, revelation is the revealing of God to man, so such divine influence certainly can be considered as another form of revelation.

A WORD OF CAUTION

Before illustrating how this form of revelation works, we need to make a point. I remember many years ago reading in the newspaper of a major power outage in New York City. Huge areas of the city were blacked out for long hours. A few days later I learned about a young boy who had been walking home at that very time. He had a stick and as he passed a line of telephone poles, he took a good solid whack at each one. At the very moment he struck one of the poles, the power went out. Frightened at what he had "done," he ran home and hid in his room. He was certain that when the police discovered his part in all this, he would end up in jail. Only later, when the power came back on, did his parents learn why he was so afraid to go out again.

As we consider such experiences, we must keep this in mind: *The simultaneous occurrence of two events does not prove that they are related or that one caused the other.*

Following his 35,000-mile journey in 1954 to the British Isles, Switzerland, South Africa, South America, Central America, and Mexico, President McKay expressed gratitude for their safe return from their travels, during which they had encountered electrical storms in mid-air, and other incidents wherein they felt divine intervention in their behalf.

DAVID O. MCKAY,
*CHERISHED EXPERIENCES
FROM THE WRITINGS OF
PRESIDENT DAVID O. MCKAY, 39*

THE HAND OF THE LORD

That said, let us reaffirm that while not all such unusual occurrences are from the Lord, *many actually are.* It is just as foolish to say that the Lord never intervenes in events as it is to say that every coincidental happening is from the Lord. There are times when, in a very natural way, things fall into place so as to provide us an answer we seek or a solution we need or to take us in a direction we need to go. And like the other forms of less direct revelation, these happen more commonly than some might think.

President Joseph F. Smith once spoke of learning to "see" the hand of the Lord in our lives:

It has not been by the wisdom of man that this people have been directed in their course until the present; it has been by the wisdom of Him who is above man, whose knowledge is greater than that of man, and whose power is above the power of man. . . . The *hand of the Lord* may not be visible to all. There may be many who cannot discern the workings of God's will in the progress and development of this great latter-day work, but there are those who see *in every hour and in every moment* of the existence of the Church, from its beginning until now, the *overruling, almighty hand of [God].*[1]

> *The news media made the events in eastern Europe appear as purely political revolutions, even though many of the oppressed have recognized it as a "religious renaissance" and have acknowledged the influence of divine intervention.*
>
> DAVID B. HAIGHT,
> *LIGHT UNTO THE WORLD*, 70

This divine influence can happen in both a *macro* and a *micro* sense. Sometimes the Lord works His will and brings about His purposes on a grand, sweeping scale, influencing events in a way that significantly alters history itself. A perfect example of this *macro* level of influence is the part the Lord played in the discovery of America and the Revolutionary War (see 1 Nephi 13:12–19).

On the other hand, the Lord also works His will on an individual scale, watching over and blessing and protecting His children in their daily lives. Sometimes, as we have seen in earlier chapters, He intervenes even in what we might think of as trivial matters. He is not some Divine Deity occasionally hurling cosmic thunderbolts at the earth from His throne on high. He is our Father, who intimately knows us and infinitely loves us, and who is not at all hesitant to use His limitless powers to bless and enrich and protect and direct us. In short, I firmly believe that if we have eyes to see, we will learn that our Heavenly Father also watches over us "in every hour and in every moment" of our existence as well.

> *I testify . . . that the miraculous power of divine intervention is among us, which is one of the signs of the divinity of the work of the Lord.*
>
> HAROLD B LEE,
> *YE ARE THE LIGHT OF THE WORLD*, 148

SCRIPTURAL AND HISTORICAL EXAMPLES OF THE LORD'S HAND

Examples of the Lord's intervention in the scriptures are so numerous as to make it nearly impossible to fully catalog them. Many of these happen in a grand and miraculous way:

- Joseph was sold into Egypt by his brothers, but the Lord, through a series of events, eventually brought him to a position where he could save his family from famine (Genesis 37, 39–46).
- The Lord gave Joshua direction on how to bring down the walls of Jericho and begin the conquest of the promised land (Joshua 6).
- Gideon was instructed to reduce his army to three hundred men, then went on to defeat a vastly superior Midianite army (Judges 7).

Other scriptural and historical examples of the Lord's influence are more personal and less spectacular, though the results may be just as profound:

- Esther was chosen from among many beautiful young women to be the queen of Persia. Years later she became an instrument in the Lord's hand to save her people (Esther 2–8).
- When Ammon told King Lamoni that he only wanted to be one of his servants, Ammon was given the one assignment on the household staff that allowed him to show forth his courage just three days later. That fortunate placement led to the conversion of Lamoni and thousands of his people (Alma 18).
- Parley P. Pratt was called to serve a mission in Canada. As he headed for Toronto, the roads were terribly muddy and his progress was slow. Deciding to ask the Lord for help, he went off the road into a grove of trees. As he entered the next town, he was approached by a stranger who asked his name, then asked Parley if he needed some money. Parley told him that he was trying to get to Toronto. Not only did the man give Parley ten dollars (a significant amount back then), but he also gave him a letter of referral to a man in Toronto who might help him in his work. That man's name was John Taylor, who later became the third President of the Church.[2]

A Woman's Shoes. Here is another example that does not involve some grand, sweeping result for the Church, but that shows the Lord's tender mercies over His individual children. Ellen Breakell Neibaur lived in Preston, England. She and her husband, Alexander Neibaur, were some of the first converts in England when Heber C. Kimball arrived in 1837. As other Saints began to immigrate to America, the Neibaurs didn't have sufficient money to go. It took them until 1845 to save enough money for passage. When they arrived in Nauvoo that fall, the Church was in the midst of a new wave of persecution, and Brigham

Young was calling on the Saints to prepare to leave for the West the following spring.

With little funds left after their voyage, the Neibaurs had to work hard to scrape together enough to get an "outfit"—wagon, team, food, and equipment—so they could cross the plains. They managed to do so, but getting the basics left no money for trail-worthy boots or shoes, so Ellen crossed the plains with her feet wrapped in rags or barefoot at times. They arrived in the Salt Lake Valley in the fall of 1848. Conditions in the valley were very difficult, and so for the next eight years they had little money for anything other than necessities. Not until 1856 did Ellen save enough money to send off to a mail-order house for a pair of patent-leather, high-button shoes, along with a pair of silk stockings. One can only imagine what a joy it must have been for her.

Though it is not specified exactly when the shoes arrived, it was not long before the October general conference of that year. That proved to be a momentous conference. On Sunday, October 5, Brigham Young announced that they had just learned there were two more handcart companies out on the plains and that the Saints had to go rescue them. Brigham called for wagons, teams, food, blankets, and clothing, *including shoes* from the Saints, to be sent with the rescue wagons. In an inspiring example of covenant and sacrifice, Ellen gave her new pair of shoes and the silk stockings to the rescue effort.

That is a wonderful story of faith and covenant keeping. After all those years of going without, she did not hesitate. She sent her shoes with the rescuers. Here, in the words of her granddaughter, is what followed:

> Customarily, the Saints in the Valley lined the streets to welcome the weary companies as they entered Salt Lake. You can imagine as Ellen stood on the street that day to greet the beleaguered handcart pioneers, was she watching faces, or was she watching feet to see whose footsteps she had lightened? Much to her surprise, when she recognized her shoes, she also realized that the woman wearing those shoes was a

dear friend of hers from England who had joined the Church after she [Ellen] had left her native country. Through her sacrifice, she had unknowingly helped to rescue the life of her dear friend.[3]

Talk about a "coincidence!" There were close to a thousand people being rescued that winter. And yet somehow, in the distribution of the clothing among them, Ellen's shoes ended up on the feet of her dear friend from England. Surely there were two women who wept that day in gratitude for this specific and wonderful blessing from the Lord.

MODERN EXAMPLES OF THE LORD'S HAND IN OUR LIVES

The following modern stories from the lives of real people show how intimately the Lord knows us and watches over his children, even those who do not hold high position in the Church. Some of these examples are really quite remarkable. Others show that the Lord intervenes even in things some might not consider worthy of an earthly parent's attention, let alone a Divine One's. Yet, they truly show "that the tender mercies of the Lord are over all those whom he hath chosen" (1 Nephi 1:20).

The Power of Two Testimonies. A woman reports that while in Deseret Industries one day, she decided to buy a Book of Mormon and give it to a friend who was not a member. She found one nice used copy and put it into her cart. But a moment later, she saw another copy that looked to be in even better condition, so she exchanged the two. Upon returning home, she decided she would write her testimony in the book before giving it to her friend. Here is her account:

> Imagine my surprise when, as I opened the book, I saw a picture of my family taken 25 years before [back when President Benson had asked members to write their testimony with a picture in a Book of Mormon and give it to

someone]. Beneath the picture was a testimony written by my father, who had recently passed away. Tears sprang to my eyes as I read his testimony and felt his presence. . . . When I found this copy of the Book of Mormon, my family lived several hundred miles away from where I was then living. After adding my testimony to my father's testimony, I gave the Book of Mormon to my friend. I then thanked Heavenly Father for the blessing that the original Book of Mormon project had given to both my friend and me. My friend felt especially touched by my father's testimony and the special "coincidence" that had occurred. She eventually gained her own testimony of the Book of Mormon and entered the waters of baptism. My testimony was strengthened . . . [by] that particular Book of Mormon finding its way back into my hands after 25 years.[4]

What is interesting in this example is that this woman was not specifically seeking help from the Lord with some challenging problem. She was not struggling with a difficult question. It was what might be called a "free gift," unsolicited and unexpected. Yet the Lord gave her a wonderful experience that not only touched the heart of her friend, but strengthened her testimony as well.

"You Are Political Prisoners." In this next example the Lord used thoughts and feelings to bring about deliverance from a difficult situation, and He did so in such a way as to build faith and strengthen testimony. The author was serving as a missionary in Germany in 1939, just prior to the outbreak of World War II.

> *The idea of divine intervention on behalf of man is often scoffed at by the skeptic.*
>
> HUGH B. BROWN,
> "ETERNAL QUEST," 83

Elder Wallace D. Montague reported that he and two other missionaries were walking down a street in Dresden when they were arrested by the police. They were taken to a nearby precinct and questioned for two hours. When they asked for permission to tell other missionaries where they were, one officer sneered and said, "You are political prisoners. You are going no place."

That phrase struck great fear in their hearts. It was common knowledge that people taken by the Gestapo were never heard from again. The missionaries were transferred to the main prison, where they had their pictures taken with their prison numbers. Again they asked for permission to contact the mission president, but this too was denied. All personal belongings, including passports, belts, handkerchiefs, money, pens, and so forth, were confiscated, and they were marched off to individual cells. Frightened and in despair, Elder Montague sat on his cot and tried to decide what to do. The situation seemed utterly hopeless.

> All of a sudden it occurred to me: "You are in this land as a servant of Father in heaven and have come to do His will. He has promised that if you will go and do what He commands He will provide a way for that to be accomplished. The one way to get a message outside these prison walls is to pray to your Heavenly Father. They cannot stop you from praying."
>
> In humility, and a bit ashamed for not having thought of it sooner, I knelt by the prison cot and told my Father in heaven about the trouble we were in and asked for His help in order that we could continue about His work among that people.
>
> I arose from my knees, folded the bed against the wall, and immediately heard a clicking noise at the cell door. It swung open and the guard commanded: "Come out. You are released."

If the story ended there, it would be a marvelous example of how the Lord answered a missionary's prayer by intervening in the situation. But the Lord had an additional blessing for these elders that day. As Elder Montague came out from his cell, his companions were all coming out as well. They were given their possessions, warned against further proselytizing, and released.

> My heart was so full of gratitude for the "miracle" that had been performed in our behalf that I could contain myself no longer, and so we stopped at a small roadside park so that I could tell of my experience. Imagine our mutual surprise when we found that this experience had happened to each of us—as we had arisen from our knees the prison doors were unlocked.[5]*

I Will Beat You into the Valley. A well-known story from Church history bears repeating here because it provides another remarkable instance of divine intervention in events, with its accompanying revelation about God's love for His children.

Mary Fielding Smith was left a widow when her husband, Hyrum, was martyred in Carthage Jail along with the Prophet Joseph. As the Saints began the trek west, she had trouble getting enough wagons, teams, and supplies to take her and her family (about eleven people in all) to the Salt Lake Valley. Finally, in 1848, she was ready to do so, but the captain of the company to which she was assigned was upset at the idea. He was afraid that she would be a burden on the company and a constant drain on his time and energy. Irritated at his attitude, Mary told him that not only would she not ask for his help on the trek, but that she would beat him to the valley. All the way across the plains, anytime she had any difficulty, instead of helping her, he would chide her and tell her this was exactly what he had expected.

Finally, just one day from the end of the long journey, they camped at the foot of Little Mountain. Here, in the words of her son, Joseph F. Smith, is what happened:

---

* As World War II broke out, there were other cases where the Lord intervened in events to help missionaries and others escape the war zone. See, for example, Ellis T. Rasmussen and John Robert Kest, "Border Incident," *Improvement Era*, December 1943, 752–53, 793–97.

Early next morning, the captain gave notice to the company to arise, hitch up and roll over the mountain into the valley.

To our consternation, when we gathered up our cattle, the essential part of our means of transportation, for some reason had strayed away, and were not to be found with the herd. A brother of mine (John) . . . obtained a horse and rode back over the road in search of the lost cattle. The captain ordered the march to begin, and, regardless of our predicament, the company started out, up the mountain. The morning sun was then shining brightly, without a cloud appearing anywhere in the sky! I had happened to hear the promise of my dear mother that we would beat the captain into the valley, and would not ask any help from him either. I sat in the front of the wagon with the teams we had in hand hitched to the wheels, while my brother was absent hunting the others. I saw the company wending its slow way up the hill, the animals struggling to pull their heavy loads. The forward teams now had almost reached the summit of the hill, and I said to myself, "True enough, we have come thus far, and we have been blessed, and not the slightest help from anyone has been asked by us." But the last promise seemed to be now impossible; the last hope of getting into the valley before the rest of our company was vanishing in my opinion.

You have doubtless heard descriptions of the terrific thunder storms that sometimes visit the mountains. . . . All of a sudden, and in less time than I am taking to tell you, a big, dark, heavy cloud rose from the northwest, going directly southeast. In a few minutes it burst in such terrific fury that the cattle could not face the storm, and the captain seemed forced to direct the company to unhitch the teams, turn them loose, and block the wheels to keep the wagons from running back down the hill. The cattle fled before the storm down into the entrance into Parley's canyon. . . . Luckily, the storm lasted only a short time. As it ceased to rain, and the wind ceased to blow, my brother, John, drove up with our lost cattle. We then hitched them to the wagon, and the question was asked by my uncle of mother: "Mary, what shall we do? Go on, or wait for the company to gather up their teams?" She said: "Joseph (that was her brother's name), they have not waited for us, and I see no necessity for us to wait for them."

So we hitched up and rolled up the mountain, leaving the company behind, and this was on the 23rd day of September, 1848. We reached the Old Fort about 10 o'clock that Saturday night. The next morning, in the Old Bowery, we had the privilege of listening to President Brigham Young and President Kimball, Erastus Snow, and some others, give some very excellent instructions. Then, on the afternoon of that Sunday, we went out and met our friends coming in, very dusty, and very foot-sore and very tired!

> *Fear thou not: for I am with thee: be not dismayed; for I am thy God: I will strengthen thee; yea, I will help thee; yea, I will uphold thee with the right hand of my righteousness.*
>
> ISAIAH 41:10

The prediction of the widow was actually fulfilled; we beat them into the valley, and we asked no help from them either![6]

Mary Fielding Smith surely learned one lesson that day: There might be wagon masters who were not that caring and concerned about the plight of a widow and her family, but Heavenly Father had not forgotten her.

"São Paulo Has Seventeen Million People." An associate of mine who served as a mission president in Brazil some years back shared a

wonderful instance where the Lord directly influenced events so as to accomplish a tender purpose. He said that one of his new missionaries came to him from the north of Brazil. It had taken him three days on a bus to get to the missionary training center at São Paulo to begin his mission. After finishing at the MTC, this missionary went to the mission home where, as was customary, he began a day of orientation and training. That evening, the mission president assigned the new missionaries to go tracting so they could have a real "missionary experience" their first day in the mission.

This elder from the far north of Brazil went out with his assigned companion. Imagine his astonishment when the very first door he knocked on was opened by someone he knew. It was his older sister, who had run away from home four years previously. The family had not heard from her in all that time, and they had no idea where she was. It was a moment of sweet reunion. But it was more than that. The elder began teaching his sister the gospel and she became the first convert baptism of his mission.

The mission president concluded his account by saying, "It was the very first door he knocked on! And you have to remember, São Paulo has seventeen million people!"

HOW CAN WE TELL THE DIFFERENCE BETWEEN A COINCIDENCE AND THE LORD'S HAND IN THINGS?

In this chapter, I used the example of a rather strange coincidence—a young boy hit a telephone pole with a stick at the very moment power went out in the city. We have now looked at several stories from the lives of actual people that the world would call "coincidences" as well. This raises that same old question that we have revisited again and again. *How can we tell when it is really the Lord's hand in our lives or just a pure coincidence* that has no real significance?

Fortunately, in this case the answer is quite simple and straight-forward. It comes down to one simple issue. Did it fulfill some purpose of the Lord? Almost always, the answer to that question is clearly found in the situation itself—although sometimes the Lord's purposes are not seen for months or even years.

It doesn't make sense to think that the Lord would use a small boy and a stick to blank out the power of New York City. The power outage did not bring about some grand purpose—or even a small one, as far as we can tell. It was just one of those weird happenings where two different incidents happen to occur at the same time—thus they both can be set aside as pure coincidence.

Compare this example to the other cases we have cited here. In every one of those instances, the Lord's intervention had a clear purpose and accomplished something positive for at least one individual.

There is wisdom in following that pattern of questioning as we examine each individual case to determine if it was from the Lord. If we are prone to see the hand of the Lord in every small or strange coincidence, let this become our model for determining which come from the Lord and which do not.

IN SUMMARY

Through Joseph Smith, the Lord gave a promise to a group of elders returning from their missions in September 1832: "And whoso receiveth you, there I will be also, for I will go before your face. I will be on your right hand and on your left, and my Spirit shall be in your hearts, and mine angels round about you, to bear you up" (D&C 84:88).

This promise of the guiding, watching hand of God is not just for full-time missionaries. The words of one of our favorite hymns also come to mind:

> *Beneath his watchful eye,*
> *His Saints securely dwell;*
> *That* hand *which bears all nature up*
> *Shall guard his children well.*[7]

What we speak of here is a divine influence and intervention that reveal the hand of God by changing outcomes so that individuals are blessed and benefited. This is another very real form of personal revelation. And like all revelation, its purpose is to bear witness to our hearts of a Heavenly Father who is perfect in His love, mercy, and goodness. It is another powerful evidence of His reality, and that is one of the prime purposes of revelation.

As President Joseph F. Smith said: "There are those who see in every hour and in every moment of the existence of the Church, from its beginning until now, the overruling, almighty hand of [God]."[8] I believe it could be equally said, that those who have eyes to see, will recognize the overruling, almighty hand of God in their lives as well.

This concludes our section on the various forms revelation may take, ranging from the most direct to the least direct forms. We have now completed our continuum of revelation, which looks like this:

LESS

DIRECT

MORE

DIRECT

| LIGHT OF CHRIST | STILL SMALL VOICE TO THE MIND AND HEART | INTERVENTION CHANGE OF OUTCOMES | DREAMS | AUDIBLE VOICE | VISIONS | VISITATIONS FROM ANGELS/ GODHEAD |

TO THE MIND
THOUGHTS
AHA EXPERIENCE
REMEMBRANCE
VOICE IN MIND
DREAMS
ENLIGHTENMENT
DISCERNMENT
TESTIMONY

TO THE HEART
PEACE
FEELS RIGHT
BURNING
STUPOR
NEGATIVE FEELINGS
WARNINGS
DIRECTION

SECTION III

WHAT PRINCIPLES GOVERN THE GIVING AND RECEIVING OF REVELATION?

Though we may all have the right to receive revelations from on high for ourselves, to govern our conduct, to regulate us in the family relation or in any capacity we are called upon to act in the Church, yet there is but one man at a time, according to God's direct word, who receives revelations for the government of the Church and to regulate matters pertaining to its doctrines and ordinances. . . . That is in accordance with the order of heaven. "My house is a house of order," said the Lord, "and not a house of confusion." . . . If every Tom, Dick, and Harry can start up and give a revelation, and pretend to have this and that authority and power and so forth, and people are led off by such individuals, there will be confusion worse confounded, and the order of the Church be disturbed if not obliterated (Charles W. Penrose, Conference Report, April 1912, 20–21).

CHAPTER 13

FIRST PRINCIPLE:

GOD DETERMINES ALL ASPECTS
OF REVELATION

*"And it shall be in his own time, and in his own way,
and according to his own will" (D&C 88:68).*

PRINCIPLES OF REVELATION

In the first two sections of this book, we have looked at how revelation works in our lives. We discussed some basic principles we need to remember about personal revelation. Here in quick review are some of the things we learned:

- Revelation is absolutely essential to the existence of the Church and to our own eternal progression.
- The Holy Ghost is the medium through which the Father and the Son communicate light and knowledge and Their will to us.
- The voice of the Lord is most often still and small and it whispers.
- The Holy Ghost speaks to our minds (through thoughts) or to our hearts (through feelings).
- Revelation comes across a wide spectrum of experiences.
- The vast majority of personal revelation comes in quiet, undramatic, almost imperceptible ways, which can easily be missed or misunderstood.

- What is given in any form of revelation is almost always more important than how it comes.
- Often the revelation we receive from the Holy Ghost comes as enlightenment and understanding; it illuminates the mind and strengthens testimony.
- The Lord warns us of danger or problems through various ways.
- One of the forms of revelation is when God intervenes in our behalf and influences events or circumstances in a way that changes the outcome.

A FUNDAMENTAL CHARACTERISTIC OF TRUE REVELATION

With that foundation in place, we will now introduce some governing principles of revelation. They clarify how true revelation works and what factors govern the giving and receiving of it. This is critical to our understanding of revelation, for many of the questions that arise about revelation come because we do not understand, or do not remember, these governing principles.

We will begin with a principle that is so basic and so absolutely fundamental to our understanding of this process we call revelation that it serves as a foundation for all other principles. It permeates all aspects of revelation. It is so basic and so fundamental—and should be so obvious—that one might think it should require no more than passing mention. And yet it is so often overlooked, forgotten, or ignored that we need to discuss it in some detail.

The principle is simply this: *God determines all aspects of revelation.*

In Doctrine and Covenants 88, the Lord gives a wonderful invitation that is oft repeated throughout scripture:

> Draw near unto me and I will draw near unto you; seek me diligently and ye shall find me; ask, and ye shall receive; knock, and it shall be opened unto you.
>
> Whatsoever ye ask the Father in my name it shall be given unto you, that is expedient for you (D&C 88:63–64).

Then, just four verses later, the Lord adds this additional clarification: "And it shall be in *his own time,* and in *his own way,* and according to *his own will*" (D&C 88:68).

Let us explore the obvious for a moment. By definition, revelation is the giving of God's mind and will, along with other forms of light and truth, to His children. In other words, revelation always flows in one direction. It comes vertically, from God to man. It never flows in the opposite direction. Man can never reveal anything to God, because He is omniscient, which means He has *all* knowledge. God knows the past, the present and the future.* There is nothing that He does not know.

We are invited to communicate with God in the two-way process we call prayer, but when revelation takes place it is always in one direction only. So we say it again. We must always remember that Heavenly Father determines *all* aspects of the process of revelation. He decides:

> *We should recognize that the Lord will speak to us through the Spirit in his own time and in his own way. Many people do not understand this principle. They believe that when they are ready and when it suits their convenience, they can call upon the Lord and he will immediately respond, even in the precise way they have prescribed. Revelation does not come that way.*
>
> DALLIN H. OAKS,
> *ENSIGN,* MARCH 1997, 10

- To whom revelation is given.
- When it is given.
- How it is given.
- What is given.

Let us use a few examples that will illustrate how this principle works and how we often forget its importance:

---

* There are numerous scriptures that attest to God's perfect knowledge. A few of the more pertinent ones would include 2 Nephi 27:10; Alma 40:10; D&C 130:7; Moses 1:6; Abraham 2:8.

THE LORD DECIDES *TO WHOM* REVELATION IS GIVEN

Most frequently, revelation is given to the individual who is seeking it or in need of it. Sometimes, however, it is given through an individual who has a stewardship or responsibility over others. Examples of this would include the prophet receiving revelation for the Church or a bishop or stake president receiving inspiration for individual members of his unit.

As God is the God and Father of the spirits of all flesh, it is His right, it is His prerogative to communicate with the human family. God . . . has a right to dictate, has a right to make known His will, has a right to communicate with whom He will and control matters as He sees proper: it belongs to Him by right.

JOHN TAYLOR,
IN LUDLOW, *LATTER-DAY PROPHETS SPEAK*, 289

However, there are cases where we are left to wonder why the Lord would choose to give revelation to one person or group and not another. Why was the angel sent to the shepherds in Bethlehem rather than to the priests at the temple or to the people of Nazareth where Jesus was born? We can speculate about possible reasons for that, but ultimately we have to say, "We don't know." The important thing to remember is that it wasn't the shepherds' choice. It was God's choice.

In the instances that follow, it is tempting to question why the Lord proceeded the way that He did, but the answer always comes down to the same concept: "Because that is how God chose to do it."

Zacharias and Elisabeth. As a precursor to the birth of the Savior, the angel Gabriel visited Zacharias and announced that Elisabeth would conceive and have a son. Surely Elisabeth had offered as many prayers as Zacharias over the many years of her barrenness. So why didn't Gabriel visit Elisabeth first, as he did Mary? Or why not appear to both of them together so she could share in that marvelous experience? We don't know. It is the Lord's decision to whom revelation is given.

The Sons of Mosiah—Ammon and Aaron. Earlier we noted that one form of revelation comes as the Lord influences circumstances and events. The story of the sons of Mosiah and their mission to the Lamanites gives us an interesting contrast between how things developed for Ammon and how they developed for the other brothers. Ammon went to the land of Ishmael among the people of King Lamoni.

Though Ammon was taken and bound, when the king heard of his desire to live among his people he made him his servant. It was only three days later that Ammon went with the other servants to water the king's flocks and drove off the Lamanites. This had such an impact on the king that he and his entire household were converted. The king then sent out a proclamation that all his people were to listen to the preaching of Ammon (see Alma 18–19). It was an incredible missionary success story.

> *I cherish as one of the dearest experiences of life the knowledge that God hears the prayer of faith. It is true that the answers to our prayers may not always come as direct and at the time, nor in the manner, we anticipate; but they do come, and at a time and in a manner best for the interests of him who offers the supplication.*
>
> DAVID O. MCKAY,
> CONFERENCE REPORT,
> APRIL 1969, 152–53

And what was happening to Aaron and the others at this same time? Mormon records: "It was their lot to have fallen into the hands of a more hardened and a more stiff-necked people" who had "cast them out, and had smitten them, and had driven them from house to house, and from place to place" until "they were taken and cast into prison, and bound with strong cords, and kept in prison for many days" (Alma 20:30).

What a sharp contrast to Ammon's experience! When the brothers finally reunited, Ammon was shocked and "exceedingly sorrowful" because "they were naked, and their skins were worn exceedingly because of being bound with strong cords. And they also had suffered hunger, thirst, and all kinds of afflictions" (Alma 20:29).

Why such a dramatic difference? Why didn't the Lord directly intervene in behalf of Aaron and his brethren as He had done with Ammon? Was Aaron less faithful? Or less worthy? Had Ammon worked harder than his brothers? I think we can confidently say that the answer to those questions, in every case, is no. All the Lord gives by way of explanation is a simple phrase, "it was their lot" (Alma 20:30). If it was up to the missionaries, things would have been very different, but it wasn't.

There is a great principle in those four simple words, "it was their lot." When I was a boy, my mother used to help me and my two older brothers make decisions by having us "draw straws." In our case the straws were stick matches. When unpleasant chores or duties lay before us, none of us wanted what we perceived to be the worst job, and we would erupt into serious efforts to avoid the same. So my mother, ever patient, would get out three matches. She would break one in half, turn her back while she put them behind her fingers and thumb, leaving only the tips showing, then hold the three matches up for us to choose. I still remember the agony I felt when I was the first to choose. I would eye the matches carefully, trying to discern which was the shortest. When we pulled out a full match, thus escaping being the unfortunate one, we would utter cries of joy. When the "short straw" was drawn, groans of sorrow followed.

The Lord can hasten His work "in its time." (D&C 88:73; Isaiah 60:22.) Generally speaking, however, there is a divinely determined pace at which things will move. Even God's revelations come "in their time." (D&C 59:4.)

NEAL A. MAXWELL,
MEEK AND LOWLY, 89

Sometimes we seem to do the same thing in our lives. Setbacks or challenges come in our lives, and our natural tendency is to say, "Why me? What did I do to deserve this? How come I drew the short straw here?" It can happen in the reverse as well. Wonderful things happen. Some marvelous blessing comes; some windfall drops into our lives. Though less inclined to question good fortune than bad, we may still have a nagging feeling that "I don't deserve this. I haven't done anything special." In some cases, premortal choices may play a role, but sometimes the only answer seems to be, "it was our lot." It was the luck of the draw, as the saying goes. We should be careful not to impute blame or give credit when trials or good fortune are just the natural unfolding of events in this experience we call mortality.

Emma Smith and Mary Whitmer. When the opposition in Harmony, Pennsylvania, became so intense it hampered the translation of the Book of Mormon, Joseph accepted an invitation from the Whitmer family to move to Fayette, New York. Soon after, Joseph, Emma, and Oliver Cowdery moved in with the Whitmers. The Whitmers had a large family but a small cabin, so the addition of three more adults surely must have worked a hardship on Mary Whitmer, the mother in the household. David Whitmer, one of the Three Witnesses to the Book of Mormon, shared an interesting experience his mother had.

> Sometime after this [the arrival of Joseph, Emma and Oliver], my mother was going to milk the cows, when she was met out near the yard by [a] man* who said to her: "You have been very faithful and diligent in your labors, but you are tired because of the increase of your toil; it is proper therefore that you should receive a witness that your faith may be strengthened." Thereupon he showed her the plates. My father and mother had a large family of their own, the addition to it therefore of Joseph, his wife Emma and Oliver very greatly increased the toil and anxiety of my mother. And although she had never complained she had sometimes felt that her labor was too much, or at least she was perhaps beginning to feel so. This circumstance, however, completely removed all such feelings and nerved her up for her increased responsibilities.[1]

---

* Based on her description of the person and what is said later, it is clear that the "man" was Moroni dressed in normal clothing.

Nothing more is said of this experience except for the joy and comfort it brought to Mary Whitmer. However, one cannot but wonder what Emma felt when Mary returned to the house and shared that experience with the family, which we may suppose she did. How would Emma have felt when Mary Whitmer told the family that Moroni had said this privilege of seeing the plates was given because of the increase in her toil? Surely Emma had seen an increase in her toil. Her very marriage to Joseph drastically altered the load placed upon her—physically, emotionally, spiritually. Visitors came constantly to her home. Surely being the wife of the Prophet had increased her burdens. So why? Why Mary Whitmer and not Emma? The Lord has not chosen to answer those questions other than to say that it was "wisdom in me" (D&C 25:4).

> *Teach your students that one cannot "call down" the Spirit as some are prone to say. We can create an appropriate environment for the Holy Ghost to instruct us. Spiritual communication cannot be forced. We must qualify ourselves and be ready to receive the Lord's guidance and direction when He determines to provide it. No matter how urgent our personal timetable, the Lord responds according to His own will.*
>
> RICHARD G. SCOTT,
> CES SYMPOSIUM,
> AUGUST 11, 1998, 11

"I Was the Stake President." Some years ago, several of my colleagues and I were having lunch together. All of us were then serving as either bishops or stake presidents. In the course of the conversation, one of them asked this question: "Did you have any promptings from the Spirit prior to your call that something was coming?" It was interesting that it was almost an even balance. Some had been given some indication; others had none. But one of the stake presidents shared his experience. He said that he had been a recently called bishop when the stake presidency was reorganized. Because of that, when he was called in for an interview by the presiding authorities he wasn't concerned. He "knew" that as a new bishop he would be "left alone." So he recommended some names for consideration and went back home.

When he was called and he and his wife were asked to come back to the stake center, this new bishop brushed aside any idea that it was to be interviewed again. "I just thought the stake president wanted us to do something for the dinner we were having that night."

When they went in with the presiding authorities and he was called to be the new stake president, "I was stunned," he said. "I could scarcely believe it." As he and his wife left the building, he expressed to her his total surprise, to which she said, "Oh, I've known for a couple of months now." She then told him that she had had a dream three nights in a row. In the dream she had seen the two of them in the stake president's office and watched a man whom she did not know interview them and call her husband as the new stake president. She hadn't said anything to her husband because while she thought she knew what it meant, she wasn't completely sure and didn't want to be presumptuous.

Patience is tied very closely to faith in our Heavenly Father. Actually, when we are unduly impatient, we are suggesting that we know what is best—better than does God. Or, at least, we are asserting that our timetable is better than his. Either way we are questioning the reality of God's omniscience, as if, as some seem to believe, God were on some sort of postdoctoral fellowship.

Neal A. Maxwell,
Ensign, October 1980, 28

Here is the interesting thing. As he finished the story, the president frowned. "*I* was the new stake president," he said, obviously still a little frustrated. "How come my wife was the one who was given the dream?" We could speculate about that all the day long, and perhaps even come up with some very good possibilities as to why it was so. But such is only speculation. And it is fruitless, for the Lord didn't choose to explain Himself in this situation.

THE LORD DECIDES *WHEN* REVELATION IS GIVEN

In a quotation previously used, President Boyd K. Packer reminded us that we "cannot force spiritual things."[2]

On another occasion he added: "It is not wise to wrestle with the revelations with such insistence as to demand immediate answers or blessings to your liking."[3]

The timing of revelation or answers to prayers is also completely determined by the Lord. We can do things that enhance our readiness to receive revelation. We can facilitate things so revelation comes more quickly than it might otherwise. But *when* it comes is still the Lord's decision. We may *influence* the timing, but we cannot *determine* it.

In many cases, setting our own timetable, and then asking the Lord to meet our timetable, comes from our own sense of urgency in a matter. For example, we may have two job offers, one of which will soon be withdrawn if we don't answer. We may be inclined to say, "Lord, I have to know by Friday."

Another common mistake we make that is related to the timing of revelation is that we blithely move along with our lives, comfortable and content when things are going well. During such a period, we have somewhat of a casual relationship with the Lord and His Spirit. Then a crisis hits. Suddenly we are desperate for help and drop to our knees to begin pleading for God's intervention in our behalf. Because it is a crisis, there is usually great urgency involved, and we press the Lord for immediate help or guidance.

> *Perhaps our first mistake is to think that we own ourselves and also blocks of time. Of course, we have our agency and an inner sovereignty, but disciples are to sacrifice themselves to do Jesus' bidding with enough faith in God's timing to say, in effect, "Thy timing be done."*
>
> NEAL A. MAXWELL,
> *PROMISE OF DISCIPLESHIP*, 87–88

Because He is our Heavenly Father and because He loves us, there are times when He may answer those urgent pleas for help, even though we have not kept ourselves as ready or as worthy as we should have done. However, we are here to learn to walk by faith, and sometimes the only way we learn faith is to have a blessing withheld. Though we may be tempted to view this as a punishment or decide that God doesn't care, it is simply another manifestation of the principle that God, in all His wisdom and knowledge, decides when a revelation or answer to prayers should be given.

THE LORD DECIDES *HOW* REVELATION IS GIVEN

In chapters 4 to 12, we noted that the way in which revelation comes ranges from very direct and dramatic experiences to very subtle, almost indefinable feelings. It is a rich and varied process. We noted then, and we do so again, that we must take care that we don't assume that the more direct forms of revelation are of greater value and meaning to us. It is easy to almost covet the more dramatic forms of revelation, thinking that they validate our closeness to the Spirit and therefore our personal righteousness.

How revelation is given is completely the Lord's prerogative. We don't get to decide whether we will have an angel appear or receive instructions through the still small voice. The Lord chooses. The revelation may come in an audible voice, a dream, or through a sudden flash of insight as we read the scriptures.

In most cases, "his own way" is not the thunderous interruption or the blinding light, but what the scriptures call "the still small voice."
. . . Some have misunderstood this principle. As a result, some have looked exclusively for the great manifestations that are recorded in the scriptures and have failed to recognize the still, small voice that is given to them. This is like making up our minds that we will learn only from a teacher who shouts and that we will refuse to listen to even the wisest teaching when it comes in a whisper.

We need to know that the Lord rarely speaks loudly. His messages almost always come in a whisper.

DALLIN H. OAKS,
ENSIGN, MARCH 1997, 11–12

Revelation is not a menu from which we get to select what items we find most appealing.

This can be a great test of our faith. For example, a woman bears testimony on fast Sunday of a remarkable way in which the Lord answered her prayers. Someone in the audience may have been searching for months for a similar answer and has received nothing.

Another example is seen in healings. Why does one person see a miraculous healing after a priesthood blessing while someone of equal worthiness and faith receives a blessing and no deliverance from suffering comes? Those kinds of circumstances are commonly seen and are a part of life. Again and again, there is only one answer. *God sets all of the conditions for the giving of revelation, and we must learn to trust His wisdom and timing.*

This is at the very heart of learning to develop faith or, as the Lord said to Abraham, to see how we will respond as He "proves" us (Abraham 3:25). In this process, we must take care that we don't compare ourselves to others and conclude that we are more or less righteous and faithful than someone else because of what has happened to us.

It is a wicked and adulterous generation that seeketh after a sign. Show me Latter-day Saints who have to feed upon miracles, signs and visions in order to keep them steadfast in the Church, and I will show you members of the Church who are not in good standing before God, and who are walking in slippery paths. It is not by marvelous manifestations unto us that we shall be established in the truth, but it is by humility and faithful obedience to the commandments and laws of God.

JOSEPH F. SMITH,
GOSPEL DOCTRINE, 7

THE LORD DECIDES *WHAT* IS GIVEN IN A REVELATION

The same principle applies just as truly in the aspect of *what* is given through revelation as to the *who,* the *when,* and the *how.* Very often, we receive less than we hoped for. Sometimes we receive an answer that seems to go counter to what we feel is best for us.

Take Nephi, for example. It would have been much less of a challenge for him as he headed back into Jerusalem that night if the Lord had chosen to say, "Go back into the city. There you will find a drunken man passed out in the gutter. That will be Laban, and I will deliver him into your hands. You will then take his keys to the treasury and convince his servant to give you the plates. And by the way, the servant, whose name is Zoram, is a faithful man and you should convince him to come with you."

That kind of detailed direction happens rarely, if at all.* The pattern for us is typically the same as it was for Nephi. He said, "I was led by the Spirit, *not knowing beforehand* the things which I should do" (1 Nephi 4:6).

That often frustrates us. If we just knew the *why* of that prompting, it would be much easier for us to respond to it. But such is not the Lord's way.

HIS TIME, HIS WAY, HIS WILL

Think of the irony of all this. We are finite, sinful, self-centered beings who are quick to err, slow to hearken, constantly stumbling, and highly limited in our view. God is infinite, all knowing, perfect in every aspect of His nature. And yet we try to tell Him what is best for us, what we really need, what kind of solutions will benefit us the most. What are we thinking at such times as those?

No wonder the scriptures warn us again and again about trying to direct God in His doings:

- "When they are learned they think they are wise, and they hearken not unto the counsel of God, for they set it aside, supposing they know of themselves" (2 Nephi 9:28).
- "Seek not to counsel the Lord, but to take counsel from his hand. For behold, ye yourselves know that he counseleth in wisdom, and in justice, and in great mercy, over all his works" (Jacob 4:10).
- "Counsel with the Lord in all thy doings, and he will direct thee for good" (Alma 37:37).

---

* One exception could be the instructions Nephi received to build a ship capable of crossing an ocean (1 Nephi 17:8).

Of course, the greatest example of a willingness to accept God's will and purposes in all we do was set by the Savior Himself. Abinadi describes Christ's entire premortal, mortal and postmortal nature with one simple phrase: "The will of the Son being swallowed up in the will of the Father" (Mosiah 15:7).

> *Not understanding these principles of revelation, some people postpone acknowledging their testimony until they have experienced a miraculous event. They fail to realize that with most people—especially those raised in the Church—gaining a testimony is not an event but a process.*
>
> DALLIN H. OAKS,
> *ENSIGN,* MARCH 1997, 14

He becomes our model, the benchmark for which we all should strive. Facing the most intense agony in all eternity, He pled with the Father: "If it be possible, let this cup pass from me." Even the Son of God, in all of His majesty submission to the Father's will, shrank back before the task that lay before him. Then came one word that provides the perfect model of how we should pray: "*Nevertheless* not as I will, but as thou wilt" (Matthew 26:39).

IN SUMMARY

I had a simple and yet sweet experience many years ago that provided a reminder of why we need to trust in the Lord and let Him determine all aspects of personal revelation.

I was teaching in the institutes of religion in southern California. Our family was young and I was still quite new in my teaching career. One summer afternoon I went out into the backyard to get something from the garage. As I stepped out, I noticed a group of children seated in a half circle on the patio. I paused. They hadn't seen me and so I observed for a moment without interrupting them.

Cynthia, our oldest daughter, who was six at the time and recently "graduated" from kindergarten, was standing before a group of seven or eight of our own and some of the neighbor's children, none of whom had yet started school. She had one of her school books open in her hands. The children sat before her on the cement in a semicircle. They had small "lap boards" made of cardboard sheets torn from a box, and each held stubs of pencils poised over blank sheets of paper.

I couldn't help but smile. It was a warm and tender scene. Clearly, they were playing school and Cyndie was their "teacher." Fascinated, I stepped back slightly so as not to interrupt the proceedings. "Now children," she began in a most solemn voice, "I am going to teach you everything I know." She then began to share the results of her educational career to that point. She started teaching them the letters of the alphabet. And they were impressed. I could see it on their faces. This was heady stuff!

Finally I walked on, chuckling to myself at what I had just witnessed. But as I entered the garage, a thought suddenly hit me with great force. "As I stand before my religion classes and 'teach them everything I know' about the gospel, it that what Heavenly Father does? Does He stand back and watch, smiling gently at my naive innocence?"

It was a humbling moment and a powerful reminder of my relationship to the Father. A few days later I penned the following lines into my journal:

> I know that next to God and His great wisdom,
> My mind is "child," and there's much more to get.
> Like children playing school in summer sunshine,
> I barely know the basic alphabet.

CHAPTER 14

SECOND PRINCIPLE:
WE MUST ACTIVELY SEEK REVELATION

"You took no thought save it was to ask" (D&C 9:7).

AGENCY AND REVELATION

There is another principle that governs the giving and receiving of revelation that comes close in terms of its importance. It has to do with the relationship between moral agency and hearing the voice of the Lord. Most of us have a basic understanding of this concept, but its application in our quest for revelation is so important that it bears a careful review here.

We know that agency was part of Heavenly Father's plan for us from the beginning and that Lucifer's plan was rejected because he "sought to destroy the agency of man" (Moses 4:3). Although we speak of it often, we may not fully appreciate the pivotal importance of this key doctrine.

There are at least two reasons why agency is so critical to Heavenly Father's plan for us: First, free will and moral agency are directly connected to our happiness. How can anyone be truly happy if he or she is being forced to do something, even something that is good?

Second, agency also defines the very concept of morality, or rightness and wrongness. If there is no agency, how can someone be held accountable for their actions? For example, history presents many tragic cases of people being forced to do despicable things or to "convert" to this religion or that so they could become "righteous." Violence, torture, captivity, and threat of death have all been used to bring people into compliance with some desired course of action. Surely such will not be judged on the same basis as those who openly rebel against God and choose a path of sin.

Because agency is so critical to our happiness and also to our ability to prove ourselves to God, it is a sacred and fundamental doctrine of the gospel. With all of His infinite power, Heavenly Father will never force or coerce His children to do something, even if it is the best thing for them. In a similar way,

> *While the Holy Ghost may be conferred upon us, and is designed to be our guide and support, it is only restrained and manifested in its fulness in our guidance and defense in proportion to the degree to which we cultivate it and listen to its promptings. We may lose it entirely through indifference or transgression, and once deprived of its presence we are left in darkness more dense than before its reception.*
>
> ANTHONY W. IVINS,
> CONFERENCE REPORT,
> APRIL 1934, 101–2

He will not force upon us a knowledge of Him and His will. In a word, He will not force revelation upon us. A song included in the first hymnal compiled by Emma Smith expresses this clearly:

> *Know this, that ev'ry soul is free*
> *To choose his life and what he'll be;*
> *For this eternal truth is giv'n:*
> *That God will force no man to heav'n.*
>
> *He'll call, persuade, direct aright,*
> *And bless with wisdom, love, and light,*
> *In nameless ways be good and kind,*
> *But never force the human mind.[1]*

ASK AND YE SHALL RECEIVE

This principle of agency applies fully in the process of revelation. As we have shown, God has a great desire to share what He knows with

His children. His entire work and glory is focused on helping us achieve immortality and eternal life. He not only invites us to come unto Him, but He commands us to do so. This is made very clear in the scriptures. In fact, one of the most frequently repeated commandments in all of scripture is one where we are told to "ask" of God so that we may "receive"! There are more than *forty* references where that counsel is given! That kind of repetition says much about what the Lord wants us to do. Through asking, we exercise our agency and initiate the contact. Surely with more than forty invitations, we may feel completely comfortable in approaching the Father and asking Him for things in prayer. In fact, we have been commanded to do this so often, we should not feel comfortable until we are doing so on a regular basis.

"YOU TOOK NO THOUGHT SAVE IT WAS TO ASK ME"

However, asking is not enough.

We have talked before of when Oliver Cowdery came to Harmony, Pennsylvania, and began acting as scribe for the Prophet. He also desired the gift of translation, which the Lord granted to him. But he failed. In what is now section 9 of the Doctrine and Covenants, the Lord told him why this had happened.

> *The trouble with most of our prayers is that we give them as if we were picking up the phone and ordering groceries—we place our order and hang up.*
>
> GORDON B. HINCKLEY,
> *TEACHINGS OF GORDON B. HINCKLEY,* 469

The Lord said: "Behold, you have not understood; you have supposed that I would give it unto you, *when you took no thought save it was to ask me*" (D&C 9:7).

We may be tempted to be a little critical of Oliver and ask ourselves how he could have missed something that seems so obvious. However, many of us also make this mistake as we seek inspiration and revelation from the Lord. We think that asking is sufficient. What Oliver learned that day is a lesson for all of us. *Obtaining revelation is not a passive experience.* We don't just toss off a prayer, then sit back and wait for the answer to come. We must choose to actively participate in the revelatory process. Asking is how the process begins, but it is not how it ends.

In twelve of those forty-plus scriptural instances noted above, the commandment to "ask" is coupled with other verbs. For example, in the Sermon on the Mount, the Savior used three different imperative verbs. In each case He coupled the commands with a promise: "*Ask,* and it shall be given you; *seek,* and ye shall find; *knock,* and it shall be opened unto you" (Matthew 7:7).

There is almost an ascending order in those three commands. *Asking* is primarily a verbal action. *Seeking* implies a higher level of involvement—when we seek we begin to do something; the word implies an earnestness that commits both the mind and the heart, the intellect and the emotions. Finally, *knocking* suggests some actual physical action. The implication is also that once the door is open, we will move through it, for that was the purpose in our knocking. The Lord drew on that latter imagery in one of the letters to the seven churches in Asia included in the book of Revelation. He said: "Behold, I stand at the door, and knock: if any man hear my voice, and open the door, I will come in to him, and will sup with him, and he with me" (Revelation 3:20).

> *We watch. We wait. We listen for that still, small voice. When it speaks, wise men and women obey. We do not postpone following promptings of the Spirit. . . .*
>
> *Never, never, never postpone following a prompting.*
>
> *As we pursue the journey of life, let us learn the language of the Spirit. May we remember and respond to the Master's gentle invitation: "Behold, I stand at the door, and knock: if any man hear my voice, and open the door, I will come in to him."*
>
> THOMAS S. MONSON,
> *ENSIGN,* MAY 1985, 68, 70

It is interesting to look at the verbs the scriptures use when the Lord encourages us to seek further light and knowledge from Him:

- "*Meditate* upon these things; *give thyself wholly* to them; that thy profiting may appear to all" (1 Timothy 4:15).

- "Whoso would *hearken* unto the word of God, and *would hold fast unto it,* . . . would never perish" (1 Nephi 15:24).
- "*Feast upon* the words of Christ; for behold, the words of Christ will tell you all things what ye should do" (2 Nephi 32:3).
- "*Lay hold upon* the word of God, which is quick and powerful" (Helaman 3:29).
- "A commandment I give unto you that *ye search these things diligently*" (3 Nephi 23:1).
- "*Treasure up in your minds continually* the words of life" (D&C 84:85).

Meditate, hearken, hold fast to, feast upon, lay hold upon, search diligently, treasure up—these are not passive verbs. They are action words. They require us to do something. And there is the challenge. Verbal action is not enough. We must *do* much more than that. Oliver was told that if he wanted the gift to translate he was to "ask in faith" (D&C 8:1). *Faith is a principle of action.* "True faith always moves its possessor to some kind of physical and mental action."[2]

"STUDY IT OUT IN YOUR MIND"

As He so often does, the Lord didn't just mildly rebuke Oliver. He also taught him what he should have done. "You took no thought save it was to ask me," the Lord said. "*But,* behold, I say unto you, that you must study it out in your mind; *then* you must ask me if it be right" (D&C 9:7–8).

The "but" in that sentence could be replaced with concepts like "however," "instead of," or "you should have." In essence the Lord was saying, "Oliver, *instead* of just asking, you should have done something else first. You must study it out in your mind, make a decision, then ask me if it be right."

"IF IT BE RIGHT"

The words *decision* and *decide* are not used in that passage, yet they are clearly implied. Note the language: "You must study *it* out in your

148

mind and ask me if *it* be right." What are the antecedents for those two "its"? The first "it" seems to refer to the issue or problem confronting us. In Oliver's case, those were issues of translation—perhaps how to use the Urim and Thummim or how to render a specific passage. In our case it could be whatever challenge or problem we are facing.

But the second "it" is not the same as the first one. That "it" implies that after studying it out in our minds, we make a decision. We come to some kind of conclusion about what we should do, then take *that* to the Lord and ask Him if "it"—our decision—be right.

Here is a practical example of how studying an issue out in our minds and then making a decision before asking the Lord if it is right can be applied to real-life issues.

Choosing whom to marry is one of the most important decisions we make in mortality and for eternity, so it is one of the most important places to apply the lesson taught to Oliver. Unfortunately, too often we let our hearts drive this decision. The Lord doesn't say study it out in your heart. It is "study it out in your mind." So while romance provides the attraction and the driving motivation, we have to do more than let our hearts lead us here. Hollywood and the media don't help, for they constantly portray heart-driven romance as the accepted way to make such determination, and they typically show it happening somewhere between twenty-four and forty-eight hours. So how do we study this issue out in our minds so we can make a wise decision, then take it to the Lord?

Don't rush the courtship. When we begin the courting process we always seek to appear at our very best. We watch our manners and our words. We go to great lengths to make a positive impression. Even when we are tired or irritated, we suppress those feelings and put on our best face. But this can only be maintained for a limited time. That is why "whirlwind" courtships are so dangerous. (Someone has noted that tornados can be very exciting, but they also leave a lot of destruction in their wake.) So as the couple spend more meaningful time together, they start to get more comfortable with each other. The artificiality and pretense begin to fade and the real persons come more and more to light so that they come to know who and what they really are.*

Use the time of courtship to get to know the partner. It isn't enough to just spend time together, it has to be time that provides opportunities to get to know the other person. This isn't done only by going to movies or playing video games together or being in large groups all the time. Spend time with his family.** Do their values harmonize with yours? If not, does he hold to those same values? How does he treat his parents? His siblings? Work together on significant projects. Do more than just go to sacrament meeting together and hold hands. Volunteer to baby-sit someone's children together. How helpful is he during that time? Does he sit in front of the television and leave all the work to you? If so, that's probably an indicator of what's coming in the marriage.

You may not think of this as "studying" in the usual sense of the word, but in courtship it fits very nicely the requirement to "study it [the issue "Is he the one I should marry?"] out in your mind." There is an old and wise saying that goes something like this: "If you want to know what a person is really like, don't listen to what they say. *Watch what they do. See what they are.*" President David O. McKay put it this way: "During courtship, keep your eyes wide open; but, after marriage, keep them half shut."³

Keep the physical expressions of your love within tightly controlled bounds. This is not just to avoid the tragedy of immorality, as important as that is. This is part of the being wise in your "study" of his potential as an eternal mate. When physical affection dominates the relationship, several damaging things happen. First of all, time spent in physical romance robs time from the interactions that are far more important to our decision-making process. Second, during physical affection our

---

* Incidentally, this is one of the things that makes Internet matchmaking so fraught with risk. All of the initial interaction is without any opportunity to watch the "whole" person and interact directly with him or her.

** To avoid the awkwardness of he/she and him/her, I have used the masculine form, but both genders are implied throughout.

emotions are raised to a high pitch. This pushes out rational and more balanced thinking. It is easy to confuse these emotional "highs" with true love. Third, by nature the aspects of a physical relationship often affect the male differently than they do the female. This frequently introduces stress into the courting process, because he may push for more physical affection and she begins to wonder if that is all he cares about.

Pray constantly. All through the courtship process, don't just pray if this person is the right one, or if they would make a "good" husband or wife. Pray that the Lord will open your spiritual eyes, as well as your emotional ones, so you can "look upon the heart" and not just on the "countenance" (see 1 Samuel 16:7). Pray that the Lord will show *you* what you need to do to become the kind of person who will attract the kind of person you want to marry. Pray for wisdom and insight and the Lord's blessings.

Decide and then seek confirmation. Too often young adults have the unrealistic expectation that when they find the right one, the Lord will give them some wonderful sign that will let them know for sure. This is *your* decision, not the Lord's. He stands ready to help and advise and guide, but *you must choose.* Stop waiting for lightning to strike, for bells to ring, for electricity to shoot through your whole being. Get the Hollywood model of love out of your heads. Note the counsel of Elder Boyd K. Packer on this matter:

> While I am sure some young couples have some special guidance in getting together, I do not believe in predestined love. If you desire the inspiration of the Lord in this crucial decision, you must live the standards of the Church, and you must pray constantly for the wisdom to recognize those qualities upon which a successful union may be based. *You must do the choosing,* rather than to seek for some one-and-only so-called soul mate, chosen for you by someone else and waiting for you. You are to do the choosing. You must

be wise beyond your years and humbly prayerful unless you choose amiss.[4]

IN SUMMARY

There are many other forms of "doing" that will facilitate the process of receiving and recognizing the voice of the Lord—searching the scriptures, humbling ourselves, following the promptings when they come, and many more. Throughout the remaining chapters of this book, these other things will be discussed individually.

If the Lord determines all aspects of revelation, there may be occasions when He chooses to send revelation to us when we have not been specifically seeking or where all the conditions have not been met. By the same token, He may choose to withhold answers even when all of the conditions have been faithfully fulfilled. Revelation is His gift to give as He sees fit or to withhold as He sees fit.

One of my daughters coined a phrase that aptly summarizes what we have said in this chapter. She said, "I have found that very often I get revelation *on the move*." By this she meant that though she may ponder and pray and study and decide, the revelation doesn't actually come until she is up and implementing the decision she has made. Sometimes she feels that it isn't right and changes what she will do. More frequently, it is while she is *doing* something that the quiet confirmation that this is the right thing comes.

When we learn to actively ask, seek, and knock, the promise of the Lord is clear and wonderful:

> If thou shalt ask, *thou shalt receive revelation upon revelation, knowledge upon knowledge,* that thou mayest know the mysteries and peaceable things—that which bringeth joy, that which bringeth life eternal (D&C 42:61).

CHAPTER 15

THIRD PRINCIPLE:
MOST REVELATION COMES INCREMENTALLY

"I will give . . . men line upon line, precept upon precept,
here a little and there a little" (2 Nephi 28:30).

SIMPLE YET PROFOUND

A third principle that helps us better understand how the process of personal revelation works is simple, clear, and easily understood. Although several places in the scriptures are often quoted by the Brethren, it is in the Book of Mormon that we find the principle stated most clearly and completely:

> For behold, thus saith the Lord God: I will give unto the children of men line upon line, precept upon precept, here a little and there a little (2 Nephi 28:30).

It doesn't get much plainer than that. In His infinite wisdom, *God's pattern of revelation is to give light and truth in small increments, or portions, over a period of time.* It needs no further definition and explanation than that given by the Lord.

However, within that simplicity there are profound practical implications for us as we seek to better understand how the Lord deals with His children. These implications are worthy of further exploration.

WHY DOES GOD CHOOSE TO TEACH US LINE UPON LINE?

We cannot always understand God's dealings with His children. Sometimes He explains the "whys" of His actions, but often He does not. We must always keep in mind the Lord's reminder to Isaiah: "For my thoughts are not your thoughts, neither are your ways my ways, saith the Lord" (Isaiah 55:8).

This principle of receiving revelation line upon line and precept upon precept is clearly part of God's plan. It is part of His doing things "in his own time, and in his own way" (D&C 88:68).

Elder David A. Bednar, while serving as president of Ricks College in Idaho, spoke on this pattern of revelation, giving a caution about some false expectations we may have:

> If you and I would learn to discern the difference between our own emotions and the promptings of the Holy Ghost, then we must come to recognize the Lord's pattern and process for giving us spiritual knowledge. And the phrase ". . . line upon line, precept upon precept . . ." describes a central feature of the Lord's pattern.
>
> I believe many of us unknowingly accept a faulty assumption about the Lord's pattern. And this faulty assumption then produces erroneous expectations about how we receive spiritual knowledge. And that faulty assumption and our misinformed expectations ultimately hinder

---

My testimony, obtained a long time ago on the street corners of England, has grown line upon line and precept upon precept until I can now stand and testify as a special witness of the Lord Jesus Christ that our Savior lives. He is the Son of God our Eternal Father. My life has never been the same since I anchored my soul to the truths of the restored gospel of Jesus Christ.

M. RUSSELL BALLARD,
*WHEN THOU ART
CONVERTED,* 36

---

our ability to recognize and respond to the promptings of the Holy Ghost. . . .

Most typically we receive a series of seemingly small and incremental spiritual impressions and nudges, which in totality constitute the desired confirmation about the correctness of the path we are pursuing.[1]

The writings of the prophets do give us at least some answers as to why the Lord chooses to work with us in this manner. One possibility is that this follows the pattern of how we learn and grow in mortality.

> *When the Lord gives us "line upon line" and "precept upon precept" about Himself and His plans, many ignore these great gifts. Instead of lines, some demand paragraphs and even pages. When God provides "here a little, and there a little" . . . some want a lot—now!*
>
> NEAL A. MAXWELL,
> *NEAL A. MAXWELL QUOTE BOOK,* 288

How We Learn Physically

President Joseph Fielding Smith taught an important principle about how we learn things in this life:

> The individual seeking knowledge goes to school for several years. He learns line upon line and precept upon precept. *There is no other way.* Perhaps he may think it would be an excellent thing could he go to school, say for one year, and accomplish everything, but *all knowledge comes in the same way,* that is, gradually through study and by faith. In the establishment of the Church, Joseph Smith had to be instructed a little at a time. If the Lord had revealed to him the fulness of the plan of salvation with all its covenants and obligations at one time, he would have been overwhelmed as with a flood and could not have endured. So it is with us in all other matters of learning. We must plod along growing in understanding and power day by day.[2]

When we are born, except for a few automatic, instinctive functions, all else has to be acquired through individual learning—individual in the sense that no one else can do it for us. That learning process almost universally involves small, step-by-step development requiring significant amounts of time. At first, our spirit (or mind, as some might call it) does not know how to control a physical body. We can want something, but we have no way to carry out that choice. We are completely dependent on others to sustain us until we gain mastery of the body. It is not enough just to want. *We have to learn how to make our body obey our will!*

That is the very nature of our learning. It comes step-by-step, one increment at a time. Simple skills build on each other until we can make our body follow complex commands. A child can barely raise her head at the beginning, but soon learns to roll over, to sit up, and to scoot about. It is a never-ending process of exploration and experimentation followed by learning and control. Scooting leads to crawling. Crawling is followed by standing up to furniture.

It not just learning *how* to do things, but allowing the body to develop as well. Muscles have to be strengthened; the bones have to grow and develop. The first faltering steps quickly steady. Almost before we are aware, walking progresses to running, then jumping, skipping, skating, basketball, and ballet. Step-by-step that newborn spirit learns how to control the body, and the body grows and strengthens and develops. That is how we learn.

Seldom will you receive a complete response all at once. It will come a piece at a time, in packets, so that you will grow in capacity. As each piece is followed in faith, you will be led to other portions until you have the whole answer. That pattern requires you to exercise faith.

RICHARD G. SCOTT,
ENSIGN, MAY 2007, 9

Even the Savior was not exempt from this learning process. Before coming to earth, He was the premortal Jehovah, a member of the Godhead. In modern revelation, we learn that "He [Jesus] received not of the fulness at the first, but received grace for grace; . . . [and] continued from grace to grace, until he received a fulness" (D&C 93:12–13). Luke described it this way: "And the child grew, and waxed strong in spirit, filled with wisdom: and the grace of God was upon him" (Luke 2:40).

How We Learn Mentally and Spiritually

The same step-by-gradual-step is true in mental development as well. One does not study calculus in kindergarten. A parent does not tap a child on the head to teach him how to read and write or to play the piano. Here too it is line upon line, precept upon precept. In most cases it takes years before higher level skills are mastered and education is completed.

Again, free will and agency are not sufficient. Simply wanting mastery doesn't do it. Agency increases as we gain mastery. Then we can both choose *and* do. There is no way around it.

One man wryly put it this way: "I would love to run a marathon. I think it would be a great accomplishment. But that's not enough. Oh, I could take my body to the starting line and command it sternly: 'All right, body! Here we go. Twenty-six miles, three hundred eighty-five yards. Do it!'" He then chuckled ruefully. "My body would roll on the ground, howling with laughter, and say, 'Who are you talking to, sir?'"

What is true in the physical and mental realms is equally true of spiritual growth. Wouldn't it be wonderful if one prayer brought full spirituality, if one grand act of unselfishness made us a saint, if one reading through the scriptures brought scriptural mastery? Spiritual mastery involves the same slow process of learning and development as does physical and mental learning. Desire here is not sufficient either. We cannot just want to be spiritual, to be righteous, to be perfect. It involves a lifetime of trial and error, learning and growth, moving from a spiritual crawl to spiritual mastery.

Learning and growing through small, incremental steps will gradually, almost imperceptibly, enlarge our capacity and ability and thus allow us to do more and more in increasingly efficient and effective ways. This is what is meant by growth and development. And this principle holds true in regard to receiving revelation. As we respond to revelation, we learn and grow and increase our capacity to receive more.

Agency and Learning

A second reason why the Lord chooses to reveal things to us in small increments, "here a little and there a little," has to do with the doctrine of agency. It is a gift fundamental to our happiness and well-being, and it is also a key factor in the plan of salvation. And agency is everywhere intertwined with learning and development.

Mortal man is a dual being, a spirit child of God tabernacled in a physical body. Endowed with agency, he is placed here in mortality between opposing forces. The influence of God on the one hand inspires, pleads, and urges him to follow the way of life. On the other hand is the power of Satan tempting him to disbelieve and disregard God's commandments. The consequences of his choices are of the all-or-nothing sort. There is no way for him to escape the influence of these opposing powers. Inevitably he is led by one or the other. His God-given free agency gives him the power and option to choose. But choose he must.

MARION G. ROMNEY,
CONFERENCE REPORT,
OCTOBER 1962, 94

Think again for a moment of our development as children. Very quickly agency comes to the forefront. We choose to master a new skill. We want it badly enough to press the body to our service. What child comes through those early developmental stages without a lot of bumps, bruises, cuts, and scrapes? Why is that so? Many times it is because the child thrusts away the protecting hands of watchful parents. "I do it myself!" is a cry that every parent hears again and again.

And in one form or another, that cry continues on into adulthood. Agency is a powerful driving force within us, even at the earliest stages of our lives. We value freedom and independence and the right to choose. How many lives have been sacrificed on the battlefield as evidence of how highly we prize our agency?

It is significant that the Lord, who has infinite power and could force everyone to do His will, takes great care never to violate our agency. He always acts in a way that we are not coerced or manipulated to any degree. It has to be so, or otherwise there could be no joy and no judgment. It is humans who constantly try to force others to comply with their will.

We are told that the very purpose of mortal life is to prove ourselves (see Abraham 3:25–26). We do this through a process we call *obedience*. If we follow a prompting or obey direction, we are giving evidence that we want to be taught and directed by the Lord. Giving us light and truth one small portion at a time is essential to that proving process and helps protect our developing agency. It allows us to move forward in both our physical and spiritual development only as we choose to do so, or choose to be obedient.

For example, God tells us of the consequences of our choices, both good and bad, and then allows us to choose. But suppose that God showed us with perfect clarity the short-term and eternal consequences of our sins just as we were about to make a bad choice. Or suppose that the very instant we made a wrong choice, we were punished by the con-sequences of those choices. That would curtail our agency dramatically. We would then not walk by faith, but by sight and from fear. It would short-circuit the proving process.

WHAT ARE WE SUPPOSED TO LEARN FROM THIS PATTERN OF REVELATION?

Now that we have examined *why* the Lord deals with us in this manner, let us now ask *what* we are supposed to learn from this process. Getting revelation one small piece at a time can be highly frustrating, but there are clearly developmental lessons for us to learn and the line upon line process helps us learn those lessons. There are probably several things we can learn, but four specific lessons seem to stand out above the others:

Incremental Revelation Helps Us Learn Patience

One of the most obvious challenges of this incremental process of revelation is that it tests our patience. When an urgent problem or challenge confronts us and we seek help from the Lord, the very urgency of our situation works counter to the attribute of patience. "This is not the time to teach me patience," we say to ourselves. "I need my answer and I need it *now!*"

But one of the core proving processes of mortality is to see if we can develop patience, for patience is a handmaiden of faith. Elder Neal A. Maxwell put it this way:

It is our stubborn use of our agency that slows us, not God's desire for delay. The eternal attributes require time for their development and expression. Instant forgiveness is not always given, though it is desperately wished for. Instant compassion is not always generated, though it is so needed. . . . And, of course, instant patience is a contradiction in terms.

NEAL A. MAXWELL,
EVEN AS I AM, 47

We . . . make the mistake of not realizing that faith and patience are to be in tandem. . . . To be *tried* really means to be *developed*, which will happen if we are meek, the trials being part of the spiritual isometrics mentioned earlier.

We certainly need to focus on faith, of course, but likewise on patience, which is so vital to succeed while living in process of time.[3]

We gain some idea of how the Lord views this attribute when we realize that the words *patient* or *patience* are used about 125 times in the scriptures. In most of these cases, the reference makes it clear that patience is a quality the Lord esteems. Take a few moments and study the following references. Note how the Lord feels about patience:

Hebrews 12:1; James 1:3–4; Mosiah 24:16; Alma 17:11; D&C 58:3; 98:1–2, 12.

Submitting to Incremental Revelation Opens the Way to More Revelation

A second lesson we can learn from this particular aspect of receiving revelation is that when we are patient and submit to the Lord's timetable of revelation, it opens the way for additional revelation. Let us look again at our theme scripture for this chapter:

For behold, thus saith the Lord God: I will give unto the children of men line upon line, precept upon precept, here a little and there a little; and blessed are those who hearken unto my precepts, and lend an ear unto my counsel, for they shall learn wisdom; *for unto him that receiveth I will give more* (2 Nephi 28:30).

Again, let us use an example from everyday life, for this principle works in day-to-day learning as well. Many children have been started on piano lessons by conscientious parents, but somewhere along the way, they decide that the benefits achieved in this very slow learning process are not worth the price required. So even against pretty strong urging by the parents, they stop the learning process. In doing so, any further progress in piano skills is immediately stopped. Therefore, of the hundreds who start piano lessons as children, only a

Put difficult questions in the back of your minds and go about your lives. Ponder and pray quietly and persistently about them.

The answer may not come as a lightning bolt. It may come as a little inspiration here and a little there, "line upon line, precept upon precept" (D&C 98:12). Some answers will come from reading the scriptures, some from hearing speakers. And, occasionally, when it is important, some will come by very direct and powerful inspiration.

BOYD K. PACKER, *ENSIGN*, NOVEMBER 1979, 21

small fraction can play the piano as adults. And of the fraction who can play the piano as adults, only a tiny percentage make the choice to stay at it to the point where they become concert pianists. These various levels of achievement are directly related to the use of individual agency.

This impact of agency on achievement is especially true in our quest for revelation. As the Lord reveals Himself and His will to us, one concept or one principle at a time, we have to choose whether to accept it or not. If we reject or ignore even small increments of light and truth, the process of receiving further light and knowledge is hindered.

We Receive Direction without Explanation

Elder Neal A. Maxwell noted that "President Boyd K. Packer has counseled us that often when we receive guidance from the Holy Ghost, *we get directions without explanation.*"[4] This is another way of saying we receive revelation in increments. First comes some form of direction. Then only as we follow that direction comes further information and confirmation. It is another lesson in the spiritual learning process— another test of whether or not we will be obedient—so let us examine it more closely.

Nephi's attempt to get the brass plates is a classic study in this interplay between agency, faith, and incremental revelation. In his experience, we can clearly see the Lord's pattern unfolding. Most of us are familiar with the details of Nephi's experience that are found in 1 Nephi 3–4, so we will only briefly summarize.

Lehi had a dream (the first step of revelation in this case) in which he was told to send his sons back to Jerusalem to get the brass plates. Note, however, that the Lord didn't tell Lehi *how* they were to do this, only that it needed to be done. The four young men used their agency and chose to do what their father requested (though for Laman and Lemuel the choice was accompanied by resentment and grumbling). Using their own intelligence and best judgment they approached Laban the first time and failed. In Laman's and Lemuel's eyes, that proved that this wasn't going to work. But Nephi had already affirmed his determination to "go and do" (1 Nephi 3:7), and so he had the idea (a second increment of revelation) to go down and collect the wealth their father had abandoned and try to purchase the plates from Laban. It was a good idea, but the second attempt also failed and nearly cost them their lives. At that point Laman and Lemuel hardened their hearts and refused to do any more. Even the personal appearance of an angel didn't soften them enough to change their minds. They had made their choice, and, for them, revelation eventually stopped. Nephi, on the other hand, chose not to lose faith. He would try again.

It is in this third attempt that we are taught the principle of "direction without explanation." He states, "I was led by the Spirit, *not knowing beforehand* the things which I should do. Nevertheless, I went forth" (1 Nephi 4:6–7).

That is incremental revelation. As he moved back into the city at great personal risk, he was being *directed* by the Spirit, but he was not given any *explanation* of what was going to happen or how it was going to turn out. It wasn't knowledge that kept him going. It was faith. That kind of incremental instruction was part of Nephi's learning experience. For example, we are told that when he was building the ship for his family, the Lord's direction on how to do so was given to him "from time to time" (1 Nephi 18:1) instead of all at once. It was Nephi's willingness to submit to such line upon line teaching that defined the rest of the history of the Book of Mormon.

We need teaching continually, line upon line, precept upon precept, here a little and there a little. Hence we have our various organizations of the priesthood, calculated to oversee, . . . to regulate, to teach, to instruct, and to enter into all the ramifications of life whether they pertain to this world or the world to come.

JOHN TAYLOR,
GOSPEL KINGDOM, 134

Remember the experience described by President Monson where he felt impressed to go visit a friend (see pages 67–68). That's all it was—a feeling or a gentle impression. If the Lord had said, "Your friend is sitting on the edge of the swimming pool in his wheelchair and he is in such despair that he is considering suicide. Go quickly and save him," it would not have required the same degree of faith and choice.

In one of our beloved hymns, we find these lines: "Keep thou my feet; I do not ask to see / The distant scene—one step enough for me."[5] Those words may be easy to sing, but they are extremely challenging to live. To choose when we cannot see the road ahead requires faith. Illuminating the road far beyond where we are currently placing our feet would greatly reduce the need for faith and thus limit our spiritual learning. President Joseph F. Smith, who served his first mission at age sixteen, described how this worked in his life:

> When I as a boy first started out in the ministry, I would frequently go out and ask the Lord to show me some marvelous thing, in order that I might receive a testimony. But the Lord withheld marvels from me, and showed me the truth, line upon line, precept upon precept, here a little and there a little, until he made me to know the truth from the crown of my head to the soles of my feet, and until doubt and fear had been absolutely purged from me. He did not have to send an angel from the heavens to do this, nor did he have to speak with the trump of an archangel. By the whisperings of the still small voice of the Spirit of the living God, he gave to me the testimony I possess.[6]

When We Follow the Direction the Lord Gives, We Receive Confirmation

Here is our fourth lesson, and it is an important one. It helps answer those nagging, ever-present questions like: But how can I know if this "direction" is really from the Lord? If we act without knowing what is down that road, couldn't we put ourselves in danger? What if Laban has his guards out looking for us? Isn't going into a big city like Jerusalem at night dangerous when I don't know what I'm supposed to be doing?

These are very common and very human kinds of reservations. We are great at talking ourselves out of things (or into things), especially when we are not comfortable in the situation. But here is the lesson. When we act based on the direction the Lord gives us, then usually we get some kind of confirming experience that shows that the direction we received was indeed from the Lord. Like Nephi, when we act in faith, when we move forward, then the Lord shows us that we did the right thing.

In Mexico, Elder Milton R. Hunter turned the plane around, then learned of another plane that had crashed. It is a pattern repeated again and again.

The Lord wants us to learn by faith. This is how we develop and grow spiritually. He isn't trying to trip us up. He doesn't set traps for us or try to trick us in some kind of test of our loyalty to Him. He wants us to learn. He wants us to come to know of His love and His power and His desire to bless us. If we meet the conditions He sets, and accept the patterns He uses, then He teaches us. There may be times when things are not clearly confirmed, or when He may withhold a confirmation or blessing from us, but generally He lets us know—often with great clarity—that it was the Spirit working with us.

This is the culmination of the line upon line, precept upon precept process. Direction is given. Agency is required. Faith is tested. Then comes the final revelation—some kind of confirmation—and we gain spiritual knowledge. In a word, we have

> *The Lord will not force himself upon people; and if they do not believe, they will receive no visitation. If they are content to depend upon their own limited calculations and interpretations, then, of course, the Lord will leave them to their chosen fate. . . .*
>
> *Remember: If there be eyes to see, there will be visions to inspire. If there be ears to hear, there will be revelations to experience. If there be hearts which can understand, know this: that the exalting truths of Christ's gospel will no longer be hidden and mysterious, and all earnest seekers may know God and his program.*
>
> SPENCER W. KIMBALL,
> *TEACHINGS OF SPENCER W. KIMBALL*, 454

learned by faith.* So we could modify the idea that we receive direction without explanation to read something like this: *The Spirit gives direction without explanation, but when we follow that direction, we typically receive confirmation that it was from the Lord.*

Surely this kind of learning experience is so valuable to our spiritual growth that this alone would justify the Lord using incremental revelation as a major pattern of revelation.

Let us conclude this chapter with an example I received from a woman concerning her decision to go on a mission. It illustrates several aspects of revelation that are typical of how the Lord works with us—incremental revelation; still, small whisperings; the withholding of an answer; a stupor of thought; and so on. She wrote this experience out for me, and I include it here with a few minor editing adjustments. I will take the liberty of inserting some commentary throughout to call attention to the process of incremental revelation:

> I had wanted to go on a mission since I was in my teens, and had moved forward with that goal, knowing that if the opportunity to marry came first, that I shouldn't postpone marriage for a mission. When I was twenty I began seriously dating a fine young man who was a returned missionary. After a time, he proposed. I, of course, began to pray earnestly, "Should I marry or should I go on a mission?" No answer came, though I prayed earnestly and repeatedly.

It would be more accurate here if she were to say, "No *clear* answer came." Sometimes no answer is an answer in and of itself.

> Though not endowed, I spent much time walking the temple grounds to put myself in tune with the Spirit. I decided to move forward in preparing my mission papers, continuing to seek revelation about this matter.

---

* Chapter 23 treats the concept of learning by faith in greater detail.

Here she was following the direction given to Oliver Cowdery. She was studying it out in her mind and she made a decision—to at least get her papers prepared.

> Still I felt no direction and so finally decided to put my papers in knowing that I could still change my mind about going on a mission. My call came and I opened it with this young man sitting by my side, and praying earnestly, "Now what?" My prayers intensified. Should I go on a mission or get married? Or perhaps neither? I prayed and studied, and pondered and wondered what was the right course. When I didn't have any feelings that I should move forward with marriage, I decided to continue on the path of a mission and wait for the Lord to intervene if this wasn't right.

Here is a good example of how a stupor of thought works. She felt like she wasn't getting an answer, but the very fact that she had no strong feelings to marry was an answer of sorts. She was having a stupor of thought on the marriage.

> The night before I went into the Missionary Training Center, I spent a great deal of time on my knees. "Heavenly Father," I said, "I can still back out, but I need to know if this is right. If you could let me know by morning if what I am doing is right, I would really appreciate it." Still nothing came. [At least nothing dramatic or clearly recognizable.] I changed my prayer to "Heavenly Father, I'm moving forward, please let me know if it isn't right." [Now she is moving forward with faith, taking that next step into the darkness without insisting that she see the path ahead.]
>
> Every morning and night during those weeks I was at the Missionary Training Center I would pray, "Heavenly Father, is this where I'm supposed to be? Am I doing the right thing? Let me know if I need to change course." For weeks nothing came. The night before I left the MTC, I felt

all panicky. Still I did not know. "Heavenly Father," I pleaded, "tomorrow, I'm getting on a plane. It really is TOO late once I'm on that plane. I can still walk out of here tomorrow morning, if a mission isn't the right thing. Please, please let me know if this if right, or at least let me know if it's not right. If I don't get an answer, I'm going to get on that plane." Morning came. Still no answer. [At least not the kind of answer she was looking for.]

It was only when the airplane reached its cruising altitude and I was sitting comfortably in my seat, when the witness finally came, strong and overwhelming, "Yes, this is the right path you have chosen. You are where you are supposed to be."

Here is a classic example of getting direction without explanation. To use Elder Bednar's phrase, she was receiving "a series of small and seemingly incremental spiritual impressions and nudges." But then, even though it took months to come, when she moved forward, following those impressions and nudges, she finally received her confirmation.

CHAPTER 16

DIVINE TUTORIALS

"All these things shall give thee experience,
and shall be for thy good" (D&C 122:7).

DIVINE TUTORIALS

The concept of line upon line and precept upon precept as a governing principle of revelation can be applied on a very basic level, that is, we may receive truth and light one small portion at a time. But we also need to remember that the Lord has a far grander and greater purpose for us than just giving us truth and light. Until we keep that grander purpose in mind, we will not fully understand incremental revelation in its fullest manifestation.

We know exactly what that grand purpose is because God Himself has told us what He intends to do for us. "This is my work and my glory—to bring to pass the immortality and eternal life of man" (Moses 1:39). There it is in His own words. Our end goal is eternal life, or life as God, our *Eternal* Father, knows it. Nothing less will do if we are willing to let Him take us in hand and, with the help of the Holy Spirit, move us along the journey that takes us to exaltation. By doing so we begin to better understand how all the elements of revelation—the still small voice, the Spirit speaking to our minds and hearts, enlightenment,

Under the Father's instruction and by Jehovah's direction, the earth and all pertaining thereto were organized and formed. They "ordered," they "watched over" and "prepared" the earth. They took "counsel among themselves" as to the bringing of all manner of life to the earth and all things, including man, and prepared it for the carrying out of the plan, which we could well liken to a blueprint, by which the children of God could be tutored and trained in all that was necessary for the divine purpose.

HAROLD B. LEE,
STAND YE IN HOLY PLACES, 234–35

a warning voice, divine intervention, confirmation, incremental learning, and so on and so on—all come together to accomplish the Lord's plan for His children.

Elder Neal A. Maxwell coined a phrase that captures this broader, holistic view of the purpose of incremental revelation.

In no dimension of the divine personality of Jesus Christ do we see His love any more fully expressed than in the *divine tutorials* given especially to His friends—those who believe in and who strive to follow Him, leaders and followers alike, rich and poor alike, men and women alike, for He is "no respecter of persons." He would not deny these enriching but stretching divine tutorials to any who follow Him, especially those who have already done much to prove their friendship for Him and are thus ready for further lessons.[1]

Tutoring is distinguished from other kinds of teaching in that it usually is done one on one (or at least in small groups) and generally it continues over an extended period of time. That very nicely describes how the Lord works with us. The changes required to prepare us for godhood may require extensive work and long-term educating.

Almost everywhere we look in the scriptures or in the history of the Church we find examples of these divine tutorials. Some clearly involve painful adversity. Most did not seek the tutoring experience. And yet, in almost every case we see an incremental development that unfolds slowly, testing faith, allowing growth, developing spiritual endurance.

There are a few examples of dramatic, "overnight" change in one's spiritual growth and learning—Enos, Alma the Younger, King Lamoni, Paul the Apostle—but these remarkable experiences are the exceptions. Most come in quieter, gentler ways, so subtle that we barely notice. Remember the Lamanites who had been born again, but "they knew it not" (3 Nephi 9:20).

In some cases, sadly the person does not submit patiently to this aspect of the Lord's way. They find the painful, slow plodding of learning unbearable and harden their hearts against it. They cry out, "Enough!" Ever honoring and respecting our agency, the Lord pulls back, the tutoring stops, and a different kind of lesson is learned.

JOSEPH OF EGYPT

Joseph learned through a series of dreams early in his youth that he was to be a leader and ruler over his family.[2] In his innocence (he was just beginning the tutoring process—although he may have been prompted in his sharing), he shared that revelation with his brothers, likely thinking they would be impressed and pleased and see some significance in the dreams, as he did. Instead, they were angry with him. Anger turned to hatred and eventually they sold him into Egypt as a slave. So much for becoming a leader over his family!

> *I have decreed in my heart, saith the Lord, that I will prove you in all things, whether you will abide in my covenant, even unto death, that you may be found worthy.*
>
> D&C 98:14

However, even in the face of a disastrous setback, he did not reject the Lord, and events quickly showed that the Lord had not abandoned him. Joseph was made of finer stuff. There was no moping around, no muttering against God's "injustice" as things seemed to go from bad to worse.

He went right on being Joseph, through one setback after another, until finally the tutoring process was completed. Pharaoh had a dream. Joseph interpreted it and eventually ended up as vice-regent to Pharaoh, which also set up Joseph's deliverance of his family and the ultimate fulfillment of those original dreams.

SAUL OF TARSUS

From the day Paul was confronted by Jesus on the road to Damascus, he committed his life to service in the kingdom. His ministry, which lasted thirty years or more, is one continuous story of faith, sacrifice, dedication, and submission. Yet, in a letter to the Corinthians, he spoke of divine tutorials of his own. In answer to apostates who were accusing him of not being a real Apostle, he gave a quick catalog of his ministry. If we stop to contemplate the reality depicted behind these simple lines, it is an incredible accounting of a man of faith who submitted his life to the Lord. He states that as part of his long ministry he was (2 Corinthians 11:23–25):

- In stripes [the lacerations made from being lashed with a whip] above measure
- In prisons more frequent
- In deaths [probably threat of death] oft
- Scourged five different times by the Jews*
- Thrice beaten with rods (what today we would call caning)
- Once stoned

---

* This is truly remarkable. The punishment for a Jew accused of heresy or other grievous transgressions was to be lashed with a leather scourge. Forty lashes were allowed, but with their usual meticulous attention to detail, the Pharisees determined to lessen that by one so as to not risk going over the allowed limit. During the scourging, the person received thirteen stripes across the breast, thirteen across the left shoulder, and thirteen across the right shoulder (see Frederic W. Farrar, *The Life and Work of St. Paul*, 1:661–64). Since Paul was a Roman citizen and could not be scourged without a trial before a Roman court, one can't help but wonder why he would submit himself to this brutal punishment five different times. Farrar suggests that by doing so, Paul maintained full fellowship in the synagogues, which were typically his first base for preaching the gospel when he entered a new city.

- Three times involved in shipwrecks
- Washed overboard and spent a night and a day in the deep

He concludes the list with:

> In journeyings often, in perils of waters, in perils of robbers, in perils by mine own countrymen, in perils by the heathen, in perils in the city, in perils in the wilderness, in perils in the sea, in perils among false brethren;
>
> In weariness and painfulness, in watchings often, in hunger and thirst, in fastings often, in cold and nakedness (2 Corinthians 11:26–27).

But that was not all, and here even Paul recognized the tutoring hand of the Lord in what had happened to him. Paul referred to what was likely some kind of physical impairment, which he called a "thorn in the flesh" (2 Corinthians 12:7). Then he said, "For this thing I besought the Lord thrice, that it might depart from me" (2 Corinthians 12:8). He was a man of faith. He had given his life to the ministry. He had paid a tremendous price in faithfulness. What miracles would not be performed in his behalf?

But for purposes that He did not disclose even to Paul, the Lord did not heed the plea for deliverance. Paul went on: "And he said unto me, My grace is sufficient for thee: for my strength is made perfect in weakness" (2 Corinthians 12:9).

Let us trust the Lord and take the next steps in our individual lives. He has promised us that he will be our tender tutor, measuring what we are ready for: "And ye cannot bear all things now; nevertheless, be of good cheer, for I will lead you along."

SPENCER W. KIMBALL,
TEACHINGS OF SPENCER W. KIMBALL, 253–54

In spite of his faith, in spite of the years of sacrifice and service, Paul still had things to learn. And because of the greatness of his heart, he did learn them. The end result of his divine tutoring fairly shouts out at us as we read Paul's concluding lines: "Most gladly therefore will I rather *glory in my infirmities,* that the power of Christ may rest upon me. Therefore I take pleasure in infirmities . . . for when I am weak, then am I strong" (2 Corinthians 12:9–10).

JOSEPH SMITH

One could write books on the divine tutoring experiences of Joseph's life. From the opening moments of the First Vision to the final gunshots in Carthage Jail, the Lord revealed Himself to Joseph line upon line and precept upon precept, and, we might add, led him along "step-by-step." It was not just *what* the Lord taught him, it was what the Lord helped him to *become.*

On two different occasions, the Prophet described the effects this lifetime of tutoring had on him:

> As for the perils which I am called to pass through, they seem but a small thing to me, as the envy and wrath of man have been my common lot all the days of my life; and for what cause it seems mysterious, unless I was ordained from before the foundation of the world for some good end, or bad, as you may choose to call it. . . .
>
> Deep water is what I am wont to swim in. It all has become a second nature to me; and I feel, like Paul, to glory in tribulation; for to this day has the God of my fathers delivered me out of them all, and will deliver me from henceforth; for behold, and lo, I shall triumph over all my enemies, for the Lord God hath spoken it (D&C 127:2).
>
> I am like a huge, rough stone rolling down from a high mountain; and the only polishing I get is when some corner gets rubbed off by coming in contact with something else, striking with accelerated force against religious bigotry, priest-craft, lawyer-craft, doctor-craft, lying editors, suborned judges and jurors, and the authority of perjured executives, backed by mobs, blasphemers, licentious and corrupt men and women—all hell knocking off a corner

here and a corner there. Thus I will become a smooth and polished shaft in the quiver of the Almighty.[3]

However, one particular aspect of Joseph's tutorial has multiple lessons for us today. When the militia and the mobs closed in on the Saints in Far West, Missouri, a tremendous tragedy was underway. Seventeen had already died at Haun's Mill. Before the winter was over, some twelve to fifteen thousand Saints would be making their way through the bitter cold as exiles from the state. In places they would leave red stains in the snow from cracked and bleeding feet. They left without recompense for their property or justice for the crimes committed against them. Many more would die before their journey was through.

Divine tutorials, whether slow and stressful or sudden and harsh, call for us to ponder, again and again, the implications of this divine perspective: "The Son of Man hath descended below them all. Art thou greater than he?"

NEAL A. MAXWELL,
IF THOU ENDURE IT WELL, 6

This period of our history raises many questions, and not just relating to Joseph. Why didn't the Lord intervene more directly to protect the Saints? Why didn't the Lord warn Joseph Smith that Colonel Hinkle was going to betray him and turn him over to the militia? It wasn't because Joseph was unworthy, or not in tune with the Spirit. But he had been warned of danger so many other times, why not this time? Instead he ended up in the horror and suffering of Richmond and then Liberty Jails.

Imprisonment of prophets was hardly a new thing, but Joseph languished in bonds in the most deplorable of conditions for over five months. Peter and John were delivered from prison by an angel on the same night they were arrested (see Acts 5:19). Paul and Silas were jailed, but they too were freed that same night, this time by a great earthquake (see Acts 16:26). Alma and Amulek were delivered when the earth shook so mightily that the walls of the prison collapsed, killing everyone but the two brethren (see Alma 14:27–28). Nephi and Lehi were encircled about by fire while they were in prison and they too were miraculously freed (see Helaman 5:23).

Surely Joseph was familiar with every one of those stories. So where were his angels? Why didn't an earthquake strike Liberty, Missouri? Where was the encircling fire that Nephi and Lehi saw?

We can't answer those questions except to say that the Lord determines all aspects of personal revelation, including the intensity and duration of tutorial experiences. A careful reading of sections 121, 122, and 123—all part of a letter written from Liberty Jail—will bring many insights as to why the Lord felt it was necessary to take Joseph there and leave him there for so long.

BRIGHAM AND HEBER

But here is another lesson to learn from that experience. While Joseph was in jail all that time, the challenge of leading an exodus of thousands of Saints to safety in the dead of winter fell to the two senior Apostles, Brigham Young and Heber C. Kimball. These were the very two men on whom would fall the task just eight years later of leading the Saints across more than a thousand miles of wilderness to the Valley of the Great Salt Lake. How's that for "in-service training"?

Often while we are undergoing our own learning experience, the Lord may be accomplishing His purposes with other people and in other settings. This is why it is foolish to think that we can fathom with our finite perspective the infinite and eternal purposes of God.

Clearly, even a calling to the holy apostleship doesn't give an individual some divine "You-Are-Hereby-Excused-from-Adversity" card.

This testing and tutoring process can be a real trial of our faith

> *When chastisements come, let them be what they may, let us always be willing and ready to kiss the rod, and reverence the hand that administers it, acknowledging the hand of God in all things.*
>
> BRIGHAM YOUNG,
> IN *JOURNAL OF DISCOURSES*, 2:280

because it is not the same with all people. Some faithful Saints face very difficult trials such as lifelong pain or one family tragedy after another. Some plead with the Lord and miracles happen. Yet at the same time, those equally faithful are not delivered. Their pleadings and striving do not result in a miracle.

We can ask ourselves questions about why such intervention happens in one case and not another. Why are some spared and some taken? Why do some suffer so much and others hardly at all? Why does life seem so unfair at times? Many times we cannot answer those questions. God determines all aspects of revelation. We don't get to choose whether we are delivered from our trials any more than we get to choose whether we have trials or not or what form they take if they are given to us. What we do get to choose is how we will respond. We can decide if we will come through those experiences with greater faith and greater patience or if we will walk away doubting the Lord's power and love. Here are a few examples of the latter reaction.

SOME WHO FALTERED

We have thus far cited examples of those who passed the test of learning, who endured the times of proving with patience and faith. Sadly, there are also numerous examples of those who couldn't bear the testing, couldn't endure the persecution, who found the forging experience too painful. They could not bear the pain of the Lord's tutoring process and left the Church.[4]

- Symonds Ryder, a prominent Campbellite preacher, was "converted" by a supposed prophecy about China that was later fulfilled. Then Joseph happened to spell his name as "Rider" instead of "Ryder" in his call to become a missionary. With his pride pricked and his ego hurting, he concluded that Joseph couldn't possibly be a prophet and left the Church. Later he was one of those at Hiram, Ohio, who tarred and feathered the prophet.
- Ezra Booth, a former Methodist minister, joined the Church when he saw Joseph heal a woman's lame arm. But when he was

called on a mission, he became upset because he had to walk the entire journey. He left the Church and began to publish anti-Mormon tracts that did considerable damage to the work.

- Another unnamed man was so upset when he saw Joseph come down from the translating room and begin to play with some children that he left the Church, saying that Joseph didn't act like a true prophet.[5]

- One of the more tragic examples of those who could not accept the tutoring, line-by-line methods of the Lord was Thomas B. Marsh, President of the Quorum of the Twelve. When his wife and another woman had an argument over some butter cream and the First Presidency ruled that his wife was in error, Thomas let his resentment and anger harden his heart. Eventually, he provided false testimony to the Missourians about Joseph and the Saints that contributed to the tragedy that followed.[6]

How many individual tutorials were being given during those early years of the Church we can only guess. The span and scope of the Lord's vision is both infinite and intimate. Even as He brought about His eternal purposes for the Church, the Lord was testing and teaching Joseph and Brigham, Hyrum and Sidney, Emma and Mary Fielding Smith and many unnamed others whose stories we do not even know.

And what of modern examples? We read some of the stories of these early Saints who lost heart and fell away, and we think, "How could they have been so foolish? How could they have given up so easily?" But the tutoring process is still a reality, and there are those who falter now as well, and sometimes for reasons just as foolish.

IN SUMMARY

These are important lessons we learn from the "line upon line, precept upon precept" principle of revelation. We are like children spiritually. First we barely toddle, and we frequently fall and bump our heads. Gradually we learn to walk and then run.

We must remember that the race we are running is for godhood.

Should we be so surprised then that the Lord doesn't grant every wish, answer every prayer, reach out and pick us up every time we fall? We have to develop our spiritual muscles, build up our spiritual wind, strengthen our spiritual endurance if we are going to win this race and claim the prize. You don't run marathons by taking a taxicab across the route several times. You don't gain patience by getting instant gratification or relief every time you call on the Lord.

Keeping the ultimate perspective in mind helps in these tutoring times. It helps us to remember what God is about. Elder Neal A. Maxwell was fond of citing words from C. S. Lewis that aptly illustrate the tutoring nature of God:

> Imagine yourself as a living house. God comes in to rebuild that house. At first, perhaps, you can understand what He is doing. He is getting the drains right and stopping the leaks in the roof and so on: you knew that those jobs needed doing and so you are not surprised. But presently he starts knocking the house about in a way that hurts abominably and does not seem to make sense. What on earth is He up to? The explanation is that He is building quite a different house from the one you thought of—throwing out a new wing here, putting on an extra floor there, running up towers, making courtyards. You thought you were going to be made into a decent little cottage: but He is building a palace.[7]

CHAPTER 17

FOURTH PRINCIPLE: WE ARE TO DEVELOP SPIRITUAL SELF-RELIANCE

"It is not meet that I should command in all things" (D&C 58:26).

TOO SPIRITUAL?

Here are some statements I have heard over the years that illustrate some of the misconceptions or misunderstandings we may have about receiving and recognizing revelation.

- One of my teachers taught us that if we are living worthily, we can receive clear direction for every question of life. We can even know what brand of toothpaste to buy.
- One way to know if something is from the Lord is after you finish praying, pause for a moment. The first thought that comes into your mind will be from the Lord.
- When I teach my class, I don't prepare anything in advance. We have prayer; then we sit and wait for the Spirit to show us what we should learn that day.
- I have decided that when it comes to important questions or issues in my life, I will never take even an initial step until I receive a clear answer from God.

The gift of revelation is of pivotal value to our eternal progression. We know that and therefore desire it. And this is right. But can we let our desire for revelation go too far? Can we try to be too "spiritual"?

The problem stems from the fact that some people require revelation as a marker or evidence that they are in good standing with God. They seek any kind of revelatory experience so they "prove" to themselves (and sometimes to others), that they really are "spiritual." Sometimes that attitude may lie behind statements like those above.

But can we be too spiritual? Clearly, if we are using "spiritual" in its true sense, that is, being worthy to receive revelation and recognizing revelation when it comes, then the answer is no, we cannot be too spiritual. On the other hand, there are many misconceptions about what it means to be

Revelations from God—the teachings and directions of the Spirit—are not constant. We believe in continuing revelation, not continuous revelation. We are often left to work out problems without the dictation or specific direction of the Spirit. That is part of the experience we must have in mortality.

DALLIN H. OAKS,
ENSIGN, MARCH 1997, 14

spiritual. Some think that spirituality must always be manifest in tears. Others lower their voice reverentially as if that alone is an indicator of spirituality. Some almost boast that the Spirit directs them in all they do. These manifestations might be called pseudo-spirituality, but unfortunately, too often these experiences are eagerly shared with others as true spiritual experiences.

In most cases, these misconceptions are driven by good intentions, not malicious attempts to be fraudulent or deceptive. But good intentions or not, if they do not conform to the Lord's pattern and principles, they are not from God. Note how clearly this is taught in the very section given to help the elders of the Church distinguish between true and false spirits:

> He that is ordained of me and sent forth to preach the
> word of truth by the Comforter, in the Spirit of truth, doth
> he preach it by the Spirit of truth or some other way?

And if it be by some other way it is not of God (D&C 50:17–18).

In other words, if the Spirit is not genuinely a part of our doings, those doings are not of God.

It is a wonderful thing to sincerely desire to be led by the Spirit, but as we have said several times thus far, part of preparing ourselves to receive revelation is a willingness to receive it on the Lord's terms and by meeting His conditions. We cannot make our own rules or set our own conditions in this important area.

A SLOTHFUL AND NOT A WISE SERVANT

In 1831, Joseph was directed to go to Jackson County, Missouri, and establish the Church there. He was accompanied by several other leaders. Upon Joseph's arrival in Independence, Missouri, the Lord revealed the specific location for the temple that was to be built there (see D&C 57:3). A short time later the Colesville Saints arrived. Eager to learn the will of the Lord for them in Zion, they asked Joseph to petition the Lord so they could learn what they should do. Section 58 of the Doctrine and Covenants was given in answer to that petition. Though given to a specific group, within that section is a principle that is another of the governing principles of personal revelation.

> *There's a fine balance between agency and inspiration. We're expected to do everything in our power that we can, and then to seek an answer from the Lord, a confirming seal that we've reached the right conclusion; and sometimes, happily, in addition, we get added truths and knowledge that we hadn't even supposed.*
>
> BRUCE R. MCCONKIE,
> *BYU SPEECHES OF THE YEAR,*
> *1972–73,* 113

It is not meet [good, desirable, proper] that I should command in all things; for he that is compelled in all things, the same is a slothful and not a wise servant; wherefore he receiveth no reward.

Verily I say, men should be anxiously engaged in a good cause, and do many things of their own free will, and bring to pass much righteousness;

For the power is in them, wherein they are agents unto themselves. And inasmuch as men do good they shall in nowise lose their reward.

But he that doeth not anything until he is commanded, and receiveth a commandment with doubtful heart, and keepeth it with slothfulness, the same is damned (D&C 58:26–29).

Here is another fundamental principle that governs the giving and receiving of personal revelation. It is taught simply and with great clarity. Like the other three principles already discussed, this principle too is rooted firmly in the doctrine of moral agency. The principle is: *The Lord expects us to become spiritually self-reliant.*

> *Spiritual independence and self-reliance is a sustaining power in the Church. If we rob the members of that, how can they get revelation for themselves? How will they know there is a prophet of God? How can they get answers to prayers? How can they know for sure for themselves?*
>
> BOYD K. PACKER,
> *ENSIGN*, MAY 1978, 91

WHAT IS SPIRITUAL SELF-RELIANCE?

What does that mean? It means that we are to use the light and knowledge we have already received to move forward with life, making choices and striving to live the gospel. It means that there may be times when we won't be told everything that we need to do. We have agency and free will. We are to use those wisely and freely to become more like God.

On the other hand, this principle is one of the most difficult to wisely apply, because the Lord has counseled us in the scriptures to come unto Him and rely on His wisdom, counsel, and direction (see, for example, Proverbs 3:5–6; Alma 37:37; D&C 6:14). We have received similar counsel from our leaders. For example:

- "Members of the Church know that the promptings of the Spirit may be received upon all facets of life, including daily, ongoing decisions."[1]
- "There is one unerring voice that is ever true. It can always be relied upon. . . . You can know by the whisperings of the Holy Spirit if you righteously and earnestly seek to know. Your own inspiration will be an unerring vibration through the companionship of the Holy Ghost."[2]
- "In secular as well as spiritual affairs, Saints may receive Divine guidance and revelation affecting themselves."[3]

But even as we consider such direction and counsel we must also remember such things as:

- "If ye will have faith in me ye shall have power to do whatsoever thing is expedient in me" (Moroni 7:33).
- "Whatsoever ye ask the Father in my name it shall be given unto you, *that is expedient for you;* and if ye ask anything that is not expedient for you, it shall turn unto your condemnation" (D&C 88:64–65).

Clearly, a balance must be struck. We have two principles of revelation, both of which have come from the Lord. We must be wise in applying them so that we strike that balance in a manner that is pleasing to the Lord and in a way that moves us forward in our spiritual progression.

For us to use our agency with wisdom, we must keep in mind the grand purpose behind all this. Remember our question in an earlier chapter. What is it the Lord is ultimately seeking to accomplish with us? The answer is clear. He is preparing us to become like Him, to inherit eternal life and partake of all that He has. In short, He is helping us prepare for godhood. The Lord is not looking to create spiritual "robots." He gives us principles to guide us, then lets us move forward on our own, learning by faith (and sometimes by trial and error). Yet even as

He does so, He continues to watch over us, blessing and directing and protecting us, sometimes in small, almost insignificant ways that confirm that "the tender mercies of the Lord are over all those whom he hath chosen" (1 Nephi 1:20; see also Moroni 10:3).

IT MATTERETH NOT UNTO ME

Before discussing the implications of the principle of spiritual self-reliance in our lives, let us take a look at another revelation that expands our understanding of the principle. It is noteworthy that this second revelation also came in Missouri, just one week after section 58 was given. Some of the elders had been appointed to return to Kirtland, and once again they came to the Prophet asking for details on "how they should proceed, and by what route and manner they should travel."[4] Obviously, the full impact of the counsel in section 58 had not yet sunk in. Here, again, they were asking for direction on what to do. But the Lord knows that we learn things slowly sometimes, and so He answered their questions:

> I will speak unto you concerning your journey unto the land from whence you came. Let there be a craft made, or bought, *as seemeth you good, it mattereth not unto me,* and take your journey speedily for the place that is called St. Louis (D&C 60:5).

Four days later, while the men were traveling down the Missouri River toward St. Louis, Joseph Smith received yet another revelation in which the Lord used similar language:

> Again I say unto you, let them take their journey in haste.
>
> And *it mattereth not unto me,* after a little, if it so be that they fill their mission, whether they go by water or by land; let this be as it is made known unto them *according to their judgments* hereafter. . . .

185

And let them journey together, or two by two, *as seemeth them good* (D&C 61:21–22, 35).

There are other places where the Lord used similar wording (for example, see D&C 62:5, 8).

When the Lord repeats something several times, He obviously is trying to teach us something of importance. In this case, we see a pattern where two things are linked together: (1) He wants us to use our best judgment and do what seems best to us; and (2) some things do not matter to the Lord.*

Trust in the Lord with all thine heart; and lean not unto thine own understanding. In all thy ways acknowledge him, and he shall direct thy paths.

PROVERBS 3:5–6

Clearly, the Lord is not suggesting that we be independent of Him, nor are we to infer that we should not ask Him for direction and guidance. In fact, in the examples given here, we should note that the Lord was not displeased with their seeking guidance from Him, that there were some things that *did* matter to him, and that he gave further instructions in response to their inquiries. While he says that how they obtained the boats or canoes to travel on the river did not matter to Him, He at the same time told them to "take your journey speedily" (D&C 60:5), and He gave specific direction on what He wanted some of the brethren to do on that journey (see verses 6–10). Further, he told them that when they exercised judgment they should couple that with "the directions of the Spirit" (D&C 62:8).

We have previously discussed how frequently throughout the scriptures we are commanded to ask, seek, and knock. Many other scriptures counsel us to trust in Him, to depend on Him for help. So again we say that we need to consider these two principles together, balancing one

---

* It was not just in Missouri that these concepts were taught. They are found throughout the Doctrine and Covenants (see D&C 38:37; 41:8; 42:72; 48:3; 58:51; 63:40; 80:3; 124:72).

against the other. Both principles come directly from the Lord and, therefore, we cannot neglect one or the other.

Elder Bruce R. McConkie discussed how these two principles—seeking guidance from the Spirit and developing self-reliance—work together in a delicate balance:

We're expected to use the gifts and talents and abilities, the sense and judgment and agency with which we are endowed.

But on the other hand, we're commanded to seek the Lord, to desire his Spirit, to get the spirit of revelation and inspiration in our lives. We come unto the Church and a legal administrator places his hands upon our head and says, "Receive the Holy Ghost." This gives us the gift of the Holy Ghost, which is the right to the constant companionship of that member of the Godhead, based on faithfulness.

And so we're faced with two propositions. One is that we ought to be guided by the spirit of inspiration, the spirit of revelation. The other is that we're here under a direction to use our agency, to determine what we ought to do on our own; and we need to strike a fine balance between these two, if we're going to pursue a course that will give us joy and satisfaction and peace in this life and lead to eternal reward in our Father's kingdom.[5]

[A person may have] a strong desire to be led by the Spirit of the Lord but . . . unwisely extends that desire to the point of wanting to be led in all things. . . . Persons who try to shift all decision making to the Lord and plead for revelation in every choice will soon find circumstances in which they pray for guidance and don't receive it. For example, this is likely to occur in those numerous circumstances in which the choices are trivial or either choice is acceptable.

DALLIN H. OAKS, *ENSIGN,* OCTOBER 1994, 13–14

Elder Boyd K. Packer also taught us about how to keep spiritual things in balance:

Things of the Spirit need not—indeed, should not—require our uninterrupted time and attention. Ordinary work-a-day things occupy most of our attention. And that is as it should be. We are mortal beings living in this physical world. Spiritual things are like leavening. By measure they may be very small, but by influence they affect all that we do. Continuing revelation is fundamental to the gospel of Jesus Christ.[6]

We must keep in mind that some things are trivial and may not need constant or detailed direction. Here is how Elder Dallin H. Oaks addressed this issue:

No answer is likely to come to a person who seeks guidance in choosing between two alternatives that are equally acceptable to the Lord. Thus, there are times when we can serve productively in two different fields of labor. Either answer is right. Similarly, the Spirit of the Lord is not likely to give us revelations on matters that are trivial. I once heard a young woman in a testimony meeting praise the spirituality of her husband, indicating that he submitted every question to the Lord. She told how he accompanied her shopping and would not even choose between different brands of canned vegetables without making his selection a matter of prayer. I think that is improper. I believe the Lord expects us to make most of our decisions by using the intelligence and experience he has given us.[7]

The same principle holds true for the teacher who routinely does not prepare anything in advance but waits for the Spirit to dictate to him what he is to do. This is "spiritual robotics." We wait for the Lord to say, "Turn here. Go there. Do that. Don't do that." The Lord made very clear in section 58 that it is a slothful and not a wise servant who seeks to be commanded in all things.

From this counsel and that given through Joseph Smith in Missouri, we may draw several principles:

- **Principle**: An important purpose of mortality is to learn to distinguish good from evil through our own experience (along with, of course, the Light of Christ).
- **Principle**: The Lord expects us to use our agency and do many things of our own free will.
- **Principle**: If we simply wait for the Lord or the prophet or our leaders to tell us everything we are to do, we are slothful and unwise.
- **Principle**: If we ask for things that are not expedient, they can turn to our condemnation.
- **Principle**: While many things are important to the Lord, some things do not matter to Him. Yet if we ask with a sincere heart, the Lord will often give us assurance and perhaps additional instructions, even if the answer to the original question is "It mattereth not."

> *Many men seem to have no ear for spiritual messages nor comprehension of them when they come in common dress. . . . .*
> *Expecting the spectacular, one may not be fully alerted to the constant flow of revealed communication.*
>
> SPENCER W. KIMBALL,
> *TEACHINGS OF SPENCER W. KIMBALL*, 457

From those principles we can then draw several practical and helpful applications that will aid us in our quest for personal revelation.

- *Application:* It is unwise to demand direction on every aspect of our life, especially on matters that are trivial. Perhaps this is a good place to note that "trivial" does not necessarily refer to something that is of relatively little importance when compared to the great things of the kingdom. For example, in this book we have shared stories of a woman who received help in fixing a washing machine (p. 66); an individual who was prompted to avoid a certain restaurant (p. 103); and a case where the Lord was involved with a pair of shoes (pp. 116–18). In the grand, eternal scheme of things, these issues or experiences could be considered as small or relatively inconsequential, but in every case the experience lifted and blessed and taught those individuals something about the Lord's tender mercies.

- *Application:* We are expected to use our own best judgment to make decisions as we seek inspiration and direction from the Lord. We can then seek spiritual confirmation of those decisions.
- *Application:* In some cases, the Lord leaves the choice up to us because either alternative is acceptable to Him.
- *Application:* We do not need to seek new revelation where the Lord or His servants have already spoken on a matter. However, we may seek confirmation of its truthfulness, as we do in other aspects of a testimony.
- *Application:* Some people seek direction in all things as a way of convincing themselves and showing others that they are highly spiritual. One of the indicators of this is when they talk too much of sacred things.
- *Application:* The more we seek and gain experience with revelation, the sooner we can become adept at distinguishing between true and counterfeit revelation. This is one way we develop spiritual self-reliance.

Part of spiritual self-reliance is that even as we seek the Spirit's direction in our lives, we should be using our best judgment in working through our problems and challenges. We have already seen that the Lord is displeased when we take no thought but to ask (D&C 9:7). Part of the testing experience (and part of the process of gaining wisdom) is using our own good sense, coupled with a sensitivity to the Light of Christ, to try to work things out, sometimes without precise and specific direction from the Lord at every step.

The story of the brother of Jared presents an excellent example of this. When he approached the Lord with the problem of how to get light into the barges, the Lord didn't give him a specific answer. He said simply, "What will ye that I should do that ye may have light in your vessels?" (Ether 2:23). This is not to suggest that the Lord did not respond. The Lord did answer the brother of Jared, but His answer was that the brother of Jared should use his own good judgment in working out the problem. Once the brother of Jared had done so, then the Lord responded again in a marvelous way by touching the stones.

The Lord made it clear that He would help, but He gave the brother of Jared an opportunity to act for himself, to use his wisdom and judgment to find a solution (see Ether 3:1–5).

I learned this principle when I was a bishop. A couple asked if they could see me one evening. This was a fine, faithful couple, one of those families that make up the backbone of a ward. They came to my home, and as soon as they entered I could tell they were somewhat troubled. The husband's company had been acquired by a large corporation, which left him without a job. After a lot of investigation and discussion with his wife, they settled on two alternatives that looked the best for his career and for their family. The one offer was especially attractive because it was something he would really enjoy doing—and the salary was higher.

But therein was part of their dilemma. They sincerely wanted to do what the Lord wanted them to do. They worried that perhaps they were letting financial considerations sway their good judgment. They explained that they had taken this to the Lord in prayer to find out what He would have them do. Weeks went by and there seemed to be no answer. They fasted two or three times. Still nothing. The need for a decision was getting more urgent as each day passed. Finally they decided to meet with their bishop and discuss it.

After listening carefully to all that they had to say, I must admit that for a few moments I was baffled. Why was getting an answer to a critical question so difficult? They were seeking earnestly. They were living as they should. What should I tell them? What *was* the Lord's will in this situation?

What happened next was a revelation, not just for them but for me as well. Suddenly, there came into my mind a phrase from the Doctrine and Covenants that I had read and marked just a few days prior to their visit. It was the very one discussed above, D&C 60:5, where the Lord said: "[Do] as seemeth you good, it mattereth not unto me." I was taken completely aback by that thought. This was a major decision for this family. Surely the Lord thought one alternative was better for them than the other.

I sat back, marveling at the feelings I was having. Could that really be the answer? I looked inwardly, asking the Lord if what I was feeling was really from Him. A deep sense of peace came into my heart. With that I looked at this wonderful couple and said, "This one is your decision. Either alternative is acceptable to the Lord." They looked shocked for a moment; then the confirmation came to them as well. They went home marveling and that night made their choice to go with the better offer. Years later they reported just how right that decision had been for them and their family.*

Somewhere in your quest for spiritual knowledge, there is that "leap of faith," as the philosophers call it. It is the moment when you have gone to the edge of the light and step into the darkness to discover that the way is lighted ahead for just a footstep or two.

BOYD K. PACKER,
THAT ALL MAY BE EDIFIED, 340

As in the story of the brother of Jared, this was not a case where the Lord left them on their own. He just chose not to answer their prayers at first. But He was involved. They felt impressed to seek counsel from their bishop; and when they followed that prompting, they received their answer.

This is an example of the balance between trusting in the Lord and

---

* By using this example, I am not suggesting that if we do not receive an answer in a timely manner, we should assume that the decision doesn't matter to the Lord. I can think of another couple with whom I counseled who had three different employment opportunities. After much prayer and one time of fasting, they got a clear and distinct prompting to accept one position. Within three months of their arrival there, he was called as the bishop of the ward.

being spiritually self-reliant that Elder McConkie spoke of earlier in this chapter.

IT IS UNWISE TO DEMAND CONSTANT DIRECTION FROM THE SPIRIT

Though such extremes are not common, most of us know someone or other who tends to attribute almost everything they do to the Spirit. Their conversations are liberally sprinkled with expressions like, "The Spirit told me to do this," or "I can't do that, because I haven't had a spiritual confirmation yet." There is nothing wrong with those kinds of expressions in and of themselves, of course, but when they become a constant pattern it seems to be symptomatic of the misconception that we must be led in all things. Requiring a spiritual experience or a witness from the Spirit for every act of life is not pleasing to the Lord.

William E. Berrett was the administrator of Seminaries and Institutes (now called the Church Educational System) for many years. In a book on the Holy Spirit, he talked at some length about those who seem to want to credit everything in their lives to the Spirit. Elder Dallin H. Oaks shared Brother Berrett's counsel in an article in the Church magazines:

Those who pray that the Spirit might give them immediate guidance in every little thing

Usually the Lord gives us the overall objectives to be accomplished and some guidelines to follow, but he expects us to work out most of the details and methods. The methods and procedures are usually developed through study and prayer and by living so that we can obtain and follow the promptings of the Spirit. Less spiritually advanced people, such as those in the days of Moses, had to be commanded in many things. Today those who are spiritually alert look at the objectives, check the guidelines laid down by the Lord and his prophets, and then prayerfully act—without having to be commanded "in all things." This attitude prepares men for godhood.

EZRA TAFT BENSON,
GOD, FAMILY, COUNTRY: OUR THREE GREAT LOYALTIES, 381–82

throw themselves open to false spirits that seem ever ready to answer our pleas and confuse us. . . . The people I have found most confused in this Church are those who seek personal revelations on everything. They want the personal assurance from the Spirit from daylight to dark on everything they do. I say they are the most confused people I know because it appears sometimes that the answer comes from the wrong source. . . . There are great dangers associated with those who profess a constant outpouring of the spirit of revelation. Frequently, those so professing place themselves above the need to listen to the counsel and direction of their priesthood leaders. Often they are above correction. It is natural for those who suppose they are having regular conversations with angels and diverse exalted beings to be a little bemused at the counsel of bishops and stake presidents. With but a bit of polish, such an attitude ripens into the cultist's mentality in which one is above the laws of both church and state.[8]

WE ARE EXPECTED TO USE THE REVELATIONS THAT WE HAVE ALREADY RECEIVED

Another application of the principle of spiritual self-reliance is that in the process of using our best judgment and making decisions, we need to look to the revelations God has already given to His children to help them govern their lives.

Joseph Smith said: "It is a great thing to inquire at the hands of God, or to come into His presence, and we feel fearful to approach Him on subjects that are of little or no consequence, to satisfy the queries of individuals, especially about things the knowledge of which men ought to obtain in all sincerity, before God, for themselves, in humility by the prayer of faith."[9]

Sometimes we are tempted to ask the Lord for a solution when a serious study of the scriptures and the words of the living prophets

194

would give us the answer we are seeking. We may not wish to expend the effort required to find our answers that way, or we may, being equally mistaken, decide that we can simply ask the Lord and He will give us what we need, even if He has given it elsewhere. Either way, this violates the principle of spiritual self-reliance. We should not expect new revelation when the Lord has already taught us the doctrine or principle that provides the answer we seek.

Someone once expressed just how important the scriptures are to the process of revelation in this way. "If you wish to talk to the Lord, get down on your knees. If you want the Lord to talk to you, open the scriptures." Of course, the scriptures don't answer all the specific questions of our lives, but they are an essential element in the revelatory process. Elder Dallin H. Oaks likened the scriptures to our own "Urim and Thummim" in assisting us to receive personal revelation.[10] And Elder Bruce R. McConkie said, "I sometimes think that one of the best kept secrets of the kingdom is that the scriptures open the door to the receipt of revelation."[11]

Here is yet another example of the balance between seeking revelation and inspiration from the Lord and developing spiritual self-reliance. The Lord expects us to immerse ourselves in the scriptures, "treasuring up the words of life continually" (D&C 84:85). This is effort required on our part. We search. We study. We seek. As we do so of our own free will and choice, then the revelation comes. The Spirit illuminates our mind or fills our heart with truth. But we are left free to implement and apply what we have learned.

> *We are expected to use the light and knowledge we already possess to work out our lives. We should not need a revelation to instruct us to be up and about our duty, for we have been told to do that already in the scriptures; nor should we expect revelation to replace the spiritual or temporal intelligence that we have already received—only to extend it. We must go about our life in an ordinary, workaday way, following the routines and rules and regulations that govern life.*
>
> BOYD K. PACKER,
> *NEW ERA*, JANUARY 2007, 4

Another manifestation of this error of wanting to be led in all things is when people constantly turn to their priesthood leaders for answers to questions or help in how to solve their problems when they could find those answers themselves. The Lord's pattern in revelation is to give each member of the Church the gift of the Holy Ghost. That gift isn't just given to bishops and stake presidents with the idea that the members would then get their revelation through them. It flows directly to us as individuals.

Some years ago, Elder Boyd K. Packer warned the Church about the importance of developing emotional and spiritual self-reliance:

> The principle of self-reliance or personal independence is fundamental to the happy life. In too many places, in too many ways, we are getting away from it.
>
> The substance of what I want to say is this: The same principle—self-reliance—has application to the spiritual and to the emotional.
>
> We have been taught to store a year's supply of food, clothing, and, if possible, fuel—*at home.* There has been no attempt to set up storerooms in every chapel. We know that in the crunch our members may not be able to get to the chapel for supplies.
>
> Can we not see that the same principle applies to inspiration and revelation, the solving of problems, to counsel, and to guidance?
>
> We need to have a source of it [inspiration and revelation] *stored in every home,* not just in the bishop's office. . . . Unless we use care, we are on the verge of doing to ourselves emotionally (and, therefore, spiritually) what we have been working so hard for generations to avoid materially.[12]

IN SUMMARY

The Lord has spoken quite clearly on the matter of developing spiritual self-reliance. He has declared that we should do many things of our own free will and choice and that if we wait to be commanded in all things, then we are slothful and unwise servants. And while He has given us the commandment to ask, seek, and knock numerous times, He has also warned that if we ask for that which is not expedient, it can turn to our condemnation. In some cases we can seek (or claim) revelation in ways that are not pleasing to the Lord.

Equally clear in the teachings of the scriptures and the modern prophets is the invitation to trust in the Lord and not rely on our own understanding. We are promised that we can be led by the Spirit in both spiritual and temporal things. This principle is taught with clarity and force, just as is the principle of spiritual self-reliance. It is in these two complementary and yet different principles of revelation that we are sometimes caught with troublesome questions.

A key to seeking revelation appropriately was given in a talk by Elder Henry B. Eyring. Speaking at Brigham Young University in September 2006, he reviewed the example of Nephi and Lehi, the sons of Helaman, who had "many revelations daily" (Helaman 11:23). "Yes, it is possible to have the companionship of the Holy Ghost sufficiently to have many revelations daily," Elder Eyring said. "It is not easy, but it is possible."

What must we do to develop our ability to receive so much? Elder Eyring indicated that we must have "faith in our Heavenly Father and in His Son, Jesus Christ." We must "be clean." And we must have "pure motive."

He continues:

> If you want to receive the gifts of the Spirit, you have to want them for the right reasons. Your purposes must be the Lord's purposes. To the degree your motives are selfish, you will find it difficult to receive those gifts of the Spirit that have been promised to you.
>
> That fact serves both as a warning and as helpful instruction. . . . God is offended when we seek the gifts of the Spirit for our own purposes rather than for His. Our

selfish motives may not be obvious to us. . . . We almost always have more than one motive at a time. And some motives may be mixtures of what God wants as well as what we want. It is not easy to pull them apart. . . . Always there is the possibility that we may have a selfish purpose that is less important to the Lord.

How can we improve our motives so we do not ask amiss, so we do not seek to have the Lord do for us what we should do for ourselves? Elder Eyring gave two suggestions:

1. "I try to suppress my desire and surrender to His."
2. "When we pray for the gifts of the Spirit—and we should—one for which I pray is that I might have pure motives, to want what our Father wants for His children and for me, and to feel, as well as to say, that what I want is His will to be done."[13]

CHAPTER 18

FIFTH PRINCIPLE:

GOD'S HOUSE IS A HOUSE OF ORDER

"Mine house is a house of order . . . and not a house of confusion"
(D&C 132:8).

REVELATION AND DIVINE ORDER

The next principle that helps us better understand the conditions for receiving and recognizing revelation is based on a simple but important doctrine. We know that the very nature of God involves absolute perfection in every attribute He possesses. He is not just full of love, His love is perfect and infinite. He is more than just; His justice is perfect in every respect. He has *all* knowledge and *all* power. It is this perfection that makes Him God and that allows us to have perfect faith in Him.

By His own declaration, one of the attributes He possesses is order. "Behold, mine house is a house of order, saith the Lord God, and not a house of confusion" (D&C 132:8; see also v. 18).* That should not be difficult to understand. The very idea of a God who is confused or disorderly is incomprehensible. And if order is one of His attributes, then

---

* For other references on order, see 1 Corinthians 14:40; Mosiah 4:27; Moroni 9:18; D&C 20:68; 41:3; 88:119; 90:15–16; 93:43–44; 107:58; 127:9.

clearly He desires that our lives reflect order as well. Further, certainly His Church and kingdom should be a church and kingdom of order.

President Joseph F. Smith clearly explained why order is essential in the Church:

> The house of God is a house of order, and not a house of confusion; and it could not be thus, if there were not for those who had authority to preside, to direct, to counsel, to lead in the affairs of the Church. No house would be a house of order if it were not properly organized, as the Church of Jesus Christ of Latter-day Saints is organized.[1]

The Latter-day Saints by this time should be well settled in the conviction that God has established His Church in the earth for the last time, to remain, and no more to be thrown down or destroyed; and that God's house is a house of order.

JOSEPH F. SMITH,
GOSPEL DOCTRINE, 381

When Jesus suggested that we make part of our prayers a petition that "Thy will be done in earth, as it is in heaven" (Matthew 6:10), that certainly would include a desire on our part to create and maintain order in all aspects of our lives and in God's kingdom.

REVELATION AND THE ORDER OF HEAVEN

From the concept of God's order, we can derive a pair of principles, with some accompanying applications, that are important to our understanding of how revelation works:

Principle: Any and all direction for the governance of the Church always flows downward from God to His called, ordained, and sustained servants and through them to the rest of the Church.

Application: The Council of the First Presidency and Quorum of the Twelve are the only ones who receive revelation and set doctrine and policy for the whole Church.

Application: When something that is supposedly for the whole Church comes to us through any other source, we can know that it is contrary to the order of God.

Application: Individuals do not receive revelation for those above them in the priesthood line.

Principle: Revelation does not move horizontally from one person to another (for example, from one bishop to another) except under strictly defined conditions; otherwise there would be great confusion in the Church.

Application: We are entitled to receive inspiration in our lives and callings so we can live better and serve others.

Application: However, unless we have a specific stewardship, that is, a priesthood or doctrinally based responsibility, over someone else, we do not receive revelation that seeks to *direct* them or *correct* them.

ORDER IN THE CHURCH

An interesting phenomenon in the Church is the frequency with which this or that sensational rumor or story gets picked up and passed on from member to member. E-mail, the Internet, and text-messaging on cell phones has only increased the speed with which these things are passed on and spread. Even though many of these stories defy logic and common sense, they are nevertheless breathlessly shared with others. They are almost always sensational and usually involve some aspect of supposed revelation—a dream, someone's patriarchal blessing, a supposed prophecy, a new interpretation of scripture or doctrine, or some marvelous "spiritual experience" had by someone in

An unusual spiritual experience should not be regarded as a personal call to direct others. It is my conviction that experiences of a special, sacred nature are individual and should be kept to oneself. Few things disturb the channels of revelation quite so effectively as those people who are misled and think themselves to be chosen to instruct others when they are not chosen.

BOYD K. PACKER,
ENSIGN, NOVEMBER 1989, 15

authority. Another characteristic of these spurious reports is that they are almost always credited to an "impeccable" source.

President Harold B. Lee gave a stirring talk to the priesthood some years ago where he warned the Church about this very kind of thing:

> It never ceases to amaze me how gullible some of our Church members are in broadcasting sensational stories or dreams, or visions, or purported patriarchal blessings, or quotations, or supposedly from some person's private diary. . . . Brethren of the priesthood, you defenders of the faith, we would wish that you would plead with our Saints to cease promoting the works of the devil. Spend your time promoting the works of the Lord, and don't allow these things to be found among those under your charge, for they are the works of Satan, and we are playing his game whenever we permit such things to be heralded about and repeated and passed about on every side.[2]

Early in the history of the Church, Hiram Page, a son-in-law of the Whitmers, found a seer stone and started receiving "revelation" for the Church. This left even faithful members of the Church, like Oliver Cowdery, confused. In a revelation directed to Oliver, the Lord not only flatly declared that these supposed "revelations" were not from Him, but He laid down three principles related to revelation that were being misunderstood:

- Satan's deceptions can imitate revelation. What Hiram Page was receiving was not from God, but from Satan (see D&C 28:11).*
- No one was appointed to receive commandments and revelations for the Church excepting Joseph Smith, the prophet of the Church (see D&C 28:2).

---

* False revelation will be discussed fully in chapters 21 and 22.

• We are not to command someone who is at our head, that is, who presides over us (see D&C 28:6).

Each year, in general, stake, ward, district, and branch conferences we are asked to sustain one man as the prophet and President of the Church. We sustain him and the fourteen other brethren of the First Presidency and Quorum of the Twelve* as prophets, seers, and revelators to the Church. These fifteen men are the governing body of the Church.

In a talk on councils of the Church, Elder M. Russell Ballard described one council that is over all others. This is a council that is not clearly understood by some members of the Church. Elder Ballard said: "The Lord's church is organized with councils at every level, beginning with *the Council of the First Presidency and the Quorum of the Twelve Apostles.*"[3]

There is the *Quorum* of the First Presidency and the *Quorum* of the Twelve, but together they form the *Council* of the First Presidency and the Quorum of the Twelve. This council meets together weekly in the Salt Lake Temple and *all matters* that affect the Church are considered by this council.**

Although he did not use its formal name, President Hinckley explained the importance of this governing body of the Church:

> The First Presidency and the Council of the Twelve Apostles, called and ordained to hold the keys of the priesthood, have the authority and responsibility to govern the Church, to administer its ordinances, to expound its doctrine, and to establish and maintain its practices. . . . Therefore, all incumbent members of the Quorum of the First Presidency and of the Council of the Twelve have been the recipients of the keys, rights, and authority pertaining to the holy apostleship.[4]

---

* The Quorum of the Twelve Apostles is also called the Council of the Twelve Apostles.

** It is interesting to note that while the Church is administered from the Church Administration Building and the Church Office Building and from other locations around the world, it is governed from the temple, the house of the Lord.

Joseph Fielding Smith said:

Let me add that when a revelation comes for the guidance of this people, you may be sure that it will not be presented in some mysterious manner contrary to the order of the Church. *It will go forth in such form that the people will understand that it comes from those who are in authority,* for it will be sent either to the presidents of stakes and the bishops of the wards over the signatures of the presiding authorities, or it will be published in some of the regular papers or magazines under the control and direction of the Church, or it will be presented before such a gathering as this at a general conference. It will not spring up in some distant part of the Church and be in the hands of some obscure individual without authority, and thus be circulated among the Latter-day Saints. Now, you may remember this.[5*]

> *I think there is one thing which we should have exceedingly clear in our minds. Neither the President of the Church, nor the First Presidency, nor the united voice of the First Presidency and the Twelve will ever lead the Saints astray or send forth counsel to the world that is contrary to the mind and will of the Lord.*
>
> *An individual may fall by the wayside, or have views, or give counsel which falls short of what the Lord intends. But the voice of the First Presidency and the united voice of those others who hold with them the keys of the kingdom shall always guide the Saints and the world in those paths where the Lord wants them to be.*
>
> JOSEPH FIELDING SMITH,
> *ENSIGN,* JULY 1972, 88

When this pattern is so clearly established as the order of the

---

* In more recent times, the First Presidency has occasionally used official press conferences to announce things.

Church, how is it that so many are enticed by these wild rumors and sensational stories and reports that are outside of the Lord's pattern of order? When we hear these things or see them passed around, we should ask ourselves two questions:

1. Did it come from the First Presidency or the combined Council of the First Presidency and the Quorum of the Twelve?
2. Did it come through the official channels of communication used by that body?

> *We may take the Bible, the Book of Mormon and Doctrine and Covenants, and we may read them through and every other revelation that has been given to us, and they would scarcely be sufficient to guide us twenty-four hours. We have only an outline of our duties written; we are to be guided by the living oracles.*
>
> WILFORD WOODRUFF,
> IN LUDLOW, *LATTER-DAY PROPHETS SPEAK*, 294

If we cannot answer yes to both of those questions, then let us first reject those things as being spurious and, second, let us do all we can to stop them from spreading in the Church by teaching the proper order of things.

STEADYING THE ARK

A second application of this principle of order has to do with priesthood lines of authority. If any member of the Church could receive revelation or direction for the Church or for a group of people or for individuals over whom they have no jurisdiction, the result would be mass confusion and disorder.

There was an incident in the Old Testament that teaches this principle. The Ark of the Covenant was the most sacred and revered object in ancient Israel. It rested within the Holy of Holies in the Tabernacle and later the temple. Even the priests who had responsibility for its care were not allowed to touch it. When it had to be moved, two staves were put through four rings on the sides of the Ark.[6] This allowed it to be moved without anyone touching it.

Centuries later, the Ark was captured by the Philistines. Later, when David became king, he determined to bring the Ark back to Jerusalem. As it was being moved by the priests back to Jerusalem, it passed through a village over a rough piece of ground. The Ark rocked back and forth and looked as if it might fall off. A man by the name of Uzzah, who was not a priest, reached out to steady the Ark. The record states, "And the anger of the Lord was kindled against Uzzah; and God smote him there for his error; and there he died by the ark of God" (2 Samuel 6:7).

I think there is no occasion for any person in this Church to fear for the destiny of the kingdom. We do not need to steady the ark, but we do need to have in our hearts a fear that we may not make ourselves worthy, that we may not hew to the line of righteousness and keep the commandments of God with that degree of valiance which will give us our exaltation in the eternal worlds.

BRUCE R. MCCONKIE,
CONFERENCE REPORT,
OCTOBER 1947, 62

To some this may seem to be a harsh response. Were not Uzzah's motivations good? Wasn't he just trying to protect something very sacred? Why then would he be punished so severely? The account is very brief and there may be other factors that are not given, but some things are clear. Uzzah was not a priest. Therefore he knew he had no right to even be close to the Ark, let alone touch it. These restrictions surrounding the Ark were well known to all of Israel. What was Uzzah thinking? The Ark was the symbol of the power and glory of God. Did he think that somehow Jehovah was not capable of preventing the Ark from being damaged? Did Uzzah think that God depended on him and him alone to save it?

It doesn't matter that Uzzah's intentions may have been good. He was unwise and went directly counter to the order that God had established. And he did so knowing that others who had approached the Ark unworthily had previously been struck down.

There is a great lesson in the tragedy of Uzzah for us today. There are those in the Church who feel like they are the only ones who can "put things right." They feel they have a special spiritual endowment that allows them to see things where there is need for correction. This may be at a local level with a bishop or a stake president, or, in some cases, they are convinced that the prophet is going astray and needs correction. And they come to this conclusion in spite of the fact that they hold no priesthood keys and are out of the proper line of priesthood authority.

Thus, figuratively speaking, they reach out their hands and try to "steady the ark." Of these kinds of people, President David O. McKay said:

> It is a little dangerous for us to go out of our own sphere and try unauthoritatively to direct the efforts of a brother. You remember the case of Uzzah who stretched forth his hand to steady the Ark of the Covenant. He seemed justified when the oxen stumbled in putting forth his hand to steady that symbol. . . . The incident conveys a lesson of life. Let us look around us and see how quickly men who attempt unauthoritatively to steady the Ark die spiritually. Their souls become embittered,

The one who receives revelation for any part of the Church, if his revelations are from God, will always be in the same direction as the general program the Lord has revealed to his prophets. In other words, the Lord will never reveal to a bishop a new program entirely contradictory to the program of the Church, even for his own ward. His revelations to the bishop, to the stake president, the mission president, will be more or less confirming and amplifying and giving further details.

SPENCER W. KIMBALL,
TEACHINGS OF SPENCER W. KIMBALL, 453

their minds distorted, their judgment faulty, and their spirit depressed. Such is the pitiable condition of men who, neglecting their own responsibilities, spend their time in finding fault with others.[7]

This is not to suggest that priesthood leaders will never make mistakes or need correction. But there is an established order in the Church to correct such mistakes when they happen. A member can bring things to the attention of a stake president, for example, if it is believed a bishop is doing something wrong. *But it is out of harmony with the order of the priesthood for an individual to command one who presides over him or her and demand that they change things in order to comply with what the individual believes is required.* To allow that would be to sow such disharmony and contention in the Church as to drive out the Spirit completely.

> *If worthy, we are entitled to receive revelations for ourselves, parents for their children, and members of the Church in their callings. But the right of revelation for others does not extend beyond our own stewardship.*
>
> JAMES E. FAUST,
> *ENSIGN,* MARCH 2002, 4

PRIESTHOOD KEYS

A clear understanding of priesthood keys is essential to understanding the order of the Church and, by extension, the order of revelation.

Priesthood keys are defined as "the right to preside and direct the affairs of the Church within a jurisdiction. All priesthood keys are within The Church of Jesus Christ of Latter-day Saints, and no keys exist outside the Church on earth."[8] Note the three key elements of the definition. Keys contain the right to *preside* and *direct,* but only within a defined *jurisdiction.* For a bishop that jurisdiction is his ward; for a stake president it is a stake. A General Authority may preside anywhere in the world as assigned by the First Presidency and the Twelve.

To maintain the Lord's order in the Church, all presiding authority flows from priesthood keys and all priesthood keys in the Church come from the First Presidency and the Twelve. When we have the Aaronic or Melchizedek Priesthood conferred upon us, we are also *ordained* to a specific office in the priesthood. Later we may be ordained to other offices in the priesthood as well—teacher, priest, elder, high priest, and so on. Priesthood keys are not bestowed when a person is ordained to an office in the priesthood, except in the case of one particular office in the priesthood. That is the office of Apostle. Men who are called as Apostles and become members of the Quorum of the Twelve have all the keys of the kingdom that are currently on the earth, which are conferred upon them at the time of their ordination to the apostleship.

This point is critical to understanding the order of the Church so we will say it again. *All priesthood keys flow from the First Presidency and the Twelve.* The right to preside and direct the affairs of the kingdom (priesthood keys) in any local or general jurisdiction always must come directly from the Apostles.

> *In secular as well as spiritual affairs, Saints may receive Divine guidance and revelation affecting themselves, but this does not convey authority to direct others.*
>
> HAROLD B. LEE,
> CONFERENCE REPORT,
> APRIL 1970, 55

Usually this transference of authority happens in a very few number of steps. For example, a General Authority, or an Area Seventy, is given an assignment from the Twelve to preside over the creation of a new stake.* That is step one. By revelation they find who the Lord wants to preside. Then by the laying on of hands, the stake president is set apart and given the keys of presidency for both the stake and for the high priests quorum in the stake (step 2). The counselors are set apart, but they do not receive keys because only one can preside. When approved and authorized by the First Presidency, the stake president can then confer the keys of presidency to a bishop (step 3). The bishop can then give the keys of presidency to a deacons or teachers quorum president (step 4). Note that, in each of these steps, the jurisdiction presided over is narrowed—from a stake to a ward to a quorum.

---

* In stake creations or reorganizations, two authorities are always assigned, but one is designated as the presiding authority. See a fuller discussion of this process on pp. 54–57.

"HORIZONTAL" REVELATION AND PRIESTHOOD KEYS

It is in the concept of keys that we see what is wrong with someone trying to "steady the ark." Someone who has not been given the right to preside and direct the affairs of the Church (which right can be directly traced to the Apostles), cannot properly correct presiding officers, reveal new doctrine, unveil a new interpretation of scripture, or command a priesthood leader to take certain action. It is contrary to the order of authority God has established.

A further extension of this principle is found in what could be described as "horizontal revelation." Well-meaning but misled individuals see things in others that they feel are not right and so they receive "a revelation" that tells someone what they are doing is wrong, or what they need to do to put things right.

However, that is outside the order of God, because the principle of priesthood authority and keys applies here as well. We will not receive revelation meant to direct (or correct) someone for whom we have no priesthood responsibility or who is not within our priesthood jurisdiction. (In this case, parental authority is included in the broader concept of priesthood authority because it is given by God.)

IN SUMMARY

Once we know and understand that the Lord has set up a system of order in the Church and that those principles of order apply in the giving and receiving of revelation, we can more wisely judge between true and counterfeit revelation.

There are at least three tests that reason can apply as a threshold check on the authenticity of revelation. True revelation will pass all three of these tests, and spurious revelation (whose source is "of men" or "of devils") will fail at least one of them.

1. *True revelation will edify the recipient.* It must therefore be in words that are coherent or in a feeling whose message can be understood by one who is spiritually receptive. . . .
2. *The content of a true revelation must be consistent with the position and responsibilities of the person who receives it.* . . .
3. *True revelation must be consistent with the principles of the gospel as revealed in the scriptures and the teachings of the prophets.* The Lord will not give revelations that will contradict the principles of the gospel. His house is a house of order.[9]

CHAPTER 19

SIXTH PRINCIPLE:
TRUE REVELATION ALWAYS EDIFIES

"And that which doth not edify is not of God" (D&C 50:23).

EDIFICATION

Our next principle could simply be called the principle of *edification.* It is closely related to the concept of God's order in the Church discussed in the last chapter. Like order, edification is also related to the very nature of God. Understanding His nature is important because revelation never works counter to the nature of God.

When some of the first missionaries went out (the Church was barely one year old at that point), they encountered various claims of spiritual manifestations. Many of these were strange, even bizarre. When they returned to Kirtland, they asked the Prophet Joseph if such manifestations could be from the Lord. He inquired of God and section 50 of the Doctrine and Covenants was given in response.

In section 50, the Lord reaffirmed that "there are many spirits which are false spirits, which have gone forth in the earth, deceiving the world" (D&C 50:2).* He then gave a precise and clear explanation of how we can tell if something is from God:

---

* False spirits and counterfeit revelation are discussed in detail in chapters 21 and 22.

Wherefore, he that preacheth and he that receiveth, understand one another, and both are *edified* and rejoice together.

And that which doth not *edify* is not of God, and is darkness (D&C 50:22–23).

In that simple statement is the key test of whether a revelation is valid, that is, whether it is from God or some other source. True revelation always edifies.*

Edify means to instruct, uplift, or build someone morally and spiritually. It comes from the same root as *edifice,* which is an imposing or grand structure. The Latin root for both words is *Ædes* (pronounced ee-dus), which was typically used in reference to a temple.[1] Therefore in its fullest meaning, to *edify* means to build or strengthen the spiritual "temple" within us.

When visions, dreams, tongues, prophecy, impressions or any extraordinary gift or inspiration, convey something out of harmony with the accepted revelations of the Church or contrary to the decisions of its constituted authorities, Latter-day Saints may know that it is not of God, no matter how plausible it may appear.

FIRST PRESIDENCY,
IMPROVEMENT ERA, SEPTEMBER
1913, 1148

This simple and yet effective measure for whether something is of God was explained more fully by Mormon:

That which is of God inviteth and enticeth to do good continually; wherefore, every thing which inviteth and enticeth to do good, and to love God, and to serve him, is inspired of God. . . .

But whatsoever thing persuadeth men to do evil, and believe not in Christ, and deny him, and serve not God,

---

* There is a caution here, however. If something does *not* edify, then we can say with surety that it is not from God. But we may have things come through our own thoughts and feelings that are uplifting and edifying. We should not automatically assume that they are a revelation from God.

then ye may know with a perfect knowledge it is of the devil (Moroni 7:13, 17).

The Apostle Paul said, "Let us therefore follow after the things which make for peace, and things *wherewith one may edify another*" (Romans 14:19).

Here is the simple principle: *Revelation from God will always edify. If something does not edify, it is not of God.*

TRY THE SPIRITS

As noted, section 50 of the Doctrine and Covenants was given at a time when there were many false spirits being manifest in the Church. Various kinds of ridiculous, bizarre, unseemly, and demeaning behaviors were popular at this time among so called "revivalist" Christian groups. Early converts to the Church either brought these behaviors with them from those other churches or sought to imitate what they felt were real spiritual experiences. Joseph Smith later described what was going on in Kirtland about this time:

> *[One] will shout under the influence of that spirit, until he will rend the heavens with his cries; while [others] moved as they think, by the Spirit of God, will sit still and say nothing. Is God the author of all this? If not of all of it, which does He recognize? Surely, such a heterogeneous mass of confusion never can enter into the kingdom of heaven.*
>
> JOSEPH SMITH,
> *HISTORY OF THE CHURCH, 4:572*

Soon after the Gospel was established in Kirtland, and during the absence of the authorities of the Church, many false spirits were introduced, many strange visions were seen, and wild, enthusiastic notions were entertained; men ran out of doors under the influence of this spirit, and some of them got upon the stumps of trees and shouted, and all kinds of extravagances were entered into by them; one man pursued a ball that he said he saw flying in the air, until he came to a precipice, when he jumped into the top of a tree, which saved his life; and many ridiculous things were entered into, calculated to bring disgrace upon the Church of God, to cause the Spirit of God to be withdrawn, and to uproot and destroy those glorious principles which had been developed for the salvation of the human family. . . .

We have also had brethren and sisters who have had the gift of tongues falsely; they would speak in a muttering unnatural voice, and their bodies be distorted; . . . whereas, *there is nothing unnatural in the Spirit of God.*[2]

Our purpose here is not to further discuss the fact that Satan promotes false revelation in the Church. We will discuss that subject in chapter 21. The point here is that these were not edifying experiences. Yet they caused confusion among the early Saints. These so-called evidences of the Spirit actually caused thoughtful men and women of common sense and spiritual maturity to view the Church with suspicion and even disgust. In their eyes, such behaviors ran counter to the very spirit of Christ. Thus some were turned away from the Church.

But that was not all. There was double damage wrought by these things. In addition to bringing "disgrace upon the Church," such demeaning and ridiculous behaviors actually led individuals farther away from the Spirit, rather than closer. As Joseph noted above, they grieved the Spirit and caused it to be withdrawn. What a sad irony! In their overzealous eagerness for some kind of proof that they were being "spiritual," these individuals actually drove the Spirit away. That is a mistake we want to avoid even today.

NOTHING INDECOROUS

In the editorial written for the *Times and Seasons,* the Prophet Joseph further commented on the bizarre nature of false spiritual manifestations:

Now God never had any prophets that acted in this way; *there was nothing indecorous in the proceeding of the Lord's prophets in any age; neither had the apostles, nor prophets in the apostle's day anything of this kind.* . . . Paul says, "Let everything be done decently and in order," but here we find the greatest disorder and indecency in the conduct of both men and women, as above described. The same rule would apply to the fallings, twitchings, swoonings, shaking, and trances of many of our modern revivalists.[3]

Note the various words and phrases used by the Prophet in these two quotations. These are not phrases used to describe something which is uplifting and spiritually strengthening. In a word these are not edifying experiences. Note Joseph's powerful declarations: *"There is nothing unnatural in the Spirit of God. . . . There was nothing indecorous in the proceedings of the Lord's prophets."*

Decorum is defined as "dignified propriety in behavior, dress, or speech."[4] Therefore to be indecorous means undignified, indecent, unnatural, or inappropriate. Those qualities are counter to the nature of God. Therefore, such experiences cannot be from God, for He does nothing counter to His own nature.

A test whereby we can know whether or not revelation is from God: 1. Is it contrary to instruction from a living Prophet? 2. Is there anything secret? 3. Does it bring harmony and peace of mind? 4. Does it square with the scriptures? 5. What have you done yourself to ask of the Lord? 6. Are you keeping the commandments? By answering this series of questions, you can know by the Spirit whether or not the information comes from God.

THOMAS S. MONSON,
*FAVORITE QUOTATIONS FROM
THE COLLECTION OF
THOMAS S. MONSON,* 104

And when we speak of God, let us remember that the Holy Ghost is a member of the Godhead. Such words as *bizarre, confusing, ridiculous, unnatural, distorted, erratic, deviant, loud, unseemly, grotesque,* and *outlandish* do not describe either the nature or the functions of the Holy Spirit. After all, His title is the *Holy* Spirit.

What is true of the Lord and the Holy Spirit will also be true of the servants of God, for they are filled with His Spirit and seek diligently to emulate the qualities of godliness in all they do.

So there is the first practical implication of the principle of edification: *Anything which comes from God will be dignified, reverent, sacred, uplifting, holy, and filled with light and knowledge, and will lead us to experience those same qualities in our own lives.*

LIGHT AND TRUTH

In those two words, *light* and *truth,* is found a second practical principle of revelation related to edification. Note what Joseph said in that same editorial on false spirits:

> One great evil is, that men . . . imagine that when there is anything like power, revelation, or vision manifested, that it must be of God. . . . They consider it to be the power of God, and a glorious manifestation from God—*a manifestation of what? Is there any intelligence communicated? Are the curtains of heaven withdrawn, or the purposes of God developed?* [5]

The purpose of any revelation is to bring us closer to God and help us become more like Him. Revelation is not given as some titillating experience designed to stimulate our emotions and simply make us feel more spiritual. The very word *revelation*—an unveiling—implies a sharing of light and truth. If light and truth are not communicated in a spiritual experience, then it is not edifying, and if it is not edifying, it is not of God.

In some ways, these strange, bizarre manifestations that Joseph describes as happening with some frequency in the early Church seem like something from the past. Do we still need to be concerned about them?

In one way, the answer to that question is no. They are not seen commonly in the Church, especially the very strange behaviors that were being brought in from other churches. But in another sense, we still need to be concerned about false spirits in the Church. Well-meaning members, especially those who may be new in the Church or less mature spiritually, sometimes undertake behaviors that they think are in harmony with the Spirit, but that are not. We need to be alert to such practices. If we are in a position of leadership, they need to be corrected. If we are not, then we should bring them to the attention of those in leadership.

Some seem relatively harmless, but if they are coming from a source other than the Spirit they cannot edify and will only add to the confusion and misunderstandings about true revelation. For example:

- At the conclusion of a Relief Society meeting, the teacher asked those present to gather in a circle and hold hands while they offered the closing prayer. (The First Presidency has counseled against any form of unusual prayer rituals, such as prayer circles.)
- Often in youth groups, such as girls' camps or youth conferences, special "spiritual experiences" are formalized and programmed by unwise leaders.
- A group of adult couples gathered together in one of the homes for a monthly fireside. Often they would sit quietly, waiting for revelation and inspiration to come. The stake president wisely counseled them to stop.
- A popular thing that still manifests itself from time to time is the "forty-day fast." A ward or branch chooses some purpose for a program of fasting, for example, missionary work, or a particular family in need, or something similar. A list is passed around in priesthood and Relief Society meetings and the members sign up for one of the forty days. Then they and their family will fast on that day. This is another example of "programmed spirituality" that goes counter to the principle that we are to do things of our own free will and choice, not because of subtle pressure or to meet some of the requirements of some program.

Those bizarre, indecorous, and weird kinds of behavior seen in the early Church may be a rarity today, but there are still forms of "false revelation" or "false spirituality" among some members. In almost every case, they are started with the intention of being more spiritual or of generating more feelings from the Holy Ghost. While they may titillate the emotions, and create an illusion of spirituality, ultimately they do not edify, and therefore they are not of God.

CONTRARY TO GOSPEL PRINCIPLES

One last application related to edification is important to note. Sometimes we see individuals seeking unwisely for spiritual experiences or answers to questions that are actually contrary to the principles of the gospel or the order of the Church. President Spencer W. Kimball taught that "if one does receive revelations, which one may expect if he is worthy, they will always be in total alignment with the program of the Church; they will never be counter."[6]

This is so obvious a principle that it should not even be necessary to state it, and yet over and over we find examples where this principle is violated. In one instance, a married man and a married woman working at the same office fell in love (as they saw

A man came in to see me and said that he had heard that some man appeared mysteriously to a group of temple workers and told them, "You had better hurry up and store for a year, or two, or three, because there will come a season when there won't be any production." He asked me what I thought about it, and I said, "Well, were you in the April conference of 1936?" He replied, "No, I couldn't be there." And I said, "Well, you surely read the report of what was said by the Brethren in that conference?" No, he hadn't. "Well," I said, "at that conference the Lord did give a revelation about the storage of food. How in the world is the Lord going to get over to you what He wants you to do if you are not there when He says it, and you do not take the time to read it after it has been said?"

HAROLD B. LEE,
STAND YE IN HOLY PLACES, 159

it). They knew that if they gave in to their love, they would lose their fellowship in the Church. So they came up with another solution. They began to fast and pray for the Lord to help them find a way out of their current marriages so they could then marry each other.

One doesn't have to ask if that is acceptable. Any right thinking person knows that God's commandment is to love our wives (and husbands) with all our hearts and cleave unto them and none else (see D&C 42:22). So how do good people get so twisted in their thinking? It is bad enough that this couple were rushing down a tragic road of self-destruction, but to ask God for help in their evil desires? How could they believe that such an approach was acceptable to God?

So here is another practical application we can derive from the concept of edification. *Something cannot be contrary to the doctrines or established order of the Church and bring us edification at the same time.* Such a thing is not possible because it is contrary to God's nature and the order the Lord has established.

As another example, let's say an individual undertakes a highly questionable or risky financial investment and, "inspired by the Spirit," seeks to bring family, friends, and fellow Church members into it as well. He may even "fervently testify that this plan has come from God," and that his motives are only to gain sufficient wealth so as to be able to bless the poor. The irony is that he himself

> *No person has the right to induce his fellow members of the Church to engage in speculations or take stock in ventures of any kind on the specious claim of Divine revelation or vision or dream, especially when it is in opposition to the voice of the recognized authority, local or general.*
>
> Letter of First Presidency, as cited by Harold B. Lee, Conference Report, April 1970, 55

really believes that. But beneath all the goodly talk, what is really driving him is self-interest and greed. And greed grieves the Spirit. And when the Spirit withdraws, darkness replaces the light. And what happens when the scheme begins to collapse like a house of flimsy cards? The individual drops to his knees and begs the Lord to intervene and save him from disaster. *And he cannot see the inconsistency in doing so!* In fact, because all of this was done in his eyes "under the direction of the Spirit," he may even feel that God is under obligation to bail him out.

When we ask for something that is counter to God's commandments, or when we seek His approval for a path that He has already clearly forbidden, we not only will not be edified, but we open the way for the darkening of our minds, and this makes us vulnerable to Satan's whisperings.

After giving the very direct commandments to ask, seek, and knock, the Lord added this warning: "If ye ask anything that is not expedient for you, it shall turn unto your condemnation" (D&C 88:65).

IN SUMMARY

The Lord has made clear the place of edification in the giving and receiving of revelation. Knowing that, our guide in these matters is to seek to follow the admonition of Paul:

> "Let us therefore follow after the things which make for peace, and things wherewith one may edify another" (Romans 14:19).

CHAPTER 20

ADDITIONAL PRINCIPLES THAT GOVERN THE GIVING AND RECEIVING OF REVELATION

"Trifle not with sacred things" (D&C 6:12).

IN REVIEW

In this section we have now examined six principles that govern the giving and receiving of revelation. They are:

- God determines all aspects of revelation (chapter 13).
- We must actively seek revelation (chapter 14).
- Most revelation comes incrementally, including through divine tutorials (chapters 15 and 16).
- We are to develop spiritual self-reliance (chapter 17).
- God's house is a house of order (chapter 18).
- True revelation always edifies (chapter 19).

There are a few additional principles, but these take less explanation, and so we will deal with them together in this chapter.

PRINCIPLE 7: THAT WHICH COMES FROM ABOVE IS SACRED

As we speak of things that do not edify and how those things influence the receiving of revelation, there is one additional area that has a direct relationship to edification. This is a principle taught three different times in the first years of the Church.

- "Remember, it [the gift to translate] is sacred and cometh from above. . . . *Trifle not with sacred things*" (D&C 6:10, 12).
- "Remember that that which cometh from above is sacred, and *must be spoken with care, and by constraint* of the Spirit*" (D&C 63:64).
- "And your minds in times past have been darkened because of unbelief, and *because you have treated lightly the things you have received*" (D&C 84:54–55).

The principle directly relates to the nature of God. The Father, Son, and Holy Ghost are perfectly holy beings. Therefore, anything that comes from them is holy and therefore sacred. Thus, *by its very nature revelation is sacred.* And we are charged to view sacred things, including personal revelation, with great reverence and care.

> *Irreverence suits the purposes of the adversary by obstructing the delicate channels of revelation in both mind and spirit. . . . Reverence invites revelation.*
>
> BOYD K. PACKER,
> *ENSIGN,* NOVEMBER 1991, 22

The Lord has made it very clear: *We cannot trifle with sacred things or take them lightly.*

To Be Seen of Men

Two allied groups who came in for blistering criticism and condemnation from the Savior during His mortal ministry were the scribes and the Pharisees (see Matthew 23). They took great pride in the exactness with which they kept the commandments of the Law of Moses, and they were quick to condemn anyone, including Jesus, who did not adhere to their strict code of obedience. But obedience is not the same as

---

* "Constrain" is the opposite of "restrain," which means to hold back. Constrain means to be directed, to be moved upon to action, to be impelled. Nephi says that he was "constrained by the Spirit" to take Laban's life (1 Nephi 4:10).

righteousness. Jesus characterized their lives with one word, "Hypocrites!" They were motivated by a desire to be "seen of men." Of them, the Lord said, "Ye . . . *outwardly appear righteous* unto men, but within ye are full of hypocrisy and iniquity" (Matthew 23:28). In a word, their "good works" were undertaken to bring glory to themselves, not to the Father. It was pride that became the driving motivation for their obedience, not faith.

When it comes to personal revelation, this very natural tendency to be seen of men takes two different manifestations. If we desire to be *seen* as a "spiritual" or a "righteous" person (as opposed to actually *being* a spiritual or righteous person), then we may be tempted to manufacture or exaggerate so-called spiritual experiences in our own minds, then unwisely share them with others. *This makes us more vulnerable to counterfeit revelation,* which may come either through false spirits or from our own emotions. Or when we have real and valid revelatory experiences, especially those of a more dramatic and direct nature, *we may be tempted to share these sacred experiences unwisely* (that is, without being so directed by the Spirit).

Both of these tendencies stem from the same root cause, which is pride, or a desire to bring glory to ourselves.

Vulnerable to Counterfeit Revelation

This first tendency generally stems from a sincere, though mistaken, idea that spiritual experiences are the outward proof of spirituality. Some individuals seek to have some of the more direct and dramatic revelatory experiences. And usually their search is accompanied by a healthy dose of impatience. They want to be more spiritual, and they want it now. So they unwisely begin to try and press the Lord. They undertake marathon gospel study programs. They begin to gather with like-minded people to discuss the "deeper" levels of the doctrine. Sometimes they go off by themselves, fasting and praying and determined not to come down until they receive something significant.

This is a dangerous double-edged sword. First of all, the root motivation behind all of this is ego. They want to think of themselves as among the spiritually elite and want to be seen of others as being especially spiritual. Second, they try to force spiritual processes, and as we have seen again and again, that is not one of our privileges with the Spirit.

These two misconceptions when mixed together are a recipe for false revelation. We open the way to be deceived, either by our own emotions or by the whisperings of false spirits. President Spencer W. Kimball gave an example of how this desire to be seen as one of the "truly righteous" may lead us into being deceived.

> *Revelation given for the personal knowledge or guidance of any person should not be given to the public, either in a civil or religious capacity.*
>
> JOSEPH F. SMITH,
> *GOSPEL DOCTRINE*, 37

> One woman, for example, claimed she was receiving revelations every day while putting up the lunches in the temple. The purported revelations were childish and silly and pertained to such little things as the Lord would never deign to control or guide. At first I said, "These are not from the Lord. He does not deal with these little things where we can make up our own minds, such as what clothes to wear or what to eat today." My observation to her did not do any good. Her "revelations" came all the more, and she knew they were from the Lord. Then I said to her, "Well, now, sister, *if* these come from the Lord, they are for you alone. Do not ever whisper them to a soul." When she quit telling about them, they ceased to come anymore. She was just glorying in her superiority over her fellow beings when she received them.[1]

Other manifestations of this delusive spirit are found in people who feel like they have to attribute every tiny feeling, or every coincidence in their lives, to the Spirit, when often what they are feeling is just their own emotions. If this is a persistent pattern that seeks to draw attention to oneself, then it is not from the Spirit. It may actually offend the Spirit, because inspiration and revelation are sacred and should not be treated lightly.

C. S. Lewis, the well-known Christian writer, captured this concept of spiritual pride in *The Screwtape Letters,* a wry and yet insightful look into human nature and the workings of the evil one. The book contains a series of letters between a senior devil, Screwtape, and his nephew, Wormwood, who is out on the firing line trying to "save" his assigned "patient," who has recently become converted to the Enemy [God]. Screwtape writes to him and shares his wisdom and experience in the game of temptation. After hearing from Wormwood that the subject has suddenly taken an alarming turn toward humility, Screwtape writes:

I see only one thing to do at the moment. Your patient has become humble; *have you drawn his attention to the fact?* All virtues are less formidable to us once the man is aware that he has them, but this is specially true of humility. Catch him at the moment when he is really poor in spirit and smuggle into his mind the gratifying reflection, "By jove! I'm being humble," and almost immediately pride—*pride at his own humility*—will appear. If he awakes to the danger and tries to smother this new form of pride, make him proud of his attempt—and so on, through as many stages as you please.[2]

> *We must be careful to remember in our service that we are conduits and channels; we are not the light. "For it is not ye that speak, but the Spirit of your Father which speaketh in you." (Matthew 10:20.) It is never about me and it is never about you. In fact, anything you or I do as an instructor that knowingly and intentionally draws attention to self . . . is a form of priestcraft that inhibits the teaching effectiveness of the Holy Ghost.*
>
> DAVID A. BEDNAR,
> ADDRESS TO RELIGIOUS EDUCATORS,
> FEBRUARY 3, 2006, 4

This form of pride is one of the most difficult to root out because the deeper the person falls into that trap, the more convinced he or she becomes that they are right. Others, including priesthood leaders who have stewardship over them, are viewed as being out of touch spiritually.

Sharing the Sacred Unwisely

A second manifestation of this desire to "be seen of men" is when we are having actual spiritual experiences and either take some of the credit for them to ourselves or share the especially sacred spiritual experiences without the "constraint of the Spirit," as it says in D&C 63:64. In other words, such experiences are wonderful, and it is tempting to want to let people know that we are "in tune." In some cases, the Spirit may even give us a gentle warning not to talk about this experience or not to focus too much attention on ourselves, but we do so anyway because we know people will be very impressed.

We are not talking about the guidance from the Spirit a priesthood leader receives concerning his flock, or that which parents may receive for the guidance of their children. Nor are we suggesting that it is improper to share the everyday less direct forms of revelation that come as thoughts and feelings.

Those times when we most offend the Spirit are when we have a particularly sacred, unusual, or significant spiritual experience. It is so remarkable and so moving for us personally, that, with sincere motives, we may feel it will bless others. But intended or not, sharing the experience still calls attention to our own spirituality. Occasionally, the Spirit will suggest that the story be shared, but as though it happened to someone else, thus eliminating the glory coming back on us. When we suggest in any way that such experiences came to us because of how we are living, it is as though we are taking some of the credit for the experience ourselves.

There is an example from the Old Testament that teaches this principle. Moses is surely one of the greatest examples of faith and obedience that we find in all of scripture. Yet in a momentary slip in which he and Aaron did not give full credit to the Lord, they lost the privilege of entering the promised land. At a place called Meribah, the Israelites were murmuring because there was no water. Frustrated with such lack of faith in those who had been eyewitnesses of remarkable miracles, Moses stood before a large rock and said, "Hear now, ye rebels; must *we* fetch you water out of this rock?" (Numbers 20:10). Moses then struck the rock twice and water came forth.

We might be tempted to view this use of the word *we* as a trivial slip, a mere trifle in light of a lifetime of faithfulness, but it was much more than that. Moses had learned at the very beginning of his ministry that to even be in the presence of the Lord he had to remove his shoes, "for the place whereon thou standest is holy ground" (Exodus 3:5). If the Lord's holiness is such that it sanctifies the very ground around Him, then how much more sacred are the powers of the priesthood and of revelation? And to even suggest that such powers emanate in any way from us is an affront to the Lord. The commandment is very clear. We are not to trifle with sacred things. That which comes from above is sacred and we cannot treat it lightly.

Of this experience, President Spencer W. Kimball said:

> Moses failed to realize that the recorder was turned on when he said to the continually complaining children of Israel, crying for the fleshpots of Egypt: "Hear now, ye rebels; must *we* fetch you water out of this rock?" He was reprimanded: "Because ye believed me not, *to sanctify me in the eyes of the children of Israel,* therefore ye shall not bring this congregation into the land which I have given them." (Numbers 20:10, 12.)
>
> Moses had integrity in great measure, but in that unguarded moment *he had presumptuously taken credit* for

the Lord's miracle and was forbidden to enter the Promised Land.[3]

The more remarkable the spiritual experience is, the greater the likelihood that when we share it, people will think, "Wow! He must really be a spiritual person." And if they express such feelings to us, it is an almost irresistible temptation to say in our hearts, "Yes, I think so too." And suddenly, we are on a very slippery slope. If it brought that kind of praise and adulation once, why not share it again? We may even be tempted to embellish the account a little, enriching this point, or leaving out that one. We can rationalize to ourselves that all of this is being done to edify and lift the people, but now we are being driven by a desire similar to the Pharisees, which is to "appear righteous unto men" (Matthew 23:28).

A warning given to Sidney Rigdon has direct application here: "And now behold, verily I say unto you, I, the Lord, am not pleased with my servant Sidney Rigdon; *he exalted himself in his heart,* and received not counsel, but *grieved the Spirit*" (D&C 63:55).

The Book of Mormon warns us again and again about the dangers of priestcraft, which is "that men preach and set themselves up for a light unto the world, that they may get gain and *praise of the world;* but they seek not the welfare of Zion" (2 Nephi 26:29).

Note the counsel of Elder Dallin H. Oaks:

> Visions do happen. Voices are heard from beyond the veil. I know this. But these experiences are exceptional. And those who have these great and exceptional experiences rarely speak of them publicly because we are instructed not to do so (see D&C 63:64) and because we understand that the channels of revelation will be closed if we show these things before the world.[4]

No wonder then that the Lord declares, "Trifle not with sacred things" (D&C 6:12), then later adds, "Remember that that which cometh from above is sacred, and must be spoken with care, and by constraint of the Spirit" (D&C 63:64).*

PRINCIPLE 8: STRONG FEELINGS DO NOT PROVE TRUE REVELATION

Here is a simple reminder about an aspect of revelation that is often overlooked by people who are seeking the gift of revelation in their lives. They somehow come to believe that if their experience is accompanied by strong feelings of conviction, then somehow that proves it must be true. As an institute teacher, I remember a young man who had received a "revelation" that he was to marry a certain young woman. When I suggested that perhaps this was his own emotions at work and not true revelation, he became quite upset. "Oh, but Brother Lund, I feel so strongly that this is from the Lord."

In another case, I remember trying to deal with a brother who wreaked all kinds of havoc in his branch by publicly criticizing the branch president and calling for his resignation. When his priesthood leaders tried to say that he was out of harmony with the order of the Church, he literally bristled with passion. "I *know* this is right," he testified with tears in his eyes. "I've prayed about it many times and received a strong confirmation that I *have* to do something to correct this problem."

Missionaries and other young people are especially vulnerable to this fallacy. They feel things very strongly, then take the strength of their emotions as proof that it must be from the Lord. This kind of circular and faulty reasoning unravels quickly when we give it some serious thought. It would be hard to find a group who felt more passionately that they were absolutely, irrevocably right than the scribes and Pharisees. In fact, they felt this so strongly that they eventually conspired together to kill Christ. Virtually every apostate who has left the Church, both in our early history and in modern times, did so because they were "so sure" that they were right and Joseph Smith (or the Church or the

---

* It is interesting to note that this counsel follows just nine verses after the declaration that Sidney Rigdon was exalting himself in his heart.

modern prophets) were wrong. Or, as yet another example, take the fanatical elements of various religious groups around the world. Some of them justify the most heinous and despicable acts of terror and violence by citing their deep conviction that they are actually serving God.

At the Last Supper, Jesus warned the Twelve about the persecutions they would face after His death. He told them that the world would hate them, just as it hated Him (see John 15:18–19). And then He made this chilling prediction: "They shall put you out of the synagogues: yea, *the time cometh, that whosoever killeth you will think that he doeth God service*" (John 16:2).

> *Implicit in asking in faith is the precedent requirement that we do everything in our power to accomplish the goal that we seek. We use the agency with which we have been endowed. We use every faculty and capacity and ability that we possess to bring about the eventuality that may be involved.*
>
> BRUCE R. MCCONKIE,
> *BYU SPEECHES OF THE YEAR,*
> 1972–73, 110

This is not to say that we never experience very strong emotions in connection with revelatory experiences. Often the Spirit does trigger strong feelings within us—joy, elation, peace, sorrow, or exultation. All of those are powerful emotions. But far more often our feelings are quiet and calm, barely noticeable amidst the other daily rush of emotions we all experience.

So here is another principle which governs our experiences with revelation. *Strong feelings about something we have experienced do not guarantee that those feelings or that experience was from God.*

PRINCIPLE 9: LEARNING FROM OUR OWN EXPERIENCE

In two places in the Doctrine and Covenants, the Lord teaches a simple principle that has application to our study of what governs the giving and receiving of revelation. This principle is suggested in two scriptural passages:

- "They who have sought me early shall find rest to their souls" (D&C 54:10).

• "He that seeketh me early shall find me, and shall not be forsaken" (D&C 88:83).

In the previous chapter, we discussed how the Lord has set up mortality as a learning experience. We also noted that central to that learning experience is acting or doing. Only as we actually do things ourselves can we develop and grow and mature. This is what it means to "learn from our own experience." Touch a hot stove and we quickly learn why our parents told us to stay away. Try a new idea at work that is highly successful, and it becomes standard procedure.

Learning from experience means that we learn both from those times when we do things right and from those times when we make mistakes. A wise man once wryly summarized that principle in this way: "Good judgment comes from experience. And experience? Well, that comes from poor judgment!"

> We must be sensitive to the Spirit. We must be tuned in, and have the courage and faith to follow the promptings of the Spirit. If we do not listen to the voice of the Spirit, there is not much purpose in the Lord's communicating to us through that channel.
>
> BOYD K. PACKER,
> TEACH YE DILIGENTLY, 358

That process certainly applies in learning about revelation. The more experience we have with the voice of the Lord, the more our ability to recognize it for what it is increases. And as we have noted previously, sometimes we learn from experiences that we think may have been from the Lord, but later prove not to be.

I earlier shared an example of when I truly believed our daughter was going to be called to Mongolia as a missionary (see pp. 76–77). Why? Because I happened to be in Asia on the very day it was announced that the first missionaries from North America were being called to Mongolia. It was a remarkable coincidence. But within a matter of hours, I learned that my "inspiration" was not from the Lord. My daughter was actually called to North Carolina.

This is how we grow in wisdom and spiritual maturity. This is part of developing spiritual self-reliance. And the earlier we begin this learning process, the stronger will be our foundation as we move through life.

Remember the Lord's counsel: "They who have sought me early shall find rest to their souls" (D&C 54:10).

PRINCIPLE 10: WE MUST ACCEPT AND IMPLEMENT WHAT IS GIVEN IF WE HOPE TO RECEIVE MORE

This final principle is a straightforward one and most people understand it well, but because it so important, we will discuss it briefly here. There are several places in scripture that teach this principle clearly. Here is a brief sampling:

- "If any man will do his will, *he shall know* of the doctrine, whether it be of God" (John 7:10–11).
- "If ye continue in my word, then are ye my disciples indeed; and ye shall know the truth, and the truth shall make you free" (John 8:31–32).
- "And they that will harden their hearts, to them is given the lesser portion of the word until they know nothing concerning his mysteries" (Alma 12:11).
- "For what doth it profit a man if a gift is bestowed upon him, and he receive not the gift? Behold, he rejoices not in that which is given unto him, neither rejoices in him who is the giver of the gift" (D&C 88:33).

Hearkening back to the principle that revelation is usually given incrementally, line upon line and precept upon precept, it becomes obvious why rejection of such revelation directly affects whether the revelation continues. If the first line is not accepted, and the first precept not followed, why would God continue to send additional lines and precepts? If a parent has been asked by a child to read them a story, who then runs off to play with a toy, the wise parent does not raise his or her voice and continue to read.

To continue to send revelation when it is not accepted would

(1) force God's word upon us and thus go counter to agency; (2) give us more than we are willing to receive or can understand and therefore work to our condemnation; and (3) allow sacred things to be trifled with or treated lightly, which goes counter to God's holy nature.

And yet there is a natural pride and stubbornness that leads us to reject or dispute things that may come but are not to our liking, that do not fit into our desires or our concept of what needs to happen. Elder M. Russell Ballard cautioned the young single adults of the Church about this very tendency:

> Most of us have had the promptings of the Spirit and then argued with the Lord as to whether or not we ought to do what we are prompted to do. Is that true? I think that happens quite often in all our lives. We get a prompting and we wrestle with the Lord as to whether or not we are going to respond to the prompting.[5]

Think again of the example of President Thomas S. Monson when he felt a prompting to go visit a friend. Had he not immediately responded that man might have ended up committing suicide. If he had delayed in any way, it would have been too late. It is no wonder that after sharing that experience, he concluded with: *"Never postpone a prompting of the Spirit."*[6]

SECTION IV

IS THERE FALSE REVELATION?
HOW DO WE RECOGNIZE IT?

Satan is here also, and is going to do all he can to keep us out of the presence of God. Satan is real; Satan is personal. He is as much a person as you and I. . . . Just as surely as the Lord, by His power, puts good ideas into our minds and entices us by them, so does Satan put evil ideas into our heads and entices us by them. I suppose we can call one "good" revelation, and the other "bad" revelation, can't we, because Satan does give revelation to us, evil revelation, to put us off the track, to lead us astray, and to ease us into sin. . . . Satan is definitely a revelator, devilish and evil as he is (Mark E. Petersen, Address to Teachers of Religion, August 24, 1954, 3–4).

CHAPTER 21

ARE THERE COUNTERFEIT FORMS OF REVELATION?

"Those things . . . are not of me" (D&C 28:11).

SATAN AND GOD'S PLAN FOR HIS CHILDREN

In the premortal existence, before the foundations of the earth were laid, "there was war in heaven" (Revelation 12:7). In ways and for reasons that have not been revealed, Lucifer was able to convince a "third part of the hosts of heaven" to follow him in an attempt to overthrow God (D&C 29:36). They were thrust out of heaven and allowed to come to earth (see Revelation 12:9).

In other words, the war that began in heaven is not over; it has merely changed battlegrounds, and it continues today with increasing fury and intensity as the Second Coming of the Lord draws closer.

We should not only study good, and its effects upon our race, but also evil, and its consequences.

BRIGHAM YOUNG,
DISCOURSES OF BRIGHAM YOUNG, 256–57

We know that revelation, in all of its marvelous variety and richness, is absolutely critical to our Heavenly Father's plan. Without revelation, we cannot "come unto Christ, and be perfected in Him" (Moroni

10:32). Without revelation, we cannot ever become like God and return to live with Him. Without revelation, this Church could not be "the only true and *living* church upon the face of the whole earth" (D&C 1:30). Without revelation, we cannot get the personalized answers we need to deal with the countless challenges, questions, crises, and setbacks of life. Without revelation, we cannot possibly know how to act more like Christ in every situation that confronts us.

Why then should it surprise us that Satan would make revelation a strategic objective in his efforts to thwart the work of God? If he can convince us that it is not real, or even confuse and deceive us about the voice of the Lord, then he has made great strides in his efforts to prevent us from entering the strait and narrow gate that leads to eternal life.

FALSE REVELATION IN THE EARLY CHURCH

Elder Boyd K. Packer wrote: "The first order issued by a commander mounting a military invasion is the jamming of the channels of communication of those he intends to conquer."[1]

Satan surely is cunning enough to understand that revelation is the means by which the Father communicates His mind and will to His children. If Satan can disrupt that communication, then he can wreak havoc in his ongoing war against God and all that is good.

Understanding the intent of an enemy is a key prerequisite to effective preparation.

DAVID A. BEDNAR,
WORLDWIDE LEADERSHIP TRAINING
MEETING, FEBRUARY 11, 2006, 5

All of us are familiar with the opposition the Church experienced during the early years of our history. Mockery, ridicule, persecution, robbery, pillage, exile, and murder were all the results of Satan's violent opposition to the Restoration. It started on the very first day of the Restoration, when Satan tried to destroy Joseph in the Sacred Grove. For Joseph and Hyrum, it ended in an upstairs bedroom in Carthage Jail.

But Satan initiated another kind of opposition during all of this.

Satan not only waged war against Joseph Smith and the Church, but he also fought a bitter battle against the very concept of revelation. If he could not *stop* revelation, he could certainly sow confusion, deception, and misdirection. Some examples from the early history of the Church illustrate just how cunning and deceptive he was.

Oliver Cowdery, Hiram Page, and a Seer Stone. Just a few months after the Church was organized, two situations arose that involved false revelation. Joseph began to arrange and copy the revelations he had received. Oliver Cowdery, who was in Fayette with the Whitmer family, wrote a letter to Joseph saying he had found an error in one of the revelations. He felt his position as Second Elder in the Church gave him the right to correct the Prophet. He felt so strongly that he was right that he wrote: "I command you in the name of God to erase those words, that no priestcraft be amongst us!"

> *There are insidious forces among us that are constantly trying to knock at our doors and trying to lay traps for our young men and women, particularly those who are unwary and unsophisticated in the ways of the world.*
>
> HAROLD B. LEE,
> CONFERENCE REPORT,
> APRIL 1970, 54

When Joseph went to Fayette a short time later, he found that Oliver had convinced the entire Whitmer family that he was right. Joseph said that it was only with great labor and perseverance that he was able to convince them that Oliver's stand was not from the Lord.[2] Shortly thereafter, a second problem occurred. Joseph wrote:

> To our great grief, . . . we soon found that *Satan had been lying in wait to deceive,* and seeking whom he might devour. Brother Hiram Page* had in his possession a certain stone, by which he had obtained certain "revelations" concerning the upbuilding of Zion, the order of the Church,

---

* Hiram Page was married to one of the Whitmer daughters and seems to have been living with the Whitmers at the time.

etc., all of which were entirely at variance with the order of God's house . . . as well as in our late revelations.[3]

Be not led by any spirit or influence that discredits established authority, contradicts true scientific principles and discoveries, or leads away from the direct revelations of God for the government of the Church. The Holy Ghost does not contradict its own revealings. Truth is always harmonious with itself. Piety is often the cloak of error. The counsels of the Lord through the channel he has appointed will be followed with safety, therefore, O! ye Latter-day Saints, profit by these words of warning.

JOSEPH F. SMITH, ANTHON H. LUND, CHARLES W. PENROSE, FIRST PRESIDENCY, IN *MESSAGES OF THE FIRST PRESIDENCY,* 6:245

Initially, when Joseph could not sway those who were influenced by these purported revelations, he inquired of the Lord in the matter. In the revelation that came as a response to that inquiry (D&C 28), the Lord responded to both situations that were causing discord. With some difficulty, Joseph was able to convince both Oliver and the Whitmers of their error. In that revelation, the Lord also laid down two important principles about revelation.

Oliver was first told that "no one shall be appointed to receive commandments and revelations in this church excepting my servant Joseph Smith, Jun." (D&C 28:2).*

Then Oliver was told, "Thou shalt take thy brother, Hiram Page, between him and thee alone, and tell him that those things that he hath written from that stone are not of me and that *Satan deceiveth him*" (D&C 28:11).

Here the Lord clearly stated that what was occurring was false revelation and that the source of it was Satan himself. It didn't matter how plausible it sounded or that it came somewhat miraculously through a so-called seer stone. Hiram Page and the Whitmers had been deceived by false revelation, even though they were some of the most faithful members of the Church at that time.

* Clearly the Lord is not speaking of personal revelation given to individuals, but of revelation given for the whole Church, which only the prophet is authorized to receive.

Missionaries and False Spirits. Just a few months later, with the Church barely a year old, Satan continued to attempt to deceive the Saints through false revelation. Parley P. Pratt and others had been out on missions and had encountered different "spiritual phenomena" that were troublesome.

> As I went forth among the different branches, some very strange spiritual operations were manifested, which were disgusting, rather than edifying. Some persons would seem to swoon away, and make unseemly gestures, and be drawn or disfigured in their countenances. Others would fall into ecstasies, and be drawn into contortions, cramps, fits, etc. Others would seem to have visions and revelations, which were not edifying, and which were not congenial to the doctrine and spirit of the gospel. In short, a false and lying spirit seemed to be creeping into the Church.[4]

Members of this church throughout the world must brace themselves for the never-ending contest between the forces of righteousness and the forces of evil.

HAROLD B. LEE,
ENSIGN, JANUARY 1973, 62

Joseph inquired of the Lord again, who responded with what is now section 50 of the Doctrine and Covenants. Once again the Lord clearly stated that these so-called spiritual experiences were from Satan.

> Behold, verily I say unto you, that there are many spirits *which are false spirits,* which have gone forth in the earth, deceiving the world.
>
> And also *Satan hath sought to deceive you,* that he might overthrow you (D&C 50:1–3).

A Discourse on False Revelation. Much later, the problem with false spirits in the Church was still prevalent enough that the Prophet felt compelled to address the issue in a lengthy editorial in the *Times and Seasons* under the date of April 1, 1842. The editorial began: "Recent occurrences that have transpired amongst us render it an imperative duty devolving upon me to say something in relation to the spirits by which men are actuated."[5]

In the editorial, Joseph listed numerous examples of false spirits influencing individuals. Some were from the Old and New Testaments, some from more recent history. Some were occurring at that time within the Church itself. He described a great variety of bizarre and unseemly behavior. Joseph noted that these various manifestations were so imitative of true and valid forms of revelation that only the Spirit of God could help distinguish between them.

THERE IS COUNTERFEIT REVELATION

The word *counterfeit* comes from two root words. The first root, "counter," means "in the wrong way; contrary to the right course; in the reverse direction." The second root, "feit" comes from the Latin *frere*, which means to make or do. Thus, a counterfeit is an imitation created with the purpose to defraud or deceive.[6] The closer the imitation is to the original, the better the counterfeit and the more effective is the fraud and deception. Detection of a good counterfeit generally requires someone who is totally familiar with the genuine original and who has had much experience in dealing with counterfeits.

> *To those in quest of spiritual light, this word of counsel: Seek it only in the Lord's appointed way. . . . Never go upon the Devil's ground. Keep away from all deceptive influence. One may believe in hypnotism, without being a hypnotist. . . . In like manner, one may believe spiritualism real, without becoming a spiritualist, without attending "seances," without consulting "mediums," without putting trust in planchettes, ouija boards, automatic pencils, false impersonations, or in any way encouraging the advances of designing spirits, who thus gain an ascendancy over their victims, leading them into mazes of delusion, and often into depths of despair. Go not after them.*
>
> ORSON F. WHITNEY,
> *SATURDAY NIGHT THOUGHTS,* 311–12

In light of this definition, these false spirits can be legitimately described as "counterfeit revelation." Such revelation is opposite or contrary to true revelation, and its purpose is to reverse the Lord's work and take people in a direction opposite from the true way.

Just as true revelation can involve a broad spectrum of experiences, so too can false revelation. In each case Satan seeks to pass these experiences off as being from God. Note the words of Elder Packer in the accompanying box. The possibility of false revelation is such that we must be "ever on guard" against it. False revelation is not something that happens only rarely. It is an ever-present possibility.

MODERN EXAMPLES OF COUNTERFEIT REVELATION

While we may not today see some of the bizarre and outlandish behaviors that were present in the early Church, false spirits and other forms of counterfeit revelation are nevertheless present today. It is a mistaken idea—and therefore from Satan himself—that there will always be something dark and sinister about false revelation. We say again, the idea of a counterfeit suggests something so close to the original that it is difficult to tell the difference. What follows are only a few ways we may see false revelation today.

Be ever on guard lest you be deceived by inspiration from an unworthy source. You can be given false spiritual messages. There are counterfeit spirits just as there are counterfeit angels. . . .

The spiritual part of us and the emotional part of us are so closely linked that it is possible to mistake an emotional impulse for something spiritual.

BOYD K. PACKER,
ENSIGN, JANUARY 1983, 55–56

OUR OWN EMOTIONS AS A FORM OF COUNTERFEIT REVELATION

Unfortunately, confusing our emotions with the Spirit is a form of false revelation that surfaces all too often. As Elder Packer said above, "The spiritual part of us and the emotional part of us are so closely linked, it is possible to mistake an emotional impulse for something spiritual." On another occasion, he said, "In your emotions, the spirit and the body come closest to being one."[7]

We noted earlier that the Lord defines the "spirit of revelation" as when the Spirit speaks to our minds through our thoughts and to our hearts through our feelings (see D&C 8:2–3). Since our spiritual selves are closely tied with the center of our emotions, this creates a problem for us. It is an easy thing to mistake strong emotions for spiritual promptings. And the opposite is true as well. Sometimes we think a true spiritual prompting is "just us" being our normal selves.

> *If we are faithful in keeping the commandments of God His promises will be fulfilled to the very letter. . . . The trouble is, the adversary of men's souls blinds their minds. He throws dust, so to speak, in their eyes, and they are blinded with the things of this world.*
>
> HEBER J. GRANT,
> *GOSPEL STANDARDS,* 44–45

This confusion can rise sharply if the feelings we are experiencing are connected to something very important to us or that we want very badly. When we strongly desire something, our emotions can rise to a fever pitch, which only makes us more vulnerable to mixing our emotions up with spiritual promptings.

A fairly common expression of this error is found in the courting process. A young man and a young woman begin to date each other. Everything is fine until one of the individuals begins to sense that their dating partner is not as excited or committed to the relationship as they are. When everything they try fails to correct that situation, their feelings can become both painful and intense. In this state of urgency—or, in some cases, downright desperation—what happens? They get a "revelation" that the Lord wants them to marry.*

In a way, this leads to a form of "spiritual coercion." They hope that

---

* In my experience with young adults as an institute teacher, as a bishop, and as a president of a singles stake at Brigham Young University, I came to believe that in most of these cases, the individual getting the "revelation" sincerely believed that he was receiving feelings from the Lord. It was not just a cynical, calculated form of manipulation.

the partner's desire to do the Lord's "will" in the matter will convince them to accept the "revelation" and agree to marry.

The late Carlfred Broderick, a renowned Latter-day Saint family therapist, reported that when his oldest daughter returned home from BYU after one semester, she excitedly told him that eight different boys had received a revelation that she was to marry them. She was thrilled. With tongue in cheek, Brother Broderick called this "hormonal revelation."[8]

This is a good example of how emotions can become counterfeit revelation. Though Dr. Broderick was clearly having some fun with the example of his daughter, in a much more serious tone, he went on to note that in many cases even married individuals can be misled *by their feelings,* which they think are from the Lord. In some cases such feelings can lead to adulterous relationships, but even when the two individuals may restrain themselves, the "emotional divorce" often leads to a dissolution of the marriage.

> I am impressed over and over again with how easily some Latter-day Saints permit themselves to get into poten- tially destructive situations because they know that only *good* people are involved and that the love they feel is pure and "special." I am particularly impressed with the frequency with which they claim that they felt the "Spirit" guiding them.[9]

Another too frequent example of this is when fine people try to jus- tify their involvement in a financial scheme by convincing themselves that it is "inspired." In reality, they are twisting their own feelings into purported revelations; the result is to entice the unwary and the gullible to invest with them.

A less frequent example, but one that is not unheard of, is a mis- sionary who goes into the mission field and then decides not to stay. He knows that if he simply says he's going home, he will look unfaithful or unworthy. So he convinces himself that his feelings are coming from the

Lord. In one case, a missionary told me that the Lord had let him know that he had fulfilled his purpose for coming on a mission in the first three months he had been out, and that he now needed to go home to accomplish other of the Lord's purposes. In another case, an elder said that his girlfriend, who was not a member, was having serious problems at home. He said the Lord had told him he could do a greater work by returning early and converting her, then taking her to the temple.

WHISPERINGS OF THE EVIL ONE

Just as the Spirit whispers to us, Satan and his followers can also speak to us through thoughts and feelings. We see this when we are tempted to do wrong and begin to rationalize that it is not harmful. Nephi taught clearly some of the things Satan whispers to us:

- "Eat, drink, and be merry, for tomorrow we die; and it shall be well with us" (2 Nephi 28:7).
- "Lie a little, take the advantage of one because of his words, dig a pit for thy neighbor; there is no harm in this" (2 Nephi 28:8).
- "All is well in Zion" (2 Nephi 28:21).
- "There is no hell; . . . I am no devil, for there is none" (2 Nephi 28:22).

A common technique is when Satan tries to discourage good people. Faithful Latter-day Saints are not vulnerable to temptation in the same way as those out in the world are. A man or woman who has never smoked or drunk alcohol in a lifetime isn't particularly tempted to stop in a bar and have a drink on the way home from work. So Satan comes at them in a different way. And one of his most effective whispering campaigns goes something like this. "Look at all the times when you fall short of what God expects of you. Therefore, you must be failing."

This can be very effective because he is always right in that argument. We are not perfect. There are numerous areas of our life where we know we could and should be doing better. Someone once noted that there are three areas of endeavor where we can never come away saying to ourselves, "I've done everything that needs to be done, and I did them right." Those areas are: Being a parent. Being a priesthood or auxiliary leader. Being a teacher.

Therefore, it is not an uncommon thing for members, especially some of our sisters, to always be comparing themselves "upward"; that is, they find someone in the family or the ward or the neighborhood who always seems to do things better than they, or who does more than they are doing, or whose children seem better behaved, or who— . . . The list is almost endless. And the result is a constant, nagging feeling of failure, of inadequacy.

Ironically, another whispering campaign comes after he has successfully enticed us into some form of sin. Then he switches tactics and whispers such things as, "You have offended God. You are unclean and therefore unworthy to approach Him in prayer. Surely God cannot still love you after what you've done. You may as well give up, for you've put yourself beyond His reach."

All inspiration does not come from God. (See D&C 46:7.) The evil one has the power to tap into those channels of revelation and send conflicting signals which can mislead and confuse us. There are promptings from evil sources which are so carefully counterfeited as to deceive even the very elect.

BOYD K. PACKER,
ENSIGN, NOVEMBER 1989, 14

What the Spirit teaches us is that our Father is easy to please, but hard to satisfy. To illustrate what we mean by that, let's take the example of a baby. When it takes those first wobbly steps, the parents are delighted and cheer and clap. They are greatly pleased. But are they satisfied? Is that all they expect? Of course not. The child still has a lifetime of achievement to pursue. So it is with us. Our Father is pleased with any forward movement, any drawing closer to the Spirit, any act of service or obedience. He will not be fully satisfied until we have become like Him. But just because we are not perfect, that doesn't mean He is not pleased with what we are doing or the progress we are making. But Satan does not want us to have such feelings and so constantly tries to discourage us and cause us to despair.

The Savior taught that "strait is the gate, and narrow is the way, that leadeth unto life, and few there be that find it" (Matthew 7:14). That is a concept with which most of us are very familiar. But do we also remember what He said just prior to that? He called on us to "enter ye in at the strait gate," because "wide is the gate, and broad is the way, that leadeth to destruction, and many there be which go in thereat" (Matthew 7:13).

That is a sobering and yet insightful description of life. It also says much about how Satan works. There is only one, very narrow way to eternal life, but there are countless roads to destruction. And it seems that Satan doesn't much care which gate we choose to enter, or which path we choose to take, as long as he keeps us from the true gate and the narrow way. We can be an atheist, or we can be a religious fanatic—either is equally effective in keeping us off the narrow path. We can worship a crocodile, as the ancient Egyptians did, or we can worship a Corvette purchased at the nearest Chevrolet dealership. As long as we don't properly worship God, Satan wins.

And so it is with false revelation. In rare cases, Satan may appear as an angel of light (see 2 Corinthians 11:14). More frequently he whispers false messages in our ears. When we have strong feelings about something, feelings originating from him or from ourselves, he may whisper to us that they are from the Lord.

He leads people into bizarre, outlandish behavior, then convinces them that this is how the Spirit works. Thus he gets them with a double blow. They are offending the Spirit with behaviors that do not edify, and they are filled with pride and conviction that he or she is indeed one of the Lord's elite because they are so "in touch" with the Spirit.

RUMORS

Another technique Satan uses to deceive and confuse is found in the all too common tendency of some Church members to accept every wild rumor, every sensational story, and every dramatic report of some supposed "spiritual experience." This is then passed from person to person and spreads rapidly in the Church. It doesn't seem to matter that some of these reports are completely counter to common sense or that they contradict known gospel principles or established programs and policies of the Church. President Harold B. Lee spoke of these to the brethren of the priesthood some years ago:

> There are some as wolves among us. By that, I mean some who profess membership in this church who are not sparing the flock. And among our own membership, men are arising speaking perverse things. Now *perverse* means diverting from the right or correct, and being obstinate in the wrong, willfully, in order to draw the weak and unwary members of the Church away after them. . . .
>
> I should like now to make reference to some of these [perverse means]. The first is the spread of rumor and gossip (we have mentioned this before) which, when once started, gains momentum as each telling becomes more fanciful, until unwittingly those who wish to dwell on the sensational repeat them in firesides, in classes, in Relief Society gatherings and priesthood quorum classes without first verifying the source before becoming a party to causing speculation and discussions that steal time away from the things that would be profitable and beneficial and enlightening to their souls.[10]

Some of these stories are so ridiculous and so counter to plain old common sense that one would think they would die a natural death, perhaps after everyone has a good laugh. But they don't. For that reason, I choose not to give any examples here, even of the most ludicrous and unbelievable. There are sufficient examples out there. They do not need repeating here.

IN SUMMARY

In a way, all of this would be quite depressing and discouraging were it not for one important truth. God has not left us on our own in this struggle. Heavenly Father knows all that Satan does and has given us the help we need to detect him and those who speak for him. As He Himself has stated: "My wisdom is greater than the cunning of the devil" (D&C 10:43). Joseph Smith also made this abundantly clear in his famous statement:

> The Standard of Truth has been erected; no unhallowed hand can stop the work from progressing; persecutions may rage, mobs may combine, armies may assemble, calumny may defame, but the truth of God will go forth boldly, nobly, and independent, till it has penetrated every continent, visited every clime, swept every country, and sounded in every ear, till the purposes of God shall be accomplished, and the Great Jehovah shall say the work is done.[11]

The Lord has given us principles that help us know the difference between true and counterfeit revelation.

And finally, in the words of President James E. Faust:

> We all have an inner braking system that will stop us before we follow Satan too far down the wrong road. It is the still, small voice within us. But if we allow ourselves to succumb to Satan's tempting, the braking system begins to leak brake fluid and our stopping mechanism becomes weak and ineffective.[12]

CHAPTER 22

How Can We Tell the Difference between True and Counterfeit Forms of Revelation?

"O be wise; what can I say more?" (Jacob 6:12).

LEARNING TO RECOGNIZE TRUE REVELATION

If:

- There is truly counterfeit revelation, as we have now shown there is; and
- The counterfeit forms are so imitative of the real thing; as we have now shown they are; and
- These counterfeit forms are an ever-present possibility;

Then:

How do we tell the difference?

Fortunately, the Lord has not left us to work this out on our own. He has given us the principles that govern the giving and receiving of revelation (chapters 13–20). From these we can derive some practical guidelines, or tools, that help us in determining if something is true revelation or not.

What makes the guidelines truly operative, however, is that we also have the Spirit. The Spirit will help us discern between true and false

[We] should understand that directions for the guidance of the Church will come, by revelation, through the head. All faithful members are entitled to the inspiration of the Holy Spirit for themselves, their families, and for those over whom they are appointed and ordained to preside. But anything at discord with that which comes from God through the head of the Church is not to be received as authoritative or reliable.

Letter of First Presidency, August 2, 1913, as cited by Harold B. Lee, Conference Report, April 1970, 55

revelation if we earnestly seek for the Lord's guidance. The Prophet Joseph made a statement on false spirits that is worthy of repeating:

The great difficulty lies in the ignorance of the nature of spirits, of the laws by which they are governed, and the signs by which they may be known; if it requires the Spirit of God to know the things of God; . . . the spirit of the devil can only be unmasked through that medium.[1]

Here then are some guidelines and questions we can use as "markers" to help us evaluate revelatory experiences. Since they are based on principles already discussed, only brief reference will be made to these principles here.

GUIDELINE 1: IS WHAT IS "REVEALED" IN HARMONY WITH THE GOSPEL AND IN KEEPING WITH THE NATURE OF GOD INCLUDING THE ORDER HE HAS ESTABLISHED IN THE CHURCH?

God does not lie, nor does He ever contradict Himself. He never seeks to confuse or trick us by sending false spiritual messages to test us.

As a simple example: God has said: "He that looketh upon a woman to lust after her shall deny the faith, and shall not have the Spirit" (D&C 42:23). Yet one young struggling missionary told me that the Spirit told him that as long as he doesn't do anything more than watch it, there is not that much harm in pornography.

Another aspect of this has to do with the nature of God. All of God's attributes are held in perfection. He is all powerful, all knowing, perfectly loving, perfectly holy. Nothing the Father and the Son do—and nothing they have the Spirit do for them—will ever run counter to that perfect nature. Once we understand that, our desire becomes to emulate those characteristics in our own lives. And we also desire to approach God in all reverence and with a great respect for His sacred and holy nature.

A simple example: Contention is completely opposite to God's nature. Yet some missionaries and members feel "inspired" to argue or contend about religion, engaging in what someone once characterized as a "scriptural artillery duel." Sadly, they think they are being courageous and doing God's will when in actuality they are offending the Spirit.

We have earlier shown that God's house is a house of order. Here is another aspect of this guideline. Testing something against the proper order of things helps to avoid confusion and gives members a clear measure to help determine whether something is really coming through the Spirit to them.

A simple example: A well-meaning neighbor told a woman who had just given birth to a premature baby, and then lost the child, that if her husband had taken the time to give her a priesthood blessing before rushing her to the hospital, the baby wouldn't have died. The grieving mother believed her and grew bitter to think that God would punish them for such forgetfulness in a time of extremely high stress. Though she came from a strong, active home, she left Church activity for an extended period of time.*

---

* This is an actual case shared with me after I had spoken on personal revelation in a fireside. The woman who had lost the baby told me she had not been to Church for several years, then told me why. Before I could do anything more than shake my head in disbelief, she said, "But my neighbor didn't have any stewardship over me, did she?" "No, she didn't," I agreed. "Then that couldn't have been from the Lord?" I assured her that I could not believe that (1) the Lord required that couple to stop and give a blessing when she was hemorrhaging and in danger of losing her life as well; (2) that a loving Heavenly Father was punishing her; and therefore (3) her neighbor, though well-meaning, was out of order in taking it upon herself to correct this couple for what she thought they should or should not have done. The woman was weeping by then and said something like, "Thank you for teaching me that principle. That will make all the difference now."

Questions to Ask Ourselves for Evaluation:

- Does the claimed revelation contradict gospel principles or Church programs and procedures as established by the First Presidency and the Quorum of the Twelve?
- Is the purported revelation (and how it was given) in harmony with God's nature; that is, is it reverent, orderly, sacred, decorous, enlightening, sensible, natural, holy, dignified, and uplifting?
- When we hear a sensational rumor or prophecy or a new interpretation of doctrine or scripture, or a "faith-promoting" story, do we check to see if it came through established patterns of communication from those who lead the Church?
- Is someone without priesthood keys or designated authority trying to *direct* or *correct* someone for whom they have no responsibility?

GUIDELINE 2: DOES WHAT IS GIVEN EDIFY?

Moroni taught that a clear test of whether something is from God or Satan is whether it leads us to do good, to be better, in a word, to draw closer to Christ (see Moroni 7:16–18). As noted earlier, edification means to lift one spiritually, to build a stronger spiritual foundation; to make someone stronger in their discipleship. And the Lord has flatly stated: "That which doth not edify is not of God, and is darkness" (D&C 50:23).

A simple example: So-called revelations that are titillating to the senses or speculative or sensational, or that lead us to act in raucous or irreverent or inappropriate ways do not edify, and therefore are not of God.

Questions to Ask Ourselves for Evaluation:

- Does what is given in the revelation lead us to do good and to strive to be more like the Father and the Son?
- Did this supposed revelatory experience bring light and truth, enlightenment and understanding to our minds and hearts?

GUIDELINE 3: DOES WHAT IS GIVEN GO COUNTER TO THE PRINCIPLE OF SPIRITUAL SELF-RELIANCE?

In Chapter 17, we saw that the Lord has clearly stated that He is not pleased with those who must be commanded in all things. He calls such a person "a slothful and not a wise servant" (D&C 58:26). In several places the Lord has also taught that some things do not matter to Him and that we can do "as seemeth you good" (D&C 60:5).

A simple example: Taking too literally the promise that the Spirit will direct us in all aspects of our lives, one couple, sincerely desiring to be "more spiritual," would not choose which kind of cereal to eat for breakfast each morning until they had received a "confirmation" from the Spirit.

Questions to Ask Ourselves for Evaluation:

- Are we expecting to be led by the Spirit in every tiny, detailed aspect of our lives, including trivial things—such as what brand of toothpaste to buy, or what cereal to eat for breakfast—that do not matter to the Lord? (see D&C 58:26–27).
- Could this possibly be a case where the Lord is telling us that this decision is our choice, that it doesn't matter to Him, or that either alternative is acceptable to Him?
- Are we always using language such as: "The Spirit told me to do this" or "The Spirit has told me where to go" or "I don't do anything until I have a confirmation" or "I never prepare for a class. I just wait as the class begins until the Spirit tells me what to teach"?

GUIDELINE 4: DOES THE MOTIVE BEHIND THIS "REVELATION" SEEM TO BE TO GET PERSONAL GAIN, GLORY, OR BENEFIT FOR THE RECEIVER?

There will always be attendant blessings when the Lord gives us direction and guidance through the Spirit. His promise is that if we ask, we will receive, if we seek, we shall find, and if we knock, it will be opened to us (see Matthew 7:7–8). However, He also warns that we should ask only for that which is "expedient" for us, and which "is right" (D&C 88:64–65; Mosiah 4:21; 3 Nephi 18:20). Often false revelation is generated by ego; that is, even as certain individuals claim such things are coming from the Lord, the underlying motivation is to bring attention, glory, adulation, or personal gain to themselves. Of such we should be especially wary.

A simple example: A brother sharply critical of his stake president's "spirituality and worthiness" offered himself as the new replacement so that all could be "put right" in the stake.

Questions to Ask Ourselves for Evaluation:

- Does the revelation further the work of the Lord and bring glory to Him rather than glory, benefit, or personal gain to the individual receiving it?
- Does the revelation pertain to a financial scheme that is being touted as "inspired" but that will, if successful, actually bring the greatest benefit to the person who has received the "revelation"?
- Even when there might not be financial gain, does what the person is teaching or claiming to be true bring him or her personal fame, glory, importance, or adulation and therefore qualify as a form of priestcraft (2 Nephi 26:29)?

GUIDELINE 5: HAS THE LORD CONFIRMED THAT THIS PARTICULAR REVELATION COMES FROM HIM?

We have noted several times throughout this book that one of the things that typically seems to accompany true spiritual experiences is a confirmation of some kind. There are exceptions to that, but generally the Lord lets us know that revelations have come through His grace and mercy. The confirmations don't always come immediately; in some cases they may be delayed for some time, but they do come.

A simple example: The person who was questioning whether God loved her had an impression not to eat at a certain restaurant, which she ignored. Later she became very ill through food poisoning, which not only confirmed the validity of the warning but gave her the witness she was seeking that God did love her (see pp. 103–4).

Questions to Ask Ourselves for Evaluation:

- After following what we thought might be promptings of the Spirit, did we receive some kind of clear confirmation that what we received was from the Lord?
- Only the Lord knows the thoughts and intents of our hearts (see D&C 6:16). Have we received something in our mind or heart that no one else except the Lord could have known?
- After careful prayer, pondering and honest searching of the heart, does it *feel* right? (see D&C 9:8–9).
- Do I feel at peace with this decision or with accepting what was received (see D&C 6:23)?

GUIDELINE 6: CAN WE HONESTLY SAY THAT OUR GREATEST DESIRE IS TO DO GOD'S WILL?

If prayer is only a spasmodic cry at the time of crisis, then it is utterly selfish, and we come to think of God as a repairman or a service agency to help us only in our emergencies. We should remember the Most High day and night—always—not only at times when all other assistance has failed and we desperately need help.

HOWARD W. HUNTER,
*TEACHINGS OF
HOWARD W. HUNTER,* 39

One of the most important things we can do is to search our own hearts with scrupulous honesty. We must examine our motives, our desires, our actions, our conclusions. One of the things that should become a standard part of our daily prayers is not only "Thy will be done," but "Heavenly Father, help me to be sensitive to Thy voice. Help me to recognize revelation when it comes, and to distinguish it from the false voices of the world or my own emotions."

Earlier I cited the case of a young bishop who had had a remarkable experience while giving a priesthood blessing to a young mother who had suddenly fallen unconscious and had been rushed to the hospital (see page 8).

The feeling that came to him as he was speaking was so positive and so powerful that he was sure it was from the Lord. Convinced of that, he then pronounced some very wonderful and specific promises for her. Yet she passed away a few hours later, contradicting what he had said.

As he shared that with me many years later, he was still agonizing over it. When I asked what conclusions he had come to about the experience, his answer was a wonderful lesson about how we can let our own emotions get in the way. He said:

> I know without question that the feelings I had were from the Lord. But in my great desire to bless this woman and her family I put my own interpretation on what I was feeling. Now I understand that the Lord was saying to me, "It's all right. I am here. I will bless her. I am going to call her home, but this is my will. Be at peace, and let the family be at peace." But I wanted so badly to intervene and stop this husband's suffering that I assumed the Lord was saying, "I am going to heal her, so you can make her promises about staying longer in mortality."

Then came a wonderful reminder for all of us. He said, "I have never again given a blessing without being very conscious that I must speak for the Lord and not just express my own desires."

Questions to Ask Ourselves for Evaluation:

After honestly examining our own hearts can we truly say that:

- Our motives are pure, that is, that our greatest desire is to promote God's work and not some selfish purpose of our own?
- We are truly willing to accept revelation in God's "own time, and in his own way, and according to his own will" (D&C 88:68)?
- We are not seeking to "counsel the Lord" (Jacob 4:10) and tell Him how to solve our problems or what He needs to do for us?

- We are not making the same mistake as Oliver Cowdery when the Lord told him, "You took no thought save it was to ask me" (D&C 9:7)?
- We are not asking for something that is not "expedient" for us?
- We are not asking for revelation on an issue concerning which God has already told us what needs to be done?
- Our own needs are deliberately pushed way down so that what we desire most is to be in harmony with God's will?

IN SUMMARY

One of the paramount purposes of this mortal existence is to learn how to receive, recognize, and then respond to the voice of the Lord. Part of that challenge lies in distinguishing His voice from all other voices, including our own emotions, false revelation from the evil one, and the subtle siren voices of the world.

Gratefully, the Lord has given us much help in this matter. He has told us what His voice is like. He has taught us how the Holy Spirit works with us. He has given us principles to guide and direct us in this challenging quest. Most of all, He has given us the gift of the Holy Ghost to help us. Early on in this book, we suggested that a well-known scripture might appropriately be amended to read, "For God so loved the world that He gave us the gift of the Holy Ghost." Thankfully, it is the Spirit that makes the process of revelation work and helps us to distinguish His voice from all others.

SECTION V

HOW DO WE INCREASE THE LIKELIHOOD OF RECEIVING AND RECOGNIZING REVELATION?

When God communicates . . . priceless truth to us, He does it by the Spirit of Truth. We have to ask for it in prayer. Then He sends us a small part of that truth by the Spirit. It comes to our hearts and minds. It feels good, like the light from the sun shining through the clouds on a dark day. He sends truth line upon line, like the lines on the page of a book. Each time a line of truth comes to us, we get to choose what we will do about the light and truth God has sent to us. If we try hard to do what that truth requires of us, God will send more light and more truth. It will go on, line after line, as long as we choose to obey the truth (Henry B. Eyring, "A Life Founded in Light and Truth," BYU Devotional, August 15, 2000, 2).

CHAPTER 23

WHAT IS THE ROLE OF FAITH IN LEARNING TO RECEIVE AND RECOGNIZE REVELATION?

"Seek learning . . . also by faith" (D&C 88:118).

EXERCISING FAITH AND LEARNING BY FAITH

As we begin the final section of this book, it will quickly become apparent that in our attempt to answer the prime question—How do we learn to more readily receive and recognize revelation?—we will draw upon concepts and principles discussed throughout the book. That is the nature of revelation. We receive it by studying different concepts and principles of truth. Revelation is simple in form, purpose, and function but complex in its various manifestations and practical implications in our own lives.

With that, let us begin with what perhaps is the most important key in the process of personal revelation. In an oft-quoted scripture given at Kirtland in 1832, we read: "And as all have not faith, seek ye diligently and teach one another words of wisdom; yea, seek ye out of the best books words of wisdom; *seek learning, even by study and also by faith*" (D&C 88:118).

Most of us seem to intuitively understand what it means to learn by study. It involves reading, pondering, examining, experimenting, comparing, analyzing, and so forth. In other words, learning by study means learning through diligent *mental* effort.

But how do we learn by faith? What exactly does that mean? For that matter, what does the phrase "We must exercise faith" mean? We know how to exercise and strengthen the body, and we know how to exercise and strengthen the mind. But how do we exercise and strengthen faith?

If we learn something by faith, have we exercised faith and have we strengthened faith? Yes. In fact, learning something through faith may be the very essence of what it means to exercise our faith. Surely as we learn something through or by faith, we strengthen and increase our faith. So what does this have to do with personal revelation?

We have defined revelation as the process through which an individual receives light and truth from God. By its very nature then, revelation involves *learning*. In a talk titled "Seek Learning by Faith," Elder David A. Bednar spoke to religious educators at some length about the idea of what it means to learn by faith. Note how he directly linked receiving revelation to learning by faith:

> As we look to the future and anticipate the ever more confused and turbulent world in which we will live, I believe it will be essential for all of us to increase our capacity to seek learning by faith. In our personal lives, in our families, and in the Church, we can and will *receive the blessings of spiritual strength, direction, and protection* [all functions of the Holy Ghost and therefore forms of revelation] as we seek by faith to obtain and apply spiritual knowledge.[1]

UNTO THE HEART

Elder Bednar used a passage in 2 Nephi to begin his discussion on learning by faith. In the last chapter of Nephi's writings, he said: "When a man speaketh by the power of the Holy Ghost the power of the Holy Ghost carrieth it unto the hearts of the children of men" (2 Nephi 33:1). After citing that scripture, Elder Bednar said, "Please notice how the power of the Spirit carries the message *unto* but not necessarily *into* the heart."[2]

This idea that the Holy Ghost carries it only unto and not into the heart is a pivotal concept that needs further exploration. And to more fully understand the implications of what Nephi taught, we have to more fully understand how the concept of the *heart* is used in the scriptures.

The word *heart* is used about 2,300 times in the four standard works. That tells us that *heart* is a significant concept. Only a small portion of those usages refer to the heart in its physiological sense—that is, as the organ of the body that is the center of the circulatory system and the fundamental organ for sustaining life. By far the greater use of the word is figurative. One Bible scholar said the heart most often connotes such things as the center of one's personal activities; the seat of emotions and passions; the seat of the intellect, conscience, and spiritual understanding; and the seat of the determination or will.[3]

To put it another way, the heart symbolizes the inner man, the "real spiritual me"—that individual entity we call the spirit that dwells in the physical body but is so much more than the body. The heart signifies the very essence of what makes us unique in both personality and character. When we understand this broader, figurative use of *heart,* we better appreciate such passages as

- "And thou shalt love the Lord thy God with all thine heart" (Deuteronomy 6:5; see also Matthew 22:37).
- "The Lord seeth not as man seeth; for man looketh on the outward appearance, but the Lord looketh on the heart" (1 Samuel 16:7).
- "With the heart man believeth unto righteousness" (Romans 10:10).
- "Which has wrought a mighty change in us, or in our hearts, that we have no more disposition to do evil, but to do good continually" (Mosiah 5:2).
- "I, the Lord, require the hearts of the children of men" (D&C 64:22).

As noted above, the heart, figuratively speaking, is where freedom of will and freedom of choice reside. The physical body doesn't choose. It is merely the instrument for carrying out what man's mind and heart decide they want to do. This freedom of will, or right to choose, is what the scriptures call "moral agency" (D&C 101:78).

The Lord will not force himself upon people, and if they do not believe, they will receive no revelation. If they are content to depend upon their own limited calculations and interpretations, then, of course, the Lord will leave them to their chosen fate.

SPENCER W. KIMBALL,
ENSIGN, MAY 1977, 76

As we discussed earlier, agency is so central, so fundamental, and so sacred to the plan of happiness that even God, with all His endless power, will never force His will or the truths of salvation upon any of His children. He will not use His infinite power to coerce or compel us in any way, even if it would be the best thing for us. As Elder M. Russell Ballard explains:

> The choice would always be ours. As much as He wanted us to return to live with Him, He could not and would not force His will upon us. The plan had at its very foundation the principle of moral agency, which could be exercised for good or ill. That meant God was leaving it up to us to determine whether or not we would return to His eternal home through His Son, Jesus Christ.[4]

In short, *God will not force the human heart.*

GUARDIANS OF THE HEART

With that quick review of the heart and agency, let us return to Nephi's comment about the Holy Ghost carrying the word *unto* but not *into* the hearts of men. Elder Bednar, who was speaking to teachers of religion, explained how this principle works in teaching: "A teacher can explain, demonstrate, persuade, and testify, and do so with great spiritual power and effectiveness. Ultimately, however, the content of a message and the witness of the Holy Ghost *penetrate into the heart only if a receiver allows them to enter.*"[5]

Why does the Holy Ghost only carry something *unto* the heart? Perhaps an analogy will help. If the heart is the symbol of the inward person, the "real spiritual me," and if God will never force Himself upon us, then we could say that God has, by divine decree, *made us the guardians of our own hearts.* Or, to put it slightly differently, *each of us is the gatekeeper of our own heart.*

In life each of us erects a fence around our hearts. We do this naturally as we move through childhood into adulthood. As we grow in understanding, we learn that inside of us is a center of being that is sensitive to the world around us. This center learns that we can experience physical pleasure and pain, as well as mental and emotional pleasure and pain. We learn that people can say or do things that make us feel better about ourselves, or they can say or do things that are hurtful and humiliating. As we grow and mature, we become less likely to be open and accepting of outside influences than we were as small children. When we meet new people or face new situations, we cautiously hold back, waiting to see if this new person or circumstance is going to threaten our well-being.

Every day we do or hear things which remind us that to some degree we are all awkward, inadequate, bumbling, imperfect, inferior, and vulnerable beings. This realization is humbling at best and painful at worst. But we are influenced by more than just negative experiences. Some things that lie deep within us—dreams, aspirations, inadequacies—are so intensely personal that we guard them carefully, hiding them behind invisible barriers until we are sure that we can fully trust that if we do reveal them, doing so will not bring us pain or betray our trust.

This is what we mean when we say that each of us has a fence around our heart. However, the nature of that barrier varies considerably from person to person. In each of us is a gate that allows entry into that private place, but only we can open it. We are the ones who control whether that gate swings open to let people in or stays shut to keep them out. This right to control access to our hearts, or our inner selves, is one of the most fundamental and sacred aspects of agency.

We all have our moral agency, but if we use it unwisely, we must pay the price. President J. Reuben Clark Jr. said, "We may use our agency as to whether we shall obey or disobey; and if we disobey we must abide the penalty."

JAMES E. FAUST,
FINDING LIGHT IN A DARK WORLD, 55

To push the metaphor further, in some cases the fence erected around the heart is a low picket fence with daisies growing along it. On the gate is a welcome sign, and the gate swings open easily. Other hearts are surrounded by an eight-foot-high, chain-link fence with a padlocked gate. Instead of daisies, the fence is topped with razor wire and patrolled by guard dogs. Sometimes such formidable defenses develop because of years of hurt and betrayal. In other cases, the high fence is the result of sin and transgression.

In light of this metaphor, consider some scriptural passages worth studying to better understand how hearts may be closed: Job 41:24; 1 Timothy 4:2; 1 Nephi 7:8; 17:45; Alma 9:5; and Moroni 9:20.

Each verse describes hearts that are hidden behind high defenses and that do not respond to the Spirit. Thus the Spirit's witness and influence is carried *unto the heart.* It can only continue *into* the heart if the person chooses to open the gate and let it enter. Therein is the first key to understanding how we learn by faith. Let us put it in a simple chain of reasoning:

- Revelation is the process whereby we learn spiritual truth and gain spiritual light.
- God has chosen to use the Holy Ghost as the primary means of communicating that light and truth to others.
- The Holy Ghost communicates light and truth to us by speaking to our minds and hearts (see D&C 8:2–3).

- God will not force Himself upon us, thus taking away our moral agency.
- Therefore, the Holy Ghost can carry something *unto* our heart, but unless we open our heart to the Spirit, we will not receive or recognize personal revelation.

Expanding on this thought, Elder Bednar said:

A learner exercising agency by acting in accordance with correct principles opens his or her heart to the Holy Ghost and invites His teaching, testifying power, and confirming witness. *Learning by faith requires spiritual, mental, and physical exertion and not just passive reception.* It is in the sincerity and consistency of our faith-inspired action that we indicate to our Heavenly Father and His Son, Jesus Christ, our willingness to learn and receive instruction from the Holy Ghost. Thus, *learning by faith involves the exercise of moral agency.*[6]

> *We are all in pursuit of truth and knowledge. The nurturing of a simple untroubled faith does not limit us in the pursuit of growth and accomplishment. On the contrary, it may intensify and hasten our progress. This is so because our natural gifts and powers of achievement are increasingly enhanced by the endless growth of knowledge.*
>
> JAMES E. FAUST,
> *IN THE STRENGTH
> OF THE LORD*, 303–4

THE TRIAL OF FAITH

To better understand this concept, we need to look briefly at the doctrine of faith. We need to understand how faith works in order to see how we learn by faith and to recognize the role faith plays in revelation.

Speaking of the Jaredites, Moroni said they would not believe the things the prophet Ether prophesied unto them because "they saw them not" (Ether 12:5). Moroni then paused in his historical narrative to teach us a great principle of faith: "I would show unto the world that faith is things which are *hoped* for and *not seen;* wherefore, dispute not because ye *see not,* for *ye receive no witness until after the trial of your faith*" (Ether 12:6).

When Moroni uses the words "saw" and "see," he clearly means more than just perceiving something with the eyes. When Ether prophesied to the Jaredites about a coming Messiah and told them that if they didn't repent, they would be destroyed, they refused to believe him because he couldn't *show* them these things. In other words, he couldn't *prove* his words to them. He couldn't present evidence of his prophecy's truthfulness that they could see and experience and know for themselves. (Note such examples as Sherem [Jacob 7:7, 13] and Korihor [Alma 30:13, 15, 43].)

Such people refuse to accept any form of spiritual witness. They want evidence that is tangible. Without *seeing* those things for themselves, they refuse to believe. Other words implied in the concept of *seeing* might include *proof, testimony, assurance, experience, confirmation, witness,* and so on. Keying off the Jaredite reaction to Ether, Moroni then teaches us that faith is to hope for things *not seen, that is,* for which we have no proof, evidence, witness, experience, knowledge, and so forth.

But is Moroni suggesting that there is no proof, no confirmation, no witness? Not at all. He says only that the witness—*seeing*—comes *after* the trial of our faith. And this is the crux of the matter. This is the key to understanding faith and how it works. It is also the key to understanding how we learn by faith.

In its simplest form, faith consists of four steps. We will use an example of missionaries and an investigator to illustrate how this process works:

> *The trouble with us today, there are too many of us who put question marks instead of periods after what the Lord says. I want you to think about that. We shouldn't be concerned about why he said something, or whether or not it can be made so. Just trust the Lord. We don't try to find the answers or explanations. We shouldn't try to spend time explaining what the Lord didn't see fit to explain. We spend useless time.*
>
> *If you would teach our people to put periods and not question marks after what the Lord has declared, we would say, "It is enough for me to know that is what the Lord said."*
>
> HAROLD B. LEE,
> *ENSIGN,* JANUARY 1973, 108

PROCESS

1. *Hearing the word.* To hear some portion of the word of God is always the first step in developing faith. Paul said that faith comes by hearing the word (Romans 10:17). Alma compared the word to a seed and said we must plant a portion of the word in our hearts and then nourish it carefully so it will grow (Alma 32:27–42). The Bible Dictionary says that faith is kindled by hearing the testimony of someone who has faith.[7]

Joseph Smith taught, "Faith comes by hearing the word of God, through the testimony of the servants of God; that testimony is always attended by the Spirit of prophecy and revelation."[8] He also taught, "Faith comes not by signs, but by hearing the word of God."[9]

2. *Hope or desire.* Remember that faith is to *hope* for things that are not seen. Once we have heard some portion of the word, the next step is that, unless our hearts are hardened, we hope that it is true. To put it another way, we *desire* it to be true and want it to be part of our lives. The good news is that this does not take a huge amount of desire. Even a tiny spark of desire is sufficient to ignite the process of faith. As Alma says, it takes only a "particle of faith, yea, even if ye can no more than desire to believe" (Alma 32:27).

EXAMPLE

1. *Hearing the word.* Let's say that two missionaries are teaching a young couple with small children. After teaching them about eternal families, one of the missionaries says, "Mr. Jones, as I watch you here today and see the love you have for your wife and children, I want to tell you something very important. We bring a message that will show you how you and your family can be together forever. I testify to you with all the power of my heart that this is true. We can teach you how it is possible that not even death can separate you."

What is the missionary doing? He is sharing a portion of the word and then testifying that it is true. Why is this important? Because faith is kindled by hearing the testimony of someone who has faith.

2. *Hope or desire.* In his mind, the young father thinks, "Could this really be true? Is there really a way I could be with my wife and children forever? I *hope* it is true. And if it is true, *I want* [or *desire*] that for my family."

271

PROCESS	EXAMPLE

3. Action. Now comes the trial of faith. It is tempting at this point to demand some kind of proof or evidence that what we have heard is true. But the very definition of faith is to hope for, or desire, something *that is not seen,* that is not proven. To get that proof or evidence (Moroni's word is "witness") so that we can come to *know* for ourselves that the word we have heard is true, we must open our hearts to the Spirit so that He can come in and testify to us. And how do we open our hearts? *We must act based on the hope that what we have heard is true.* We must *do* something because faith is a principle of action. This is the trial, or test, of our faith.

Satan tempts us to demand that it be the other way around. This is the Sherem/Korihor method: "Show me! Give me proof. Then I will believe and do something." But by its definition, faith is to act *based on hope,* not on evidence.

3. Action. The father looks at the missionary and says. "What you say intrigues me. If you can show me that what you say is true, then I will listen to your message. If you can prove it to me, then I and my family will join your church." He is not saying it exactly as Korihor and other sign seekers say it, but what the father is asking for is to see before he believes. But *faith is believing so that you can then see.*

If the missionaries are wise, they will say something like this: "We cannot prove that to you—not in the sense that you mean it. But we can tell you how you can come to know for yourself, for you can receive your own witness from God that what we have taught you is true." If this father is open to the Spirit—if he is willing to open the gateway to his heart—he will ask, "What do we have to do?"

And what will the missionaries ask him to do? They will ask him and his wife to make a commitment, to *act,* to do something: Read the Book of Mormon. Pray about it. Ask God if Joseph Smith was His chosen prophet. Come to Church. Repent. Stop smoking. Pay tithing. Be baptized.

If the parents are willing to start acting on their hope and desire, they will move to the next level of learning by faith. However, if Mr. Jones insists on some kind of evidence before he will do anything, then his heart is closed and the Spirit will not give him the witness he desires.

PROCESS	EXAMPLE
4. *Confirmation or witness.* Moroni said the witness comes *after* the trial of faith, which, as stated above, is to act based on the hope within us rather than on proof or evidence.	4. *Confirmation or witness.* If Mr. Jones and his family commit themselves to accept the testimony of the elders and begin seeking to know for themselves, then they have opened their hearts and the Spirit can come *into* their hearts and bear witness.
Tithing is a classic example of how this works. Many would be willing to pay their tithing if the Lord would bless them first. But the trial, or test, of faith is to pay tithing with the hope that the principle is true and that the blessings will come. There is no way to *show* God's children that this principle works by giving them the blessings first. This is why tithing is more a principle of faith than of finance.	It may be that the full confirmation of the truthfulness of the doctrine of eternal families will come only after other testimonies— that the Book of Mormon is true, that God answers prayers, that Joseph Smith was a prophet, and so forth—but eventually those who seek truth will come to know for themselves that it is a true doctrine.
	And how have they learned this? *They have learned it by faith.* They heard the word, hoped that it was true, desired it for themselves, and then acted based on that hope so that they eventually received their own witness from the Spirit.

IN SUMMARY

In brief form, this is a summary of how faith works. It is simple and yet profound and merits careful pondering to see its full implications for us. As Elder Bednar said, "Only as an investigator's [or missionary's, or member's] faith *initiates action and opens the pathway to the heart* can the Holy Ghost deliver a confirming witness."[10]

Elder Boyd K. Packer tied faith and the flow of revelation together in this way:

The flow of revelation depends on your faith. You exercise faith by causing, or by making, your mind accept or believe as truth that which *you* cannot, by reason alone, prove for certainty.

The first exercising of your faith should be your acceptance of Christ and His atonement.

As you test gospel principles by *believing without knowing,* the Spirit will begin to teach you. Gradually your faith will be replaced with knowledge.

You will be able to discern, or to see, with spiritual eyes. Be believing and your faith will be constantly replenished, your knowledge of the truth increased. . . . You may then receive guidance on practical decisions in everyday life.[11]

Note that these quotes are also good answers to our question, "How can I learn to receive more revelation and recognize it when it comes?" As we learn to exercise faith in this manner, we receive more and more light and knowledge from God. The quote by Elder Bednar also answers the question, "How do we learn by faith?"

Examples of this process of learning by faith (and gaining greater revelation by faith) are found virtually everywhere throughout the scriptures. Learning by faith is similar to what we mean by "exercising our faith."

CHAPTER 24

WHAT ARE THE KEY STEPS IN LEARNING BY FAITH AND INCREASING OUR ABILITY TO RECEIVE REVELATION?

"Search diligently, pray always, and be believing, and all things shall work together for your good" (D&C 90:24).

KEY ATTITUDES AND ACTIONS IN THE PROCESS OF LEARNING BY FAITH

In the previous chapter, we outlined the process by which we develop and gain faith, and we used the example of a new investigator to show how that process works in our own lives. We also noted that this process answers the oft-asked question: "How do I exercise faith?"

We then discussed how this relates to the commandment that we "seek learning . . . by faith" (D&C 88:118) and how learning by faith is directly related to increasing personal revelation. In this chapter, we will focus on the key attitudes and actions we must take if we are to learn by faith. There are many scriptural examples of people learning by faith. We will examine two of those because they provide interesting scriptural models of learning by faith and because they allow us to identify the key actions in each.

MODEL NO. 1: NEPHI (1 NEPHI 1–15)

This example occurred in Lehi's family as they were commanded to leave Jerusalem and make their way to the promised land. While others in the family became involved in an ensuing conflict, we will look only at the contrast in behavior between Nephi and his two oldest brothers, Laman and Lemuel. Lehi's various revelations disrupted what was clearly a comfortable existence for the family to that point.* Since this story is well known by most, we will only highlight the key words and phrases in Nephi's response.

"Having *great desires* to know of the mysteries of God" (2:16).
"I did cry unto the Lord" (2:16).
"He did visit me, and did *soften my heart*" (2:16).**
"I *did believe* all the words which had been spoken by my father" (2:16).
"I will *go and do*" (3:7).

After the brothers finally returned from Jerusalem with the plates of brass, Lehi had his dream, or vision, of the tree of life (another marvelous revelation) and shared it with his family. Clearly the dream wasn't very flattering to Laman and Lemuel because in the dream they did not partake of the fruit of the tree (8:35). Again we learn much from Nephi's response:

"After I had *desired to know*" (11:1).
"*Believing* that the Lord was able to make them known unto me" (11:1).
"I sat *pondering* in mine heart" (11:1).
"I *desire* to behold the things which my father saw" (11:3).
"And the Spirit said unto me: *Believest* thou? And I said: Yea, thou knowest that I *believe*" (11:4–5).

---

* We know that Lehi had much "gold and silver, and all manner of riches" (3:16). Therefore, it is likely that his family lived in a nice, comfortable home. It is interesting that Nephi tells us three different times in his narrative that his father "dwelt in a tent" (2:15; 9:1; 10:16). He is clearly impressed with his father's sacrifice and obedience. Laman and Lemuel weren't the only ones who gave up a lot.

** Note that Nephi says that the Lord softened his heart. Does that imply that he too had some difficulty accepting this at first? Did he have some initial doubts or perhaps resentment?

"Blessed art thou, Nephi, because thou believest . . . wherefore, thou shalt behold the things which thou hast desired" (11:6).

In sharp contrast to Nephi, Laman and Lemuel received their father's revelations with resentment, murmuring constantly and expressing anger, rebellion, and rejection. The best insight we get about the contrast between these brothers comes from Nephi when, fresh from his remarkable vision, he found Laman and Lemuel disputing and asked them about their disagreement. Here are key phrases from their interchange:

Laman and Lemuel: "We *cannot understand* the *words* which our father hath spoken" (15:7).

Nephi: "*Have ye inquired* of the Lord?" (15:8).

Laman and Lemuel: "*We have not;* for the Lord maketh no such thing known unto us" (15:9).

Nephi: "How is it that ye do not *keep* the commandments of the Lord?" (15:10).

Nephi: "Because of the *hardness of your hearts*" (15:10).

Nephi: "If ye will not harden your hearts, and *ask [the Lord] in faith, believing* that ye shall receive, with *diligence in keeping [His] commandments,* surely these things shall be made known unto you" (15:11).

Nephi's willingness to open his heart and Laman and Lemuel's decision to keep theirs closed and tightly guarded profoundly influenced the entire history of Lehi's people. Nephi *learned by faith* and went on to have many great revelations and to lead his people in righteousness. By contrast, Laman and Lemuel just kept extending the fences around their hearts higher and higher until they not only lost the Spirit themselves but also took generations of their posterity with them into spiritual darkness.

THE KEY ELEMENTS OF GAINING REVELATION THROUGH FAITH

As illustrated by Nephi, gaining revelation through faith involves several important elements. We will only note them here and then discuss them in more detail later. They can be summarized with five key attitudes and actions:

1. First we must **DESIRE**. This means that above our personal wishes and needs, we must want to be in harmony with the Lord's will and be taught of Him.

2. Then we must **SEEK** by inquiring and asking of the Lord. But seeking is not enough.

3. We must, at the same time, **BELIEVE** that the Lord lives, that He can hear us, and that He will respond. Believing is a condition of the heart.

4. Along with our searching in a believing way, we must **DO** something. We must *act*. Faith is a principle of action. We must act based on faith and hope in order to receive confirmation.

5. When we have done this, the Lord promises that we will **RECEIVE**—light, truth, knowledge, help, answers to prayers, blessings, and so forth.

Perhaps it would help if we diagrammed this process as a flowchart showing how these steps interact with each other. It would look something like this:

$$\text{DESIRE} \longrightarrow \begin{array}{c}\text{SEEK \&}\\\text{BELIEVE}\end{array} \longrightarrow \text{DO} \longrightarrow \text{RECEIVE}$$

MODEL NO. 2: OLIVER COWDERY (D&C 6, 8–9)

One of the principles that govern the giving and receiving of revelation is that we must actively seek for revelation and participate in the revelatory process. In chapter 14 we examined what Oliver Cowdery was taught about how to receive revelation. Like Nephi, he provides another classic model of how we learn by faith and increase personal revelation. Because we have already looked at that model, here we will only note specific things the Lord said that directly relate to our five-step model. I would encourage you to take a few minutes now and carefully study the references for each key attitude or action and see how they relate to learning by faith. (All references are from the Doctrine and Covenants.)

- Desire (6:8, 20, 27)
- Seek (6:11, 14; 8:1, 10)
- Believe (6:13, 19–20, 36; 8:1, 8, 10–11; 9:8, 11)
- Do (6:9, 13–14, 18–20; 9:3, 6–8)
- Receive (6:14–17, 23; 8:1–3; 9:8–9, 14)

This is an amazing confirmation of the process of gaining revelation, or learning by faith. In Doctrine and Covenants 6, 8, and 9, there are only 63 verses. And yet in those verses we have:

- 13 uses of the words *ask* or *inquire*
- 8 uses of the word *desire*
- 6 uses of the word *witness*
- 13 uses of the word *do,* as well as several charges to do various things
- 9 uses of the word *receive*
- 7 uses of the words *faith* or *believe*

In the midst of this very intense tutorial on how to learn by faith, the Lord also gave Oliver (and all of us) some cautions:

"Behold thou hast a gift. . . . Remember *it is sacred and cometh from above. . . . Trifle not with sacred things*" (6:10, 12).
"*Trifle not* with these things" (8:10).
"Do not ask for that which *you ought not*" (8:10).
"You *took no thought save it was to ask* me" (9:7).

That should be enough to convince anyone that the Lord very much wants us to understand how this process of learning by faith and gaining revelation works for us.

There are many other examples of individuals who learned how to make this process work. In fact, once sensitized to the process of learning by faith, we start to see it virtually everywhere we look.

IN SUMMARY

In the talk referred to in the previous chapter, Elder David A. Bednar said:

> The responsibility to seek learning by faith rests upon each of us individually, and this obligation will become increasingly important as the world in which we live grows more confused and troubled. Learning by faith is essential to our personal spiritual development and for the growth of the Church in these latter days. May each of us truly hunger and thirst after righteousness and be filled with the Holy Ghost (see 3 Nephi 12:6)—that we might seek learning by faith.[1]

CHAPTER 25

How Do I Implement the Key Steps in My Life?

"Even as you desire of me so shall it be done unto you" (D&C 11:8).

In chapter 24, we identified five critical actions that constitute the process of learning by faith—meaning gaining greater light and truth through revelation. We will now take each of those actions and, using examples and illustrations, show their possible application in everyday life.

STEP 1: DESIRE

I Don't Want to Know. Some years ago when I was a stake president in a Brigham Young University singles stake, a young woman who was nearing her twenty-second birthday came in for some counseling. She said she felt that her life was at a standstill, that she was not accomplishing anything of real worth. She was in college but found it unsatisfying. She had been dating a boy seriously, but that relationship had ended.

After listening to her, I suggested that perhaps she ought to consider a mission. I explained that young women are not under the same obligation to serve full-time missions as priesthood holders, but in many cases the Lord lets young women know this is something He would like them to do. She admitted that a mission had been on her mind.

Having given them . . . agency, . . . Heavenly Father persuades and directs his children, but waits for their up reaching, their prayers, their sincere approach to him. . . . The Lord is eager to see their first awakening desires and their beginning efforts to penetrate the darkness. Having granted freedom of decision, he must permit man to grope his way until he reaches for the light. But when man begins to hunger, when his arms begin to reach, when his knees begin to bend and his voice becomes articulate, then and not till then does our Lord push back the horizons, draw back the veil, and make it possible for men to emerge from dim uncertain stumbling to sureness, in heavenly light.

SPENCER W. KIMBALL,
MUNICH GERMANY AREA
CONFERENCE, 1973, 74–75

"So," I suggested, "why don't you ask the Lord?" She dropped her head. "Because I don't want to go on a mission." I again reiterated that if those were her feelings, she wasn't obligated to go. "But," I continued, "perhaps this feeling of dissatisfaction with your life is the Lord's way of telling you that a mission is right for you at this point. So why don't you just ask the Lord? He may say no. Then you can move ahead with your life. But if He says this will be the best thing for you, wouldn't you want to know that?"

She wouldn't look at me, but she slowly shook her head. "I don't want to ask because I don't want to know," she said. "I guess I don't care if it is the best thing for me or not. I really don't want to go on a mission."

That was her choice, of course. The Lord wasn't going to try to force her. A year or so later, she started dating a returned missionary and they soon married in the temple. So it wasn't as if this decision of hers ended her activity in the Church.

But I can't help but wonder if she has ever asked herself questions such as, "What would have happened *had I* asked and *had He said yes* and *had I gone?* How would my life be different now? Would I have married someone else—or the same man, but after better preparation? Would I be a better mother? A better person? Would I have more spiritual blessings in my life?"

I have often pondered her words: "I don't want to know." I have also wondered how many times in my life I have closed off an opportunity for revelation because I didn't trust the Lord enough to ask.

A thought-provoking passage on desire is found in the book of Alma. After some success in his ministry, and some serious setbacks (such as the people of Ammonihah), Alma paused to reflect on his service to God. From his heart burst a great desire to do more: "O that I were an angel," he cried, "and could have the wish of mine heart, that I might go forth and speak with the trump of God, . . . and cry repentance unto every people" (Alma 29:1). One can hardly imagine a more noble and righteous desire than that. But almost immediately, Alma caught himself and said, "But behold, I am a man, and do sin in my wish; *for I ought to be content with the things which the Lord hath allotted unto me*" (Alma 29:3). Then follows this:

I know that [God] granteth unto men *according to their desire,* whether it be unto death or unto life; yea, I know that he allotteth unto men, yea, decreeth unto them decrees which are unalterable, *according to their wills,* whether they be unto salvation or unto destruction.

Yea, and I know that good and evil have come before all men; he that knoweth not good from evil is blameless; but he that knoweth good and evil, *to him it is given according to his desires,* whether he desireth good or evil, life or death, joy or remorse of conscience. (Alma 29:4–5)

> *The blessing of revelation is one that all should seek for. Righteous men and women find that they have the spirit of revelation to direct their families and to aid them in their other responsibilities. But . . . we must seek to qualify for such revelation by setting our lives in order.*
>
> Spencer W. Kimball,
> *Teachings of Spencer W. Kimball,* 126

That should give us all cause for reflection. If God so honors the principle of agency and free will that He allows the fulfillment of our desires, even if they run counter to the plan of happiness, then we must carefully examine our desires. What if what we hope and long and work for is not for our long-range good? What if we are so "in love" with a person that we are not willing to consider if he or she will have a long-term destructive effect on our lives? What if we desire a comfortable and safe calling in the Church that doesn't take us out of our comfort zone?

If we are not careful, even those striving to be faithful disciples of the Father and Son may close our hearts to any guidance or counsel from the Lord and thus lose out on great opportunities. The Lord will not force anything upon us, even if it is the absolutely best thing for us.

Elder Erastus Snow, an early member of the Quorum of the Twelve, stated it this way:

> If our spirits are inclined to be stiff and refractory and we desire continually the gratification of our own will . . . , the Spirit of the Lord is held at a distance from us. . . . The Father withholds his Spirit from us in proportion as we desire the gratification of our own will. We interpose a barrier between us and our Father, that he cannot, consistently with himself, move upon us so as to control our actions.[1]

A deep and abiding desire to surrender our will to God's will, to put our lives in harmony with the Father and the Son, is the open latch on the gateway to our hearts, as it were. Until we truly desire to let the Father and the Son take a hand in our lives, our hearts may remain closed to some things, and we will miss out on the marvelous blessings They have to give.

STEP 2: SEEK

Earnestly seeking to know the Lord and stay in harmony with His will is the second key step in the process of learning by faith. Seeking was discussed earlier as one of the foundational principles that govern the giving and receiving of revelation. It was fully developed in chapter 14, and we will make only a few additional observations. These relate specifically to the role of inquiry, or asking questions, in the process of receiving and recognizing revelation.

Note how questions have led to revelation. (In these examples, you will see that sometimes the Savior asks questions to help lead others to truth. In some cases angels ask questions of a mortal. Other times mortals ask questions of each other or of the Lord.)

- Why are you offering sacrifices? (angel to Adam and Eve)
- Whom do men say that I, the Son of Man, am? (Jesus to the Twelve)
- Art thou a king then? (Pilate to Jesus)
- Lovest thou me? (Jesus to Simon Peter)
- Which of all the churches was right? (Joseph Smith in the Sacred Grove)
- If baptism is required by the Lord, where will we get the authority to do so? (Joseph Smith and Oliver Cowdery on the banks of the Susquehanna River, May 15, 1829)
- If we are going to be judged according to our works, doesn't the next life have to consist of more than just heaven or hell? (Joseph and Sidney Rigdon after reading John 5:29, resulting in Doctrine and Covenants 76)
- If many are called to the priesthood, why are they not chosen to call down the powers of heaven? (The Lord to Joseph Smith in Liberty Jail)
- Has the time finally come for the promises of the prophets to be fulfilled that all who are worthy may receive the priesthood? (Spencer W. Kimball in the Salt Lake Temple, 1978)

If questions play such a primary role in bringing revelation, we ought to give careful thought to the questions we ask of ourselves and of the Lord. As one of my colleagues in the Seventy is fond of saying,

"It really doesn't matter what the answer is if you don't ask the right question."

Fortunately, we are invited to seek the help of the Spirit even in knowing what questions to ask. The Apostle Paul taught: "The Spirit also helpeth our infirmities: for we know not what we should pray for as we ought: *but the Spirit itself maketh intercession for us* with groanings which cannot be uttered" (Romans 8:26). Remember the mother whose unborn child had been diagnosed with severe problems? When the Spirit directed her to "pray for a miracle," a dramatic outcome resulted.

Here are a couple of simple lessons I have learned about asking the right questions.

Are they too general? Most of us ask questions of the Lord, but in many cases they may be too general. For example:

- Instead of, "What should I do to be a better person?" we ask, "What things in my life right now are most grievous to the influence of the Spirit?" Or, even more specific, "What should I do differently or better as a father (or mother)?"
- In addition to "Bless the missionaries and help lead them to the honest in heart," we ask, "Wouldst Thou please put someone in my path that I can talk to about the gospel of Jesus Christ, and wouldst Thou give me the courage to do so?"
- Instead of "Bless me as a bishop," we ask, "Of all the duties and responsibilities I have as a bishop, husband, and father, what should be my highest priority in terms of my efforts right now?"

Is there a better question? I remember once praying as a bishop about a man we were considering for a significant position in the ward. My question was, "Will this man do a good job in this calling?" I had a good feeling about it, and so we proceeded to extend the call. However, he informed us of a special family challenge that precluded him from serving at that time. Later, as I wondered why things hadn't worked in accord with my feelings, the thought came to me, "The answer to the question you asked was yes. He would do a good job. A better question

286

would have been, 'Is this the man we should call to this position *at this time?*' "

Here are some questions that I have learned from those who seem closest to the Spirit and that I have found to be especially helpful in inviting the Spirit:

- As I think about my experience today in this meeting, what things has the Spirit taught me that *weren't* said?*
- Before I kneel and ask Heavenly Father for help, what is it I *really* want from Him?
- What gift of the Spirit would help me deal with the specific weakness I am trying to overcome?
- In what areas of my life am I still striving to have it "my way?"
- What do I think about when I don't have to think about anything? What does that say about my heart?
- What do I fear most in life? How can the Lord help me face and overcome that fear?
- What things give me the greatest joy in life? How do they compare with those things that give the Father and the Son their greatest joy?
- What aspect of my character do I feel makes me most like Christ? Least like Christ?

STEP 3: BELIEVE

In both models discussed in Chapter 24 (Nephi and Oliver Cowdery), *believing* was of pivotal importance. There are many ways we could illustrate how that process works in our lives, but to get at the heart of it, I am going to hold an imaginary conversation with a young woman I met as a missionary. As a second example, we'll look at senior missionary couples.

---

* When we have this question in our minds as we participate in general conference, sit in sacrament meeting, or receive priesthood training, the Spirit often teaches us things beyond what is said.

The Atheist and the Experiment

While I was serving as a missionary in a university town, a student who was a member of the Church set up a teaching appointment with her roommate, Elizabeth. She was a lovely young woman—bright, articulate, and outspoken. She listened politely until I began to tell her the Joseph Smith story. Suddenly she stopped me. "Wait a minute," she said. "Have you ever seen God?" I assured her that I had not. "Have you ever heard Him or touched Him?" Again I said no. "I don't believe there is a God," she said flatly, "and unless you can prove to me that He exists, there's not much point in our continuing this discussion."

I tried to tell her that there was a way she could come to know for herself, but she would have none of it. "No, I know all that stuff about prayer and so on, but unless you can prove to me that there is a God—let me see or hear or touch Him—then I cannot believe."

That ended our discussion, and we never saw her again. Knowing much more now than I did then, I would like to replay that conversation with what I could have said. I will use Alma's analogy of planting a seed, with all references coming from Alma 32.

Missionary: Elizabeth, I can see that you rely on knowledge that you can verify for yourself.

Elizabeth: Yes, that's right.

Missionary: Carol (her roommate) tells me that you are majoring in the physical sciences.

Elizabeth: Yes, physics and chemistry.

Missionary: So you are used to verifying things through experimentation?

Elizabeth: Yes, I am.

Missionary: Then I would like to suggest another kind of experiment. A man who lived many years ago suggested this experiment. He calls it an "experiment on the word," meaning the truths of the gospel of Jesus Christ. I'll just call it an experiment on spiritual experiences.

Elizabeth (now suspicious): It's not the same thing.

Missionary: I understand, but while it's a different kind of experiment, it is a way to verify for yourself that something is true. Are you willing to at least try the experiment? If it doesn't work, then you haven't lost anything.

(Alma says we must "give place, that a seed may be planted in [our] heart," and that we cannot "cast it out by [our] unbelief, that [we] will resist the Spirit of the Lord" (Alma 32:28). If Elizabeth says that she is not willing to conduct such an experiment, there is nothing more we can do. She has closed off her heart, and the Spirit can go no further.)

Elizabeth: How can I do this experiment when I don't even believe in God?

Missionary: Would you like to know for sure whether there is a God?

Elizabeth: Of course, but . . .

Missionary: Then that is enough. That desire is enough to get you started on this experiment.

Elizabeth: All right. So what do I have to do?

Missionary: Let's read Alma 32:27–28 together. "*Even if ye can no more than desire to believe,* let this desire work in you, even until ye *believe* in a manner that ye can give place for a portion of my words. Now, we will compare the word to a seed. . . .*" (Alma 32:27–28).

Alma suggests that we have to *do* something. It isn't enough just to want to know if there really is a God. Note the action verbs he uses here: Awake! Arouse your faculties! Desire! Give place! Don't cast it out! Experiment! You have to do something, Elizabeth. You have to make a choice to conduct the experiment with a real desire to find out.

Elizabeth: But . . .

> "Is it my duty to pray when I have not one particle of the spirit of prayer in me?" . . . Our judgment teaches us that it is our duty to pray, whether we are particularly in the spirit of praying or not. My doctrine is, it is your duty to pray; and when the time for prayer comes, John should say, "This is the place and this is the time to pray; knees bend down upon the floor, and do so at once." But John said, "I do not want to pray; I do not feel like it." Knees get down, I say; and down bend the knees.
>
> Brigham Young,
> *Discourses of Brigham Young,* 45

289

Missionary: Don't misunderstand me. At this point, we're not asking that you accept God and become a believer. We're not asking you to be baptized or give your whole life over to God. All you have to do is an experiment with the word.

Elizabeth: Which means what?

Missionary: We would like to read something together. Then we'll talk about it until you clearly understand what we are teaching you. Then we'll ask you to pray about it, to ask—

Elizabeth: Hold it right there. I don't believe in prayer.

Missionary: You don't have to believe in prayer to conduct this experiment—only be willing to try prayer as part of the test.

Elizabeth: This isn't going to work. I don't pray.

Missionary: Let's suppose my chemistry teacher asked me to prove to myself that water boils at 212 degrees Fahrenheit at sea level.

Elizabeth (laughing): Actually, we had to do that in my beginning chemistry class.

Missionary: Good. Tell me what I have to do.

Elizabeth: Well, you'll need a source of heat, a pan of water, and a thermometer.

Missionary: I don't believe in thermometers. What else can I do?

Elizabeth: Don't be ridiculous. You can't do this without a thermometer.

Missionary: Well, Elizabeth, in this case, prayer is like the thermometer. This is the most challenging part of the experiment. You cannot find out for yourself unless you are willing to at least try prayer. (He then takes a few minutes to explain how we are guardians of our own hearts and how the Spirit will never force its way in.) Are you willing to crack that gate open just a hair? Are you willing to put those guard dogs of skepticism on a leash long enough to hear us out on this? If not, then the experiment can go no further, for we cannot—and will not—force our beliefs on you. And more important, neither will your Heavenly Father. But I testify to you that if you will open your heart just wide enough to ask, that you can know for yourself. You can know that there is a God as surely as you know that water boils at 212 degrees. You don't have to take our word for it or Alma's or Carol's. You can know for yourself.

We need not carry on the conversation further, but this illustrates why a *belief* (which may at first be no more than a willingness to experiment) is one of the absolute requirements for receiving revelation. It is at the very heart of learning by faith.

Senior Missionary Couples

Now let's look at how belief might work in the lives of those of us who are already believers. If you are an older reader, I warn you in advance that this may make you squirm a little, but that's all right. There's an old saying that goes like this: The role of a good teacher is to comfort the troubled and *trouble the comfortable*.

Currently in the Church, only about one in ten couples who are in good health, and who could actually serve, go on missions. Why? They are so desperately needed. There is not a mission president in the world who is not pleading for more couples. They do such wonderful work, often accomplishing things that young missionaries cannot do. So why aren't more stepping forward?

There are two answers. The first has to do with desire. The second has to do with belief.

If health and other limiting circumstances are not a factor, a major reason couples do not serve has to do with family. Some may have children who are struggling, and they think they need to stay close by to care for them. Sometimes aged parents need care, and they feel that they are the only ones who can provide that care, even when other siblings are around to help. More commonly, the thought of leaving grandchildren for a year or two is simply too painful to consider.

This is a *desire* problem, just as with the young woman who didn't want to ask the Lord about her mission. We don't want to leave. We don't want to give up what we now enjoy. But as Elder Snow said above, when we put the gratification of our own will ahead of the Lord's will for us, we lose blessings.

How does belief play a role in this choice? Well, the second major reason couples do not step forward is anxiety about what a mission will mean in their lives. One or both spouses are afraid of the mission experience. They fear the unknown. It will mean uprooting their lives, going to new places, meeting new people, dealing with new challenges, facing less comfortable and pleasant conditions. This is understandable. Will they be up to it? What about family? What about that child who is struggling? What will he or she do without you?

Here is what is interesting to me. My wife and I have had the privilege of conducting mission tours in many different missions around the world. We have met hundreds of senior couples serving in dozens of different callings. With few exceptions, they testify—frequently with tears in their eyes—that going on a mission has been one of the best decisions of their lives. We have met numerous couples who were serving their third, fourth, or fifth mission. Many of those missions were in difficult and challenging circumstances, but the experience was so uplifting, so beneficial to them, that they "re-upped," as we used to say in the army. Are these couples just more courageous? Do they not have grandchildren or struggling children or aged parents at home?

> *With any major decision there are cautions and considerations to make, but once there has been illumination, bear the temptation to retreat from a good thing. If it was right when you prayed about it and trusted it and lived for it, it is right now. Don't give up when the pressure mounts.*
>
> JEFFREY R. HOLLAND,
> *ENSIGN,* MARCH 2000, 7

I used to think it was just that they had a more adventuresome spirit. But I've come to a different conclusion. These are couples who were willing to *believe* that what the Lord wanted for them was the best thing for them. They were willing to experiment and ask the Lord what He wanted them to do.* Because of that, they are having marvelous,

---

* In some cases, a couple may ask it this is what the Lord wants them to do at this time and the answer will be, "No, not at this time."

life-altering experiences. They will testify of the unique and remarkable blessings that have come to them, their families, and their grandchildren because they planted the seed of willingness in their hearts and asked the Lord, "Is this what Thou wouldst have us do?"

Here are some other examples of places where our faith to believe is being tested:

- Many young single adults are postponing marriage until they complete their education because it will mean too much of a sacrifice to do otherwise.
- Young couples marry but postpone having children until they have completed their schooling or are comfortably established in their careers or have paid for their homes and automobiles.*
- Many active young men turn down mission calls because they interfere with their life, interrupt their education, or scare them. They do not believe that a mission experience is the best thing for them.
- An individual falls in love with someone who the parents (or others who deeply care for the individual) can see is going to bring unhappiness and misery to the relationship. But the individual pushes aside all advice and counsel. The individual *knows* what is best and will not listen.

As we deal with the circumstances that life so often presents, let us remember the powerful counsel from Moroni: "Hearken unto the words of the Lord, and ask the Father in the name of Jesus for what things soever ye shall stand in need. *Doubt not, but be believing,* and begin as in times of old, and come unto the Lord *with all your heart*" (Mormon 9:27).

---

* When to have children and how many children to have is an intensely personal decision between the couple and the Lord. All I am suggesting is that in many cases, the Lord is not brought into this decision. The couple decides what is best for them, not asking whether their decision is in harmony with the Lord's will.

STEP 4: DO

In the *Lectures on Faith,* many of which were given by Joseph Smith in the School of the Prophets in 1834–35, the Prophet taught that there are three things required for a person to have faith:

> Let us here observe, that three things are necessary in order that any rational and intelligent being may exercise faith in God unto life and salvation. First, the idea that he actually exists. Secondly, a *correct* idea of his character, perfections, and attributes. Thirdly, an actual knowledge that the course of life which he is pursuing is according to his will.[2]

The first two seem achievable for most of us, but the third one seems counterintuitive. It seems more logical that we first have faith and then be led to live a good life. The Prophet suggests that it is the other way around—that living as we should actually increases our faith.

When I was newly married, I had an experience that helped me understand what Joseph Smith was trying to teach us. I was still working through my undergraduate studies. My wife had graduated in elementary education and taught one year, but then our first daughter, Cynthia, arrived, and my wife stopped teaching to care for her. I was working full time at the Utah State Mental Hospital as an attendant as well as taking a full load at school. It was a challenging time. I worked afternoon or midnight shifts while I carried a full load of classes. We were eager to finish schooling as quickly as possible.

When I was hired at the mental hospital, I was assigned to what was known as the maximum-security ward. Male patients with any kind of criminal record ended up on our ward. We had the dregs of society, and I found myself growing cynical about human nature and society. Looking back, I like to blame what happened partially on that and also on the long hours each day I put in at work and school. But that is probably because we like to blame our failings on things outside ourselves.

Whatever the cause, I was in a spiritual down cycle. I was not praying regularly or studying my scriptures.

Cynthia was about nine months old at this time. One night when I happened to be home, we put her to bed as usual. About 9:30, as we were retiring for the night, we heard a strange sound coming from her bedroom. We rushed in and found that she had come down with a sudden and severe case of croup. She was fighting for every breath with deep, raspy gasps that frighten any parent, especially those who have never seen this condition before.

I took her out of her crib and was holding her up, trying to ease her breathing, while my wife called the doctor. When she explained what was happening, the doctor told her to have me go immediately into the bathroom and turn on the hot water, filling the air with moisture.

I remember this as vividly as though it happened just a few days ago. As I sat there in that steamy bathroom, looking down at this precious little girl who was struggling mightily for every breath, this thought came to me: "You're an elder in the Church. You hold the Melchizedek Priesthood. Why don't you bless her?"

It was a terrible thought because at that moment my spiritual standing with the Lord came keenly into my mind. I knew where I was right then, and I was ashamed. And so, filled with sadness, I didn't bless her that night. We went to the doctor's office and got a steamer and some medication. Fortunately, everything turned out all right. But that night, I vowed to myself that I would not be caught like that again.

I hadn't hesitated to bless my daughter because I doubted God's ability to heal her. I also knew that God determines when and how or if He will choose to intervene (see Chapter 13) and that I had to accept His will. I had complete faith in His power. What I doubted was *myself*. I knew, though I hadn't expressed it to myself in these exact terms, that my life was not pleasing to God at that point. And that left me weak in the faith and doubting my ability to call down God's help in our behalf even if it was His will to bless my daughter at that time.

It is in *doing* that we increase faith and open the heavens to us. This kind of *doing* surrenders not only our will to God but our lives as well. It is putting things right. It is knowing that generally our lives are pleasing to Him.

STEP 5: RECEIVE

This final key is the culmination of the process rather than one of the steps in achieving it. It is what happens when we fulfill the first four requirements. We will say no more of this final principle here because it has been covered in earlier chapters and will be the subject of following chapters as well.

After setting down the conditions for drawing down the powers of heaven, the Lord makes a promise:

> Let virtue garnish thy thoughts unceasingly; *then shall thy confidence wax strong in the presence of God* [because we know that our lives are pleasing to Him]; and the doctrine of the priesthood [priesthood is power] shall distil upon thy soul as the dews from heaven.
>
> The Holy Ghost shall be thy constant companion (D&C 121:45–46).

That is the end promise of the process. When we desire, seek, believe, and do, we receive faith. Then we receive greater revelation. This is how the Lord works with us. This is why He reminds us: "I, the Lord, am bound when ye do what I say; but when ye do not what I say, ye have no promise" (D&C 82:10).

CHAPTER 26

Why Isn't God Answering Me?

"O God, where art thou?" (D&C 121:1).

A CRY OF ANGUISH

One of the darkest times in the history of the Church was during the last few weeks of 1838 and the first months of 1839. The extermination order issued by Missouri governor Lilburn W. Boggs unleashed the Missouri militia and associated mobs upon the Saints in northern Missouri. The horror of Haun's Mill, the fall of Far West, the arrest and imprisonment of Joseph Smith and many other Church leaders, and the expulsion of more than twelve thousand Latter-day Saints from the state in the midst of winter dominated those dark days. And at the very time when the Saints most needed the Prophet's inspired and calming leadership, he was cast into a filthy, unheated cell beneath a building with the deeply ironic name of Liberty Jail.

On March 20, 1839, after almost four months of imprisonment under the most wretched and ghastly of conditions, the Prophet put on paper the wrenching and anguished cry that he was feeling in his heart:

O God, where art thou? And where is the pavilion that covereth thy hiding place?

How long shall thy hand be stayed, and thine eye, yea thy pure eye, behold from the eternal heavens the wrongs of thy people and of thy servants, and thine ear be penetrated with their cries?

Yea, O Lord, how long shall they suffer these wrongs and unlawful oppressions, before thine heart shall be softened toward them, and thy bowels be moved with compassion toward them? (D&C 121:1–3).

Though our words may not be so eloquent or our cause not nearly so critical, at some point we all feel that same anguish and ask those same questions: "Oh, God, I have prayed and prayed for Thy help. Why is there no answer? Why do the heavens seem like they are sealed against me? What am I doing wrong that Thou art not responding? How long will this go on? Why is this happening to me?"

Eventually, the Lord did answer Joseph's pleading prayer and gave him answers to his questions, but this came only after months of personal suffering and separation and after the Saints had been driven from Missouri.

This becomes especially painful for the faithful—those who deeply believe in a Heavenly Father who knows and loves His children. If the pleas were for something evil, it would not be difficult to understand why there is no response. But what if the cause is just? What if it is a cry to ease the terrible pain of a loved one? What if we seek relief from wrongdoing or oppression? What if our desire is to make a decision that is in harmony with God's will? Why won't He help us in something so simple?

WHY ISN'T GOD ANSWERING?

It is impossible for a finite mind to grasp the infinite wisdom and knowledge of God or to fully fathom His motives and purposes. So it is likely not possible to fully answer the question "Why doesn't God answer our earnest prayers?" However, from revelation the Lord has given us, and from pondering about our own experiences, we can provide at least some possible answers to this question. What follows is only a sampling of answers. No attempt is made to place them in any order of importance. This is simply an exploration of possible answers.

Perhaps the Timing Is Not Right

One possible reason for a delayed answer is that the Lord does have an answer prepared, but certain things must happen before it will come to pass. For example, suppose a person has been pleading with the Lord for help in finding employment. What if there is a position that would be just right for that person, but it is currently filled? The Lord knows that in another month or so this position will open. It is not likely that He will either (1) compel the person who has that position to move sooner than planned or (2) tell you why He is not answering your prayer right now.

> *Even in decisions we think are very important, we sometimes receive no answers to our prayers. This does not mean our prayers have not been heard. It only means we have prayed about a decision that, for one cause or another, we should make without guidance by revelation.*
>
> DALLIN H. OAKS,
> *LORD'S WAY*, 36

Remember that one of the first principles we learned about the giving and receiving of revelation was that God determines all aspects of revelation, including *when* it is given. Part of our learning experience in this life is the development of patience. That is a major component of faith. So let us be careful that we do not assume that no answer is a "no" answer.

Some Things Do Not Matter to the Lord

We discussed this at some length in chapter 17. There are really two applications of this principle. First, we are told that we are not to ask the Lord for things that are trivial. Some people, thinking that they are being spiritual, may seek direction on such minor things as which brand of food to buy or on personal matters that do not affect their spiritual standing with the Lord.

The second application is that in some cases the alternatives we are considering are both equally acceptable to the Lord. His decision not to answer our prayer may be His way of saying, "This one is your choice."

Elder Dallin H. Oaks explains this principle clearly:

> What about those times when we seek revelation and do not receive it? We do not always receive inspiration or revelation when we request it. Sometimes we are delayed in receiving revelation [for example, when the timing is not right], and sometimes we are left to our own judgment and understanding based on study and reason. We cannot force spiritual things. It must be so. Our life's purpose to obtain experience and to develop faith would be frustrated if our Heavenly Father enlightened us immediately on every question or directed us in every act. We must reach conclusions and make decisions and experience the consequences in order to develop self-reliance and faith.[1]

Our Hearts May Not Be Right

This is not as comfortable an answer as some of the others. It certainly is more complicated and thus will take more time to explain.

In answer to the Prophet's cries from Liberty Jail, the Lord taught Joseph how to control the powers of heaven (see D&C 121:34–46). The Lord said many are called, but few are chosen. This may have application in broader contexts (for example, called to eternal life but not chosen for it), but the context here is called to control the powers of heaven but not chosen (or able) to do so (v. 36).

Here is the Lord's answer to the question "And why are they not chosen?" He explains that the answer lies in a specific condition of the heart: (There's that concept of the heart again.) "Their hearts are set so much upon the things of this world, and aspire to the honors of men" (v. 35). When that condition is present, other problems flow from it.

What is interesting is how the Lord shows what other problems develop when our hearts are (1) set upon the things of the world; and (2) aspire to the honors of men. Here is what follows:

- *We seek to cover our sins.* (Why do we seek to hide our sins from others? Because we want them to think well of us. We want people to think we are better than we are. We want the praise and honor of men.)

- *We seek to gratify our pride and vain ambitions.* (How do we gratify our pride? By the accumulation of things such as praise and honor. When we sense that others are looking at us with envy, then our pride is gratified or fulfilled.)

> *We live in an age of materialism, a materialism which has enthroned worldly things and . . . that has cast a shadow even over our spirituality.*
>
> J. REUBEN CLARK,
> *BEHOLD THE LAMB OF GOD,* 217

- *We exercise control, dominion, or compulsion over the souls of others in unrighteousness.* (Why do so many of us seek to control or compel others to do our bidding—even to the point of enslavement in some cases? First, because it gives us a sense of self-importance—another gratification of our pride. Second, doing so can also help us gain the things of the world more quickly than if we rely only on ourselves.)

What is the result of these three behavioral patterns in our lives? The Lord's answer is explicit. "The heavens [with all their power] withdraw themselves; the Spirit of the Lord is grieved; and when it is withdrawn, Amen to the priesthood or the authority of that man. . . . Hence many are called, but few are chosen" (vv. 37, 40).

On the other hand, when we

- Become more focused on the things of God than the things of the world
- Aspire more to God's acceptance and praise than the praise of men

301

Then we seek to

- Repent of our sins, rather than covering them
- Gain God's honors and acceptance by becoming more like Him
- Become kinder, more tolerant, and more filled with love for others

When we do that

- The heavens draw closer
- The Spirit of the Lord is pleased, and this brings an increase in power and authority with God.

When we face a crisis and approach the Lord for help, one reason we may not receive an answer is that we have not yet learned "this one lesson": the root cause lies within our own hearts.

> *Do we turn away the still, small voice? Do we do things that offend the Holy Ghost? Do we allow influences into our homes that drive the Spirit from our homes? The type of entertainment that we permit into our homes will certainly have an impact on the power of the Holy Ghost.*
>
> JOSEPH B. WIRTHLIN,
> *ENSIGN,* MAY 2003, 28

We May Be Asking for Something That Is Not Right for Us

As noted several times throughout this book, the Lord said in the Doctrine and Covenants: "If ye ask anything that is not expedient for you, it shall turn unto your condemnation" (D&C 88:65). The Savior made a similar promise to the Nephites, but note the qualifier He added there as well: "Whatsoever ye shall ask the Father in my name, *which is right,* believing that ye shall receive, behold it shall be given unto you" (3 Nephi 18:20; see also Mosiah 4:21).

Sometimes the answer from the Lord is no because what we're asking for is not right for us.

We May Already Have an Answer but Just Don't Recognize It

One of the three aspects of personal revelation is *recognizing* it when it comes. Some forms of revelation are so subtle, so indirect, and so hard to define that when they come we may not recognize them at all. Sometimes the answer may have already come, but it didn't come in a way that we were expecting, or it came in a way that we didn't recognize it as coming from the Lord.

This may also happen in cases where we have been earnestly seeking for help and the answer comes in small incremental changes (line upon line). They are so small that we don't at first recognize that something is happening. In other cases an event occurs that seems totally unrelated to the issue about which we were praying. We may even give up and assume the Lord's answer is no or that we didn't get an answer. Only some time later—months perhaps, sometimes even years—do we look back and see that the event was a turning point.

The Lord May Be Saying That He Trusts Us to Use Our Best Judgment

In a general conference address, Elder Richard G. Scott spoke of prayer and suggested another possible response to our question regarding unanswered prayers:

> What do you do when you have prepared carefully, have prayed fervently, waited a reasonable time for a response, and still do not feel an answer? You may want to express thanks when that occurs, for it is an evidence of His trust. When you are living worthily and your choice is consistent with the Savior's teachings and you need to act, proceed with trust. . . . When you are living righteously and are acting with trust, God will not let you proceed too far without a warning impression if you have made the wrong decision.[2]

303

To Answer Our Prayers the Lord Would Have to Limit Someone Else's Agency

We have talked much about the sacred nature of free will and moral agency. It is so critical to our happiness and progression that God, even in His infinite power and knowledge, will not force the human heart. This principle often brings sorrow and suffering into the world because many choose to do evil, and that almost always directly affects others.

Sometimes to get an answer to our prayers, what we pray for would require the Lord to force another person to do something against his or her will. He will not do that. He may intervene in ways that soften the heart or change the mind, but He will not force or coerce us in any way. We have to remember that *life isn't just about us.*

Many faithful, righteous parents have undergone the bitter sorrow of seeing a child turn away from the gospel and fall away "into forbidden paths" (1 Nephi 8:28). The parents may offer years of fervent, heart-wrenching prayers. They may remain faithful and true to their covenants. With little or no change in their child, they may wonder if their faith is strong enough.

We must always factor in agency. Considering the heartbreak Lehi and Sariah faced with some of their children, Lehi's counsel takes on special meaning: "Wherefore, men are free according to the flesh. . . . And they are free to choose liberty and eternal life, through the great Mediator of all men, or to choose captivity and death, according to the captivity and power of the devil" (2 Nephi 2:27).

He Has Answered, But We Haven't Accepted It

Another possible answer to our question of why God doesn't seem to be answering our prayers may stem from our unwillingness to accept what the Lord gives us.

I had this experience as a bishop. A returned missionary in the ward had been home about a year. He came to me one day and said that he was struggling to know what to do with his life. He felt that he was going nowhere. He had a construction job and was making good money, but he felt that construction wasn't what he wanted to do as a career. After a couple of counseling sessions, I said: "I feel impressed to say to you that what the Lord wants you to do is sell that new pickup truck you recently bought, break off the relationship with the girl you are currently dating, and go to college."

For a moment, he just looked at me, clearly shocked. Then he shook his head sadly. "I couldn't do that, Bishop," he said. "If I sell my truck, I'll lose a lot of money on it. And I really love this girl. And besides, why should I go to college? I've got a good job. Isn't there something else I can do?"

Some years ago Elder Boyd K. Packer gave a talk in general conference about the need to develop spiritual self-reliance. In that talk, he made an observation that applies here:

> We seem to be developing an epidemic of "counselitis" which drains spiritual strength from the Church much like the common cold drains more strength out of humanity than any other disease. . . .
>
> There are many chronic cases—individuals who endlessly seek counsel but do not follow the counsel that is given.
>
> I have, on occasions, included in an interview this question:
>
> "You have come to me for advice. After we have carefully considered your problem, is it your intention to follow the counsel that I will give you?"
>
> This comes as a considerable surprise to them. They had never thought of that.[3]

In the model on learning by faith and increasing our ability to receive revelation, we noted that one of the key steps was to *do*. Part of doing is *responding* appropriately to what the Lord counsels us to do. If we don't, the flow of further inspiration and revelation will be significantly restricted.

We May Be in the Midst of a Divine Tutorial

In chapter 16 we explored the concept of what Elder Neal A. Maxwell called "divine tutorials." A careful reading of that chapter may provide the answer to our question. We may not get an answer to our prayers because the Lord is about something much greater in our lives than we can see at the moment.

Years ago I was in a Church history class at Brigham Young University. We had studied the Missouri persecutions, the exile from Nauvoo, the sacrifices of the Saints as they made the arduous journey across the plains to the Rocky Mountains—especially of the Willie and Martin handcart companies.

After we rehearsed that catalog of adversity and suffering, one of the students asked this question: "Why was the way so hard? I know they were being tested, but did it have to be so relentless, so intense?" The professor's answer showed tremendous insight into the purposes of God. He said: "What you have to realize is this. There was a great work to be done, and these people were just common folk. They weren't great crusaders or proven heroes. However, by the time they reached the valley, many of the physically weak had died, and almost all of the spiritually weak had apostatized. So what Brigham Young had left to work with was pure steel."

Two verses of a beloved hymn capture this concept of testing and refining:

When through the deep waters I call thee to go,
The rivers of sorrow shall not thee o'erflow,
For I will be with thee, thy troubles to bless,
And sanctify to thee thy deepest distress.

When through fiery trials thy pathways shall lie,
My grace, all sufficient, shall be thy supply.
The flame shall not hurt thee; I only design
Thy dross to consume and thy gold to refine.[4]

What may appear to be indifference on God's part may actually be one of the great evidences of His love for us. Like so many other Saints before us, we may simply be in the midst of an intense divine tutorial.

We May Give Up Too Soon

One last possible answer to our question about unanswered prayers comes from a parable given by Jesus and recorded by Luke (see Luke 18:1–6). The parable is often called the parable of the unjust judge. This lesson is so important to our understanding of how prayer sometimes works that we will explore it at some length.

This parable is unusual in a couple ways. First, the Savior stated what lesson we are to learn from the parable before He even gave it: "And he spake a parable unto them to this end, *that men ought always to pray, and not to faint*"* (Luke 18:1).

Second, the story, though simple and only four verses long, raises some interesting—almost troubling—questions.

> There was in a city a judge, which feared not God, neither regarded man:
>
> And there was a widow in that city; and she came unto him, saying, Avenge me of mine adversary.
>
> And he would not for a while: but afterward he said within himself, Though I fear not God, nor regard man;
>
> Yet because this widow troubleth me, I will avenge her, lest by her continual coming she weary me (Luke 18:2–5).

When children want something badly from their parents, we use various expressions—some of them slang terms—to describe what they do. We say, "They *pestered* me until I couldn't stand it anymore" or "They *bugged* me until I gave in" or "They *hounded* me until I said yes" or "I said yes just to *get them off my back.*"

But is this what the parable is suggesting? Do we pester the Lord

---

* *Faint* is an old English word that carries an additional meaning to that of losing consciousness. It means to lose heart, to get discouraged, and to give up.

until He throws up His hands and gives in? Surely that is not how God works with us.

There is a deeper question triggered by this parable. In the Sermon on the Mount, the Savior taught that we are not to use vain repetitions in our prayers because "your Father knoweth what things ye have need of, *before* ye ask him" (Matthew 6:8). This is an important point to keep in mind. With His infinite knowledge of all things, we can never come to God in prayer and surprise Him. And if that is so, why would He request that we not only pray to Him but also that we persist in prayer? If He already knows what we need, why should we have to ask Him at all, let alone ask Him again and again?

> *There are two kinds of people: Those who say to God, "Thy will be done," and those to whom God says, "All right, then have it your way."*
>
> C. S. Lewis,
> *Great Divorce,* 75

Another name given to this parable is the parable of the importunate woman. The word comes from the verb *to importune.* This word conveys exactly the opposite meaning of *to faint.* To importune means "to press or beset with solicitations; demand with urgency or persistence."[5] Jesus told His disciples that the parable is meant to teach us that we should importune the Lord.[*]

The request that we importune God with great persistence cannot be to satisfy some petty whim of His. Nor can it be that He wants us to jump through some theological hoops in order to prove our submissiveness. That is completely counter to His nature and purposes for us. So the first conclusion we can draw is: The commandment to importune the Father is not for His benefit. *It is for ours.*

That leads us to the next question. What is it about importuning that

---

[*] That specific word is not used in Luke, but after the Saints were driven from Jackson County in 1833, in a revelation telling the Prophet how to deal with the situation, the Lord likened their situation to the parable of the unjust judge and then told them three times to "importune" the civil authorities for redress (see D&C 101:81–89).

has such great spiritual benefit that the Lord would specifically encourage us to do so?

To better understand why the Lord has asked that we pray always and not faint, let us walk through what happens to a person of faith when he or she (1) faces a major crisis or turning point in life, (2) begins to pray earnestly for help from God, but (3) receives no answer from the Lord.

When nothing seems to be happening, a natural reaction is to ask ourselves why. There are at least three possible answers.

> *If one rises from his knees having merely said words, he should fall back on his knees and remain there until he has established communication with the Lord who is very anxious to bless, but having given man his free agency, will not force himself upon that man.*
>
> SPENCER W. KIMBALL,
> *TEACHINGS OF SPENCER W. KIMBALL*, 124

- *The answer is no.* In a way that is not a comforting answer, but it is understandable and therefore more easily accepted. We decide that the Lord simply isn't going to grant us our request for whatever reason, and so we just have to accept it. We conclude that no answer means the answer is "no."
- *The problem is with God.* When nothing happens and the situation has great urgency, some individuals get highly frustrated. They turn bitter or angry and conclude, "Either God doesn't hear me or, if He does, He doesn't care." Being weak in the faith, they turn a little bitter. "Well, that's fine. I'll show Him! I'll just stop believing in Him. I don't need Him."* *Thus they harden their hearts, locking the gate against any spiritual influences.*
- *I must be the problem here.* This reaction most often comes from people of faith, people who not only deeply believe in God but

---

* Ironically, this tendency frequently happens with those who turn to God only in a crisis. They go years without praying to him. Then, when a crisis hits, they immediately plead for help. If it doesn't come soon, they are quick to project the blame away from themselves and onto God. Even more ironic is the petty satisfaction they get from thinking that somehow they are punishing God for not treating them properly.

also have a solid understanding of His attributes. They know that He is perfect. Therefore they have to conclude that He cannot be the source of the problem. That leaves only one other possible conclusion. If God is not the problem, then *I* must be the problem.

If we come to this last significant conclusion, interesting things begin to happen. We begin to ask questions of ourselves, questions like "What I am doing wrong? What is there in my life that is blocking the Spirit?" This triggers an inward search, a spiritual inventory, as it were. We begin to assess and evaluate where we are in our relationship to God. More important, we begin to change.

[Some people] regard God as an airman does his parachute: it's there for emergencies, but he hopes he'll never have to use it.

C. S. LEWIS,
PROBLEM OF PAIN, 94

We move from questioning the situation to self-examination. Self-examination brings remorse and a resolve to do better. This humility softens our heart and opens it even more to the influence of the Spirit. With that change of heart, the very nature of our prayers begins to change as well. Our prayers will begin to fill with greater power, deeper yearnings, and more righteous petitions. President Spencer W. Kimball eloquently described this pattern of prayer:

Have you prayed? How much have you prayed? How did you pray? Have you prayed as did the Savior of the world in Gethsemane or did you ask for what you want regardless of its being proper? Do you say in your prayers: "Thy will be done"? . . . Or, did you pray, "Give me what I want or I will take it anyway"? Did you say: "Father in Heaven, I love you, I believe in you, I know you are omniscient. I am honest. I am sincerely desirous of doing right. I know you can see the end from the beginning. You can see the future. . . . Tell me, please, loved Heavenly Father, and I

310

promise to do what you tell me to do." Have you prayed that way? Don't you think it might be wise? Are you courageous enough to pray that prayer?[6]

Therein lies the great lesson of the parable of the importunate woman. Importunity, as the Lord suggests it, initiates a tremendous process of spiritual growth. The very exercise of questioning, then seeking and humbling ourselves, and finally submitting our will to His, becomes spiritually enlivening and spiritually empowering. Knowing this, is it any wonder that sometimes the Lord withholds an answer from us for a time?

Be thankful that sometimes God lets you struggle for a long time before that answer comes. Your character will grow; your faith will increase.

RICHARD G. SCOTT,
ENSIGN, MAY 2007, 9

That is the principle taught in the parable of the unjust judge. We don't persist in prayer to change God's mind. We persist in prayer to change our hearts.

THIS KIND COMETH NOT OUT

An additional perspective related to importuning needs to be addressed, if only briefly. It comes from another teaching moment by the Savior. One day a father brought a child who was having seizures. The father begged the Savior to bless his son, saying that he had taken him to the disciples, but they couldn't heal him. Jesus blessed the child and immediately the boy was healed (see Matthew 17:14–18).

Afterward, the disciples, troubled by their inability to heal the child, asked Jesus, "Why could not we cast him out?" (Matthew 17:19). The Savior said that it was because they didn't have sufficient faith. But then He added a significant comment: "Howbeit [nevertheless], *this kind goeth not out but by prayer and fasting*" (Matthew 17:21).

Some challenges, some circumstances, and some conditions are of such magnitude and are so serious that an extra measure of spiritual power is required to overcome them. The Savior suggests that in such cases prayer alone is insufficient. To it we can add fasting. There is something about fasting that generates greater spiritual power and deeper spiritual sensitivity. Perhaps it comes from deliberately and consciously putting the flesh in subjection to the spirit. One obvious benefit of fasting is that the pangs of hunger constantly remind us of the issue at hand. We find ourselves praying about it all day long, not just in the morning and evening.

In short, fasting is a way to intensify the process of importuning the Lord. It generates the power we need to finally bring down the powers of heaven in our behalf.

Selling a House

How fasting coupled with prayer can bring the answers we seek is illustrated by the following story shared by a man concerning an urgent situation in which he found himself. I am a little hesitant to share this experience because, while it is a wonderful example of the power of fasting, some may think such remarkable results will always come if we just fast long enough. As we previously noted in Chapter 13, we must always remember the principle that it is God who determines all aspects of revelation, including when it comes, what is given, to whom it is given, and how it is given.

> It was a time in our marriage when our family was growing and our house was becoming less and less adequate to accommodate them. We determined to build a new home. A friend of ours was both a contractor and a real estate agent. When he learned of our decision, he offered to lower some of his fees if we would both list our old home with him and let him build the new one too. It was an attractive offer so we decided to do it.
>
> Just the way the financing worked out, we had six months to sell our home, pay off the construction loan, and start our new mortgage. Our builder assured us that he could do that. So we signed. However, the bank had made

it clear that if we couldn't sell our current home, we would end up having three loans come due September 1. We decided to go for it and signed the papers early in March.

At first things looked good. As the new house was begun, we put our current home on the market. Numerous people came through to see the home. Many expressed an interest, but time after time nothing came of it. By June the traffic through our home had dropped off sharply. For the first time I started to get nervous. The interest rates had gone up almost two full points, which meant if we missed the September 1 deadline, in addition to the three mortgages, our new mortgage would cost significantly more.

By July, virtually nothing was happening. We tried everything, including many fervent prayers. By August, just weeks away from the deadline, we hadn't seen a potential buyer in over a month. Now both my wife and I were starting to feel sick to our stomachs. Never had we prayed so earnestly for anything. We knew the Lord could help us but began to wonder why He wasn't doing so. Had we made a terrible mistake and was He now going to let us suffer the consequences?

Then one day I read the story about the man with the epileptic son. The Master's words almost leaped off the page at me. "This kind goeth not out but by prayer *and* fasting." That was on a Sunday. That night I told my wife that beginning the next day I was going to start fasting. I was aware of the counsel that we are not to fast for more than 24 hours at a time, so I told her I was going to fast for a day, then go off it for a day, then fast another day, and go off it for a day, and that I was going to keep that up until I got an answer one way or the other. I decided that even if the answer was that we had been foolish and now had to live with our decision, knowing that much would help us cope with what was to come.

I fasted Monday, Wednesday, and Friday and nothing happened. But on Saturday morning, I got a call from our agent/builder. A real estate agent had called with an offer! They weren't just interested in seeing the house again. They had an offer. We set up an appointment with their realtor at 5 o'clock that afternoon. We were absolutely ecstatic. It had worked! We had an answer! A wonderful answer!

Imagine our astonishment when our agent called again an hour or so later. "You're not going to believe this," he said, "but we have a second offer." That afternoon, after only three days of fasting, we sat at our table with two different realtors. Both buyers were so determined to purchase the home that they bid each other up and we ended up getting $1,500 more than our asking price!

> *The Lord has instituted this law [of the fast]; it is simple and perfect, based on reason and intelligence, and would not only prove a solution to the question of providing for the poor, but it would result in good to those who observe the law. It would call attention to the sin of over-eating, place the body in subjection to the spirit, and so promote communication with the Holy Ghost, and insure a spiritual strength and power which the people of the nation so greatly need.*
>
> JOSEPH F. SMITH,
> *GOSPEL DOCTRINE*, 237

What a fascinating story. The couple didn't need two buyers. They would have been thrilled with one buyer and taking $1,500 *less* than they were asking. After weeks of not seeing anyone, this answer was not just remarkable; it was a small miracle. Why had the Lord blessed them so abundantly? We cannot say for sure, but I truly believe that this was the Lord's way of not only answering their prayers in a marvelous way but also of teaching them about the benefits of not giving up their importuning the Lord.

A CAUTION

Before every reader starts fasting every other day as this man did, let me again offer a word of caution. Remember the first governing principle we learned about how revelation works: *God determines all aspects of revelation, including the when, who, what, and how.* An ancillary principle that we have stated several times is that we cannot force the things of the Spirit. Sometimes the Lord asks us not to persist in our petitions to Him. We learn this from two specific examples drawn from the lives of great prophets.

A thorn in the flesh. In an earlier chapter we noted a comment by the Apostle Paul about a personal problem he had that he referred to as a "thorn in the flesh." He does not give us any detail about what it was, but it seems to have been some personal physical affliction that hampered him in the work of the ministry. Here is what he says about it:

> And lest I should be exalted above measure through the abundance of the revelations, there was given to me a thorn in the flesh . . . lest I should be exalted above measure.
>
> For this thing I besought the Lord thrice, that it might depart from me.
>
> And he said unto me, My grace is sufficient for thee: for my strength is made perfect in weakness (2 Corinthians 12:7–9).

Here was a man of great faith who had sacrificed much in the service of the Lord, importuning God for relief, and yet God's answer was, "No, I'm not going to grant this request." Then comes the gentle suggestion, "My grace is sufficient." In other words, there was no sense in further petitioning. The Lord was not going to change His mind on this one.

Trouble me no more. Here was another tutoring experience for the Prophet Joseph Smith:

> *Genuine faith makes increasing allowance for . . . individual tutorials. In view of these tutorials, God cannot . . . respond affirmatively to all of our petitions with an unbroken chain of "yeses." This would assume that all of our petitions are for that "which is right" and are spiritually "expedient." (3 Ne. 18:20; D&C 18:18; D&C 88:64–65.) No petitioner is so wise!*
>
> NEAL A. MAXWELL,
> *ENSIGN*, MAY 1991, 90

I was once praying very earnestly [importuning] to know the time of the coming of the Son of Man, when I heard a voice repeat the following: Joseph, my son, if thou livest until thou art eighty-five years old, thou shalt see the face of the Son of Man; therefore, *let this suffice, and trouble me no more on this matter* (D&C 130:14–15).

We are invited to pray and not faint—to importune the Lord—but we need to stay sensitive to the Spirit. At times the Lord says, "Don't press me any further on this one. For reasons I will not share with you, I have chosen not to answer your request at this time."

These times become a test of patience and faith. When in our extremities, we cry out to the Lord to "let this cup pass from us," we, like the Savior, need to learn to bow our heads and say, "Nevertheless not as I will, but as thou wilt" (Matthew 26:39).

CHAPTER 27

INCREASING MY ABILITY TO RECEIVE AND RECOGNIZE REVELATION
I. SOURCES OF INNER NOISE

"Be still and know that I am God" (D&C 101:16).

BRINGING IT ALL TOGETHER

In this section we are seeking to answer the final question: *How do I increase my ability to receive and recognize revelation in my life?*

We have noted before that there are no pat answers, no set formulas, and no detailed recipes we can put in our pocket to pull out whenever we have a question. This thing we call revelation is a miraculous process, but for the most part it doesn't feel like a grand, dramatic crusade. It is a day-to-day, month-to-month, year-to-year learning experience. From time to time there may be bursts of grandness and exciting experiences. Mostly, revelation is the quiet, almost imperceptible process of growing and becoming.

We started out our study of revelation by looking at what the voice of the Lord is like and summarized it by saying that usually *the Spirit speaks to us in a still, small voice that whispers to our minds and hearts.*

It is rarely dramatic or sensational. Mostly, it is gentle and soft, more like the stirring of a spiritual breeze across our face, or like the first coolness of the evening after a hot, stifling day. And that is the challenge. It is one thing to receive revelation; it is quite another to recognize it when it comes.

BE STILL AND KNOW

In the same verses that state that the Holy Ghost speaks to our minds and hearts, the Lord said that this "spirit of revelation" is how Moses knew that he was to lead the people of Israel through the Red Sea. In that context, it is interesting to note Moses' words. The children of Israel were unarmed, their backs were to the water, and Pharaoh and his armies were bearing down upon them. As the people were nearing hysteria, Moses said: "Fear ye not, *stand still,* and see the salvation of the Lord" (Exodus 14:13). In his classic commentary on the Bible, Adam Clarke rendered that verse as: "Be *quiet,* and do not render yourselves wretched by your fears and your confusion."[1]

The expulsion of the modern Saints from Jackson County differed from the flight of Moses and Israel, but the Saints received a similar charge. The Lord said, "Be still and know that I am God" (D&C 101:16; see also Psalm 46:10).

This commandment has great importance for our study, for what we are trying to do is learn how to listen to and recognize the still, small voice when it comes to us. Our crises are rarely as desperate or dangerous as those of ancient Israel or the modern Saints in Missouri, but our challenge is essentially the same. How do we become *still* so we can better hear the still, small voice?

This is a challenge because in the first part of the twenty-first century our lives are filled with noise—physical noise, spiritual noise, and emotional noise. Our lives are filled with all kinds of things that create a state of inner noise within us. And we mean more than just sin and transgression.

Some sources of spiritual noise, or spiritual static, are pretty obvious. Some are subtler and harder to recognize. Here is a list of some of the things that seriously affect the ability of our spiritual senses to pick up thoughts and feelings that come from the Lord.

Personal Unworthiness

The general problem of unworthiness is the most common source of inner noise and the most deafening. Sin so dulls our spiritual senses—leading to what the scriptures call "hardness of heart," "blindness of mind," "dullness of hearing"—that we are no longer sensitive to the whisperings of the Spirit. Nephi described his brothers as "past feeling" (1 Nephi 17:45). Paul described some in the early Church as having their consciences "seared with a hot iron" (1 Timothy 4:2). Christ described some of the Jews of His time by saying their "heart is waxed gross, and their ears are dull of hearing, and their eyes they have closed" (Matthew 13:15).

We could write a whole volume on the effects of sin on our ability to hear the voice of the Lord, but since readers of this book will already clearly understand that concept, we will pass on to other sources of inner noise.

Pride

This is another condition of the heart. We aspire to the honors of men, for example, because of pride. We set our hearts on the things of the world because they help us feel superior to others. When Lehi saw the great and spacious building, which represented the pride of the world (see 1 Nephi 12:18), it was filled with "both old and young, both male and female; and their manner of dress was exceedingly fine" (1 Nephi 8:27).

It is interesting how often pride is linked with riches and the wearing of "fine apparel" (see, for example, Jacob 2:13; Alma 1:6, 32; 4:6–8; 5:53; Mormon 8:36). After speaking of the "wise, and the learned, and they that are rich, who are puffed up because of their learning, and their wisdom, and their riches," Nephi, in one of the most scathing denunciations found in scriptures, states, "Yea, *they are they whom [the Lord] despiseth*" (2 Nephi 9:42).

Pride parades itself in many different guises: self-righteousness; self-aggrandizement; racial, religious, or class prejudice; unrighteous

Among the Latter-day Saints, the preaching of false doctrines disguised as truths of the gospel, may be expected from people of two classes, and practically from these only; they are:

First—The hopelessly ignorant, whose lack of intelligence is due to their indolence and sloth, who make but feeble effort, if indeed any at all, to better themselves by reading and study; those who are afflicted with a dread disease that may develop into an incurable malady—laziness.

Second—The proud and self-vaunting ones, who read by the lamp of their own conceit; who interpret by rules of their own contriving; who have become a law unto themselves, and so pose as the sole judges of their own doings. More dangerously ignorant than the first.

Beware of the lazy and the proud; their infection in each case is contagious.

JOSEPH F. SMITH,
GOSPEL DOCTRINE, 373

dominion; demeaning others; and so forth. President Ezra Taft Benson defined it this way:

One of Satan's greatest tools is pride: to cause a man or a woman to center so much attention on self that he or she becomes insensitive to their Creator or fellow beings. It's a cause for discontent, divorce, teenage rebellion, family indebtedness, and most other problems we face.[2]

He added:

Pride does not look up to God and care about what is right. It looks sideways to man and argues who is right. Pride is manifest in the spirit of contention. Was it not through pride that the devil became the devil? Christ wanted to serve. The devil wanted to rule. Christ wanted to bring men to where He was. The devil wanted to be above men. . . .

Pride is characterized by "What do I want out of life?" rather than by "What would God have me do with my life?" It is self-will as opposed to God's will. It is the fear of man over the fear of God.[3]

320

Contention

Here is another *heart* condition that is worthy of separate mention because it can be so devastating to our ability to receive and recognize the voice of the Lord. When the resurrected Savior visited the Nephites in the Land Bountiful, one of the first things He taught them was that "he that hath the spirit of contention is not of me, but is of the devil" (3 Nephi 11:29). Likewise, even before the Church was organized, Joseph Smith was told that one of the reasons for the Restoration was so that there would not be "so much contention" (D&C 10:63).

Clearly, there is something about contention that is particularly toxic to our ability to call down the Spirit on our behalf. Sometimes missionaries or well-meaning Latter-day Saints make this mistake. Thinking they are defending the kingdom, they get embroiled in vigorous and often angry debates. They begin shooting scriptural shafts, trying to knock their opponent out of the saddle so they can declare victory. Actually, they lose not only the Spirit in such contests but also a round to Satan.

Even everyday disagreements or little frictions can desensitize us to the Spirit. Elder B. H. Roberts cites an incident from the life of Joseph Smith that happened while he and Emma were staying in Fayette, New York, at the Peter Whitmer farm. The experience was shared by David Whitmer, who was present when it happened:

> One morning when [Joseph] was getting ready to continue the translation, something went wrong about the house and he was put out about it. Something that Emma, his wife, had done. Oliver and I went up stairs and Joseph came up soon after to continue the translation, but he could not do anything. He could not translate a single syllable. He went down stairs, out into the orchard, and made supplication to the Lord; was gone about an hour—came back to the house, asked Emma's forgiveness and then came up stairs

where we were and then the translation went on all right. He could do nothing save he was humble and faithful.[4]

Busyness

Today our lives have become complex and crammed with activities and demands. For many people, virtually every waking moment is programmed with something. Our brains are engaged constantly with work, family, Church, recreation, and entertainment. We surround ourselves with noise—television, radio, video and computer games, MP3 players, and so forth. We have background music in stores, on elevators, in the workplace, at home, and even in some restrooms. We walk or jog with earphones and music playing in our ears. We also fill our lives with activity noise—sports, music, school, arts, dancing, travel, camps, conferences, and a hundred other things.

Where do we find time to stop and be still? When can we let our brains disengage and relax and contemplate life? Previous generations that did much more hard physical labor than we do nevertheless had many tasks that engaged only part of their brains. Walking behind a team of horses and a plow, hanging out the wash on a line, taking the carriage into town, canning a hundred quarts of fruit in a day. These got the work done but also allowed thinking time. "Inspiration comes more easily in peaceful settings. Such words as quiet, still, peaceable, Comforter abound in the scriptures."[5]

We are free from much of the drudgery and hard work of our ancestors. We drop a load of clothes in the washing machine, turn a button, and go do something else. We stick a frozen dinner in the microwave and take it out piping hot four or five minutes later. But what are we doing with our extra time? We are cramming it full with things, and many of those things create noise in our lives.

Youth are especially influenced by this new culture of ours—except they don't think of it as new. It is all they've known. The digital age, with its music and videos and computers and computer games and text messaging and Internet, has inundated them with what often approaches both visual and sensory overload. "Noise"* is so much a part of their lives that someone recently quipped that if the Lord wanted to get a revelation to some of our youth, He would have to say, "We interrupt this broadcast to bring you the following message."

I am not suggesting that advances in technology and convenience are bad, nor am I advocating that we return to simpler times. But these advances have not simplified our lives; rather, they have complicated them. Earlier we cited a statement by Elder Packer about the still, small voice. He warned that because of the whispering nature of that voice, "*if we are preoccupied* we may not feel it at all."[6]

A society that grows more and more preoccupied with the sheer complexity and busyness of life can't help but have an effect on our ability to receive and recognize revelation.

Irreverence

In chapter 20, we noted that one of the basic governing principles of revelation is that we must treat sacred things with care. We must not trifle

I ask you to think about all of the time you spend in front of your computer, maybe surfing the Internet, or plugged in to video games, or watching some of the inane programs and sports contests on television. I am not anti-sports. I enjoy a good football or basketball game. But I have seen so many men and women become addicted to sports or the Internet or video games. I know far too many people who are controlled by the noise and opinions they have constantly coming into their lives and minds. I believe their lives would be richer and more rewarding if at least occasionally they would get up from watching a game that will be forgotten tomorrow, get up from surfing one more web site, and spend a little time reading and thinking and simply Being Still.

GORDON B. HINCKLEY,
WAY TO BE! 105–6

with them or take them lightly. When we do, we stifle the process of

---

* By calling it *noise,* I don't mean to suggest that it is bad, just that it constantly impinges on our senses, competing for our attention.

revelation, for such irreverence grieves the Spirit and causes Him to withdraw.

Reverence is both an attitude and a set of behaviors. The attitude is that we have a deep awareness of the greatness, majesty, holiness, and perfections of God. This fills us with a permeating respect and love that influences how we act.

In his general conference talk in October 1991, Elder Packer spoke of the relationship between reverence and revelation. He titled his talk "Reverence Invites Revelation." He said, "Irreverence suits the purposes of the adversary by obstructing the delicate channels of revelation in both mind and spirit."[7]

A classroom teacher can lose the Spirit by treating sacred things in a humorous manner. During the partaking of the sacrament, people may casually pop the bread into their mouths while engaged in whispered conversation with the person next to them. Our chapels are often filled with a low rumble of chatter. These may not be great and glaring errors, but even small things can directly affect the state of inner quietness we need to receive revelation.

Elder Packer went on to warn us about some of his concerns:

> For the past several years we have watched patterns of reverence and irreverence in the Church. While many are to be highly commended, we are drifting. We have reason to be deeply concerned. . . .
>
> Our sacrament and other meetings need renewed attention to assure that they are truly worship services in which members may be spiritually nourished and have their testimonies replenished and in which investigators may feel the inspiration essential to spiritual conversion. . . .
>
> When we [come] for Sunday meetings, the music, dress, and conduct should be appropriate for worship. Foyers are built into our chapels to allow for the greeting and chatter that are typical of people who love one another. However, when we step into the chapel, we *must!*—each of us *must*—watch

ourselves lest we be guilty of intruding when someone is struggling to feel delicate spiritual communications.[8]

Another manifestation of our casualness toward sacred things and our drift away from reverence is the number of people who arrive late to our meetings. We even commonly joke about Mormon Standard Time.

Not long ago I was visiting a sacrament meeting in another stake. Because I was seated on the stand, I could watch the congregation come in. Out of curiosity, I began to keep a rough count of those who came in after the meeting had begun. I was saddened that more than half the congregation arrived after the starting time. Some were late enough that they missed the administration of the bread.

As I watched this happening, I saw something else. When someone came in late, heads would turn to see who it was. People would smile in greeting, and in some cases whispered hellos would be exchanged. With our penchant to take the most convenient seats available, most of the outside places on the pews were already taken. People already seated had to stand up and move in, or the latecomers had to climb over them. What became painfully obvious was that this behavior distracted from the reverence of the meeting. We are not just talking about the young or new in the faith. This habit is found among some of the strongest members of our wards.

Reverence invites revelation. Irreverence in whatever form creates inner noise.

The Cares of the World

In the parable of the soils, Jesus said the cares of the world could choke out the seed of the gospel, even though the seed and the soil were both good. These cares are not necessarily bad things. In some cases, they may even be good things. Caring for a young family is a noble endeavor and of great worth in the plan of the Father, yet it can be so time-consuming and emotionally demanding that we may be distracted from being as sensitive to the Spirit as we should be. Loss of employment, health problems, caring for aged parents, and sorrow over a child's transgression could be included in the definition of the cares of the world. Each of these, both the good and the bad, can press in upon our minds and hearts so heavily that we become consumed to the point that we are filled with a different kind of inner noise and do not allow sufficient time for the Spirit.

Having Our Wants Too High

Another source of inner noise that can be highly desensitizing occurs when our desires and wants are so high that our own emotions begin to drown out the soft whisperings of the Spirit and we do not truly open our hearts to the will of God. Remember that one of the heart conditions Joseph was warned about in Liberty Jail was having hearts set so much upon the things of the world.

Many worldly things can become attractive to us. We want love, comfort, pleasure, status, fame, success, wealth, and education. We want to have things done our way, to have people like us, and to enjoy many other wonderful and commendable things. But if our desire for those things becomes so compelling that the things of God take a secondary position, we are creating inner noise in our hearts. Not only will this cause the Spirit to draw back, but also, even if the Holy Ghost tries to speak with us, we will be deafened by our own demands.

IN SUMMARY

There are other sources of spiritual, or inner noise, but this is sufficient to make our point. The voice of the Lord is still and small, and it whispers. If we are to hear and recognize it, we must develop a quality of inner quiet and deliberately suppress the sources of spiritual noise in our lives.

Here again is the Lord's simple counsel: "*Be still,* and know that I am God."

CHAPTER 28

INCREASING MY ABILITY TO RECEIVE AND RECOGNIZE REVELATION
II. REDUCE THE INNER NOISE AND DRAW CLOSER

"Their ears are dull of hearing" (Matthew 13:15).

A FAMILY PARTY

Now that we have seen some of the major causes of inner noise, let us discuss what we can do to reduce that kind of noise and create a state of inner stillness, or inner quiet. Some years ago I had an experience that provides a useful analogy in this regard.

We were having an extended family party at our home. About twenty people—mostly adults and teens with one or two older children and a couple of infants—were gathered in the large downstairs family room. In a nearby room, a children's video was booming. Down the hall other children were laughing and playing games. In the family room, half a dozen conversations were going on simultaneously.

I was sitting across the room from my niece and her mother, who were seated together on a couch. We were separated by perhaps ten or fifteen feet. She was attending Brigham Young University at the time, and so I asked her how things were going there. As she responded, her mother broke in and said, "Tell him about that experience you had in your religion class." That immediately caught my interest, so I leaned forward. My niece is somewhat soft-spoken, and with all the noise I was having difficulty hearing her.

What could I have done to make sure I heard her? As I look back on it now, I can see four possibilities:

- I could have asked her *to speak more loudly*. Obviously that option wouldn't apply if we were talking about revelation. It is not our privilege to request louder—more distinct and more recognizable—forms of revelation from the Lord.
- I could have turned down or *eliminated some of the other noise* by turning off the movie, sending the kids outside, and so forth.
- I could have *moved closer* to her.
- I could have *concentrated and focused* on her and what she was saying, trying to screen out some of the other noise.

That provides a simple pattern for us to follow as we seek to increase our ability to receive and recognize the voice of the Lord when we live in a world filled with noise and distraction.

REDUCE THE NOISE

In the previous chapter, we identified seven important sources of inner noise: unworthiness, pride, contention, busyness, irreverence, the cares of the world, having our wants too high.

To turn down the noise, we reduce the power and influence of those seven qualities in our lives.

If we are guilty of serious transgression, the road will be challenging and extended. It may require counsel from a bishop. It may involve leaving friends or romantic interests. It may involve professional counseling. But the way is still repentance. Fortunately, we are not left alone in this process. When we even begin to turn back to the Lord, we begin to open our heart to the Spirit. And the Spirit will help us win the battle.

For those who are struggling with the more common failings that grieve the Spirit, the same course of action is required. Do we speak too harshly to our children? Are we too concerned with the things of the world—clothes, cars, position, fame? Is watching television more important than spending time with our spouse and children? Are we spending an inordinate amount of time playing video games? Is our language offensive to the Lord? Do we speak unkindly of our spouse? Do we shade the truth just a little when contracting business? Do we let our frustrations boil over when we are on the freeway and mutter unkind comments or uncomplimentary names about other drivers?

All of us do things that create spiritual noise in our lives. Let us be sensitive to them. Let us ask the Lord what things we need to change and then change them!

The example of Joseph Smith mentioned earlier is a good model. The moment he sat down to translate, he knew something was wrong and he recognized what it was. He didn't think it was Emma's problem and wait for her to change. He immediately went downstairs, prayed to the Lord, and then apologized to Emma. He reaffirmed his love for her. Only then was he able to return to the work of translation.

DRAW CLOSER

Another application we can draw from the analogy of our family party is that we need to draw closer to the Lord. At the party I could have moved my chair or had my niece move hers closer to me. So it is with us. We need to do things that either move us closer to Him or draw the Spirit closer to us. As we talk about how to do that, we will find little that is new or surprising. These are things we already know, but we often forget what a tremendous impact they can have on revelation.

Another way to think of this is that the things we listed under the sources of spiritual noise in the previous chapter could be considered to be things that *grieve* the Spirit. Why are they so grievous? Because they deaden and harden the mind and heart. Thus, when the Spirit tries to bring us light and truth, He can only come *unto* the heart, not *into* it (see 2 Nephi 33:1).

Now we will look at things that please the Spirit and cause Him to draw closer. These things are gate openers and heart softeners. They allow the Spirit to draw closer because we use our agency to open more widely the gateway to the heart and allow Him to come *into* it, not just *unto* it.

Humility and Meekness

The condition of humility and meekness is closely connected to our ability to receive and recognize revelation. It is, of course, the opposite of pride. Often when the scriptures talk about a "softening" of the heart, they refer to a pushing aside of pride, a willingness to submit our will to the Lord's.

The ultimate expression of humility is to acknowledge God's divine perfections as being so infinitely superior to our own attributes that we, of our own free will, surrender our hearts to Him. As Abinadi noted, in the Savior we have the perfect model for humility, for "the will of the Son [was] swallowed up in the will of the Father" (Mosiah 15:7).

Note how the Lord values this attribute and especially how often He links it directly to an increase in revelation:

> *Humility is that quality that permits us to be taught from on high through the Spirit or to be taught from sources whose origin was inspiration from the Lord, such as the scriptures and the comments of the prophets. Humility is the precious, fertile soil of righteous character. In it the seeds of personal growth germinate. When cultivated through the exercise of faith, pruned by repentance, and fortified by obedience and good works, such seeds produce the cherished fruit of spiritual direction.*
>
> RICHARD G. SCOTT,
> CES SYMPOSIUM,
> AUGUST 11, 1998, 11

- *"Be thou humble;* and the Lord thy God shall lead thee by the hand, and give thee answer to thy prayers" (D&C 112:10).
- "They did fast and pray oft, and did *wax stronger and stronger in their humility, . . . yielding their hearts* unto God" (Helaman 3:35).
- *"Because of meekness and lowliness of heart* cometh the visitation

330

of the Holy Ghost" (Moroni 8:26).

- "Walk in the *meekness* of my Spirit, and you shall have peace in me" (D&C 19:23).
- "I, the Lord, am not pleased with my servant Sidney Rigdon; *he exalted himself in his heart,* and received not counsel, but grieved the Spirit" (D&C 63:55).

As the Lord communicates with the meek and submissive, fewer decibels are required, and more nuances are received.

NEAL A. MAXWELL,
*NEAL A. MAXWELL
QUOTE BOOK,* 288

Some expressions of humility could include:

- A willingness to patiently accept the divine tutorials the Lord may choose to put us through.
- Carefully avoiding "righteous" behavior only "to be seen of men" (Matthew 23:5).
- The recognition that while we may have been given special blessings or talents (wealth, intelligence, physical beauty, artistic ability, and so forth), these are gifts from the Lord and are to be used to bring glory to Him, not just to ourselves.
- Putting our wants way down on our list. Notice that I don't say push our wants *away.* Pushing our wants way down means that we trust in God sufficiently to say "Thy will be done" and truly mean it—not just mean it but *want it.* Our desire becomes to be in harmony with God's desire.

Prayer and Fasting

In chapters 24 and 25, we looked at the processes for learning by faith and using faith to increase our revelation. Earnestly seeking was one of the key actions discussed there. A major part of that seeking happens through prayer. In chapter 26, we further explored the power of asking as we looked at what is known as importuning the Lord.

Because both chapters 24 and 25 give much information on the power of prayer in helping us draw closer to God, we will not duplicate that information here. We will only note that prayer, fasting, and revelation are closely intertwined. (The following references teach this relationship clearly: 1 Nephi 10:17; 15:8; 2 Nephi 32:8; Alma 17:3, 9; D&C 6:11, 14; 19:38; 42:14.)

One thing we can specifically pray for is the gifts of the Spirit. President George Q. Cannon wrote:

> How many of you, my brethren and sisters, are seeking for these gifts that God has promised to bestow? How many of you, when you bow before your Heavenly Father in your family circle or in your secret places, contend for these gifts to be bestowed upon you? How many of you ask the Father, in the name of Jesus, to manifest Himself to you through these powers and these gifts? Or do you go along day by day like a door turning on its hinges, without having any feeling on the subject, without exercising any faith whatever; content to be baptized and be members of the Church, and to rest there, thinking that your salvation is secure because you have done this? I say to you, in the name of the Lord, as one of His servants, that you have need to repent of this. You have need to repent of your hardness of heart, of your indifference, and of your carelessness. There is not that diligence, there is not that faith, there is not that seeking for the power of God that there should be among a people who have received the precious promises we have.[1]

Feast upon the Word

We all recognize the role the scriptures play in receiving revelation. They are like a well of living water that we can return to again and again. They provide a rich source of enlightenment, instruction, truth, comfort, solace, direction, warning, and confirmation. Tens of thousands of Latter-day Saints can testify of how they have been blessed by the scriptures.

As noted earlier, someone has said, "If you want to speak to the Lord, get down on your knees and pray. If you want the Lord to speak to you, *open your scriptures.*" There is no question but what the written word becomes an important catalyst to revelation. Many of the revelations in the Doctrine and Covenants came as answers to questions that arose as Joseph and others were studying the scriptures. Note the promises offered if we use the scriptures in our search for gospel knowledge:

- "Thy word is a lamp unto my feet, and a light unto my path" (Psalm 119:105).
- "All scripture is given by inspiration of God, and is *profitable* for doctrine, for reproof, for correction, for instruction in righteousness: That the man of God *may be perfect,* thoroughly furnished unto all good works" (2 Timothy 3:16–17).
- "Hear the pleasing word of God, yea, the word which *healeth the wounded soul*" (Jacob 2:8).
- "They had waxed strong in the knowledge of the truth; for they were men of a sound understanding and *they had searched the scriptures diligently,* that they might know the word of God" (Alma 17:2).
- "First seek to obtain my word, and then . . . if you desire, you shall have my Spirit" (D&C 11:21).

Just as Oliver Cowdery was chided for taking no thought save it was to ask, so it is with us. If we want to draw on the "virtue of the word" (Alma 31:5) to help us in our quest for inner stillness, let it not be said of us that we took no thought save it was to *read* the scriptures.

A few verses tell us to read the scriptures (see Alma 33:14; 3 Nephi 27:5), but more often we are asked to do more than just read. Note the power of the verbs used in the following passages:

- "This book of the law shall not depart out of thy mouth; but *thou shalt meditate therein day and night*" (Joshua 1:8).

- *"Feast upon* the words of Christ" (2 Nephi 32:3).
- "Whoso would *hearken unto* the word of God, and *would hold fast unto it"* (1 Nephi 15:24).
- *"Lay hold upon* the word of God" (Helaman 3:29).
- "Yea, a commandment I give unto you that *ye search these things diligently"* (3 Nephi 23:1; see also Mosiah 1:7).
- *"Treasure up in your minds continually* the words of life" (D&C 84:85).

If we will energetically pursue [a study of the scriptures] in a determined and conscientious manner, we shall indeed find answers to our problems and peace in our hearts. We shall experience the Holy Ghost broadening our understanding, find new insights, witness an unfolding pattern of all scripture; and the doctrines of the Lord shall come to have more meaning to us than we ever thought possible. As a consequence, we shall have greater wisdom with which to guide ourselves and our families.

SPENCER W. KIMBALL,
TEACHINGS OF SPENCER W.
KIMBALL, 135

Elder Bruce R. McConkie made this promise:

I think that people who study the scriptures get a dimension to their life that nobody else gets and that can't be gained in any way except by a study of the scriptures. There's an increase in faith and a desire to do what's right and a feeling of inspiration and understanding that comes to people who study the gospel—meaning particularly the standard works—and who ponder the principles, that can't come in any other way.[2]

The Sacramental Covenants

Virtually every week throughout the year, active Latter-day Saints receive a remarkable promise about revelation and the Holy Spirit. That promise is contained in the covenants of the sacrament.

A covenant is a contract between the Lord and us. It involves a two-way promise. We covenant or promise to do certain things, and if we fulfill those covenants, the Lord promises to give us special blessings in return. To put it another way, it is as if covenants contain an if-then clause.

We find that structure in the sacrament prayers as well. Though we do not actually find the words *if* and *then* in the prayers, they are implied. It is contractual language. The prayers can be found in the Doctrine and Covenants (see 20:77, 79) and the Book of Mormon (see Moroni 4:3; 5:2). Here are the covenants we make:

If we are willing to:

1. Take upon us the name of Christ,
2. Always remember Him, and
3. Keep His commandments, which He has given us;

Then we are promised that we:

May have His Spirit to be with us.

Few passages in all of scripture offer a more direct promise concerning the Holy Ghost. When it comes to drawing closer to the Lord so we can better receive and recognize His voice, the promises don't get much better than that.

However, when the Savior introduced the sacrament to the Nephites after His resurrection, He added a solemn warning. It gives some indication of how sacred the sacrament is in the eyes of the Lord:

> And now behold, this is the commandment which I give unto you, that ye shall not suffer any one knowingly to partake of my flesh and blood unworthily, when ye shall minister it;
>
> For whoso eateth and drinketh my flesh and blood

Little wonder that weekly, when we partake of the sacramental bread, we ask to have the Spirit always with us. Only then are we safe. Otherwise, without the Spirit, we are left to ourselves. Who would ever want to solo anyway?

NEAL A. MAXWELL,
CES SYMPOSIUM, 1991, 3

unworthily *eateth and drinketh damnation to his soul.*
(3 Nephi 18:28–29; see also Mormon 9:29)

The Apostle Paul gave a similar warning to the Corinthian Saints
(see 1 Corinthians 11:27–29).

The root meaning of the word *damnation* is "condemnation."[3] That
is sobering, for which of us ever feels completely worthy to partake of
the emblems of the Savior's body and blood? While we have this marvelous promise found in the sacramental covenant, there is also a solemn
warning against taking that covenant lightly.

So just how scrupulous should we be in deciding whether we are
worthy each week? The consequences are serious enough that the question deserves careful thought. Elder Melvin J. Ballard gave some specific
and helpful counsel in this regard:

> I suggest that perhaps some of us are ashamed to come
> to the sacrament table because we feel unworthy and are
> afraid lest we eat and drink of these sacred emblems to our
> own condemnation. [But] we want every Latter-day Saint to
> come to the sacrament table because it is the place for self-
> investigation, for self-inspection, where we may learn to rec-
> tify our course and to make right our own lives, bringing
> ourselves into harmony with the teachings of the Church
> and with our brethren and sisters. It is the place where we
> become our own judges.
>
> There may be some instances where the elders of the
> Church could say, properly, to one who, in transgression,
> stretches forth his hands to partake of the emblems: "You
> should not do this until you have made restitution"; but
> ordinarily we will be our own judges. If we are properly
> instructed, we know that it is not our privilege to partake of
> the emblems of the flesh and blood of the Lord in sin, in
> transgression, or having injured and holding feelings against
> our brethren and sisters. No man goes away from this

Church and becomes an apostate in a week or in a month. It is a slow process. The one thing that would make for the safety of every man and woman would be to appear at the sacrament table every Sabbath day. We would not get very far away in one week—not so far away that, by the process of self-investigation, we could not rectify the wrongs we may have done. If we should refrain from partaking of the sacrament, condemned by ourselves as unworthy to receive these emblems, we could not endure that long, and we would soon, I am sure, have the spirit of repentance. *The road to the sacrament table is the path of safety for Latter-day Saints.*[4]

Two words associated with virtually every scripture that talks about the sacrament are *remember* and *remembrance.** Both sacramental prayers state that we are partaking of the bread and water in "remembrance" of His body and His blood. Then we make a specific covenant to "always remember him" (D&C 20:77, 79). To the Nephites, He used language similar to our modern sacramental prayers (see 3 Nephi 18:7, 11).

It is in remembrance that we fulfill the covenant. We should covenant as we partake that during the coming week, we will diligently strive to remember Christ throughout the day and let thoughts of Him influence our behavior. Think what such a simple remembrance would do for profanity, muttering unkind things on the freeway, watching pornography, and so forth.

But we should also make a special effort to remember Him during the actual ordinance, with particular effort during the sacramental hymn, the sacramental prayers, and when we partake of the bread and water.

If we *always* remember Him, as we covenant to do, then He extends this promise: we will *"always"* have His Spirit with us (D&C 20:77).

---

* For example, in the gospel accounts of the Last Supper given by Matthew, Mark, and Luke, only Luke's account has the Savior using the word *remembrance.* But in the Joseph Smith Translation, "remember" or "remembrance" is restored to both of the other two accounts.

Deepen Our Reverence

In the previous chapter, we discussed some common manifestations of irreverence among good and faithful members of the Church. If we wish to draw closer to God and to the Spirit, then we must eliminate those manifestations in our own lives. Here are some simple things we can do:

Determine that we will not speak lightly of sacred things, such as passing on jokes that demean sacred things or make light of the Savior, the Father, or the doctrines and principles of the gospel. This is what is meant by the charge to avoid light-mindedness.

A related injunction in the scriptures refers to "much laughter" or an "excess of laughter" (D&C 59:15; 88:69). This clearly is not suggesting that we go around with long faces or forced soberness. In the same verse where "much laughter" is cautioned against, the Lord asks that we do things with "cheerful hearts and countenances" and that we have "a glad heart and a cheerful countenance" (D&C 59:15).

Over the years I think I have come to better understand what concerns the Lord about "an excess" of laughter. This understanding typically has happened to me at parties or other social gatherings. The mood is light and happy. People are having a good time. Then someone tells a humorous experience or story. It is not inappropriate in any way. It is received with merriment and laughter. That reminds someone of another story. Then another and another. As that proceeds, something subtle begins to happen. The stories become a little more questionable. The laughter becomes forced and loud, even raucous. The mood undertakes an almost imperceptible change, and the original spirit of fun and fellowship becomes more strained and artificial. At those times, I have wondered if that is why the Lord has said that "much laughter" is a sin (D&C 59:15).

As for reverence in our meetings, I have learned a wonderful lesson from the example set in our General Authority and Area Seventy training sessions held before each general conference. The meetings officially start at 8:00 A.M. in an auditorium in the Church Office Building.

However, the first of the brethren start arriving as early as 7:15. Even the last one to arrive is always there by 7:30 or 7:35 at the latest.

The association among the brethren is warm and open. Many have returned from service in international areas, so there is much greeting of old friends and associates, much renewing of previous ties. But even though as many as two hundred brethren eventually gather in the room, their greeting is always done in an appropriate way—not subdued but not loud or unrestrained either. As members of the Twelve arrive, they circulate among the group, shaking hands and extending greetings.

The fellowship among the brethren continues until about 7:45. Then, and usually without any signal, the talking stops, and everyone takes a seat. For the next ten to fifteen minutes, we sit quietly and listen to the prelude music. Even with that many people, the only sound is that of the quiet and reverent music. I personally can begin to sense the pushing back of the normal press of things in my mind. It is as if something inside the heart begins to gently settle and grow more "still." Finally, the person conducting the meeting stands (often around 7:55 A.M.), and the meeting begins. The result of that quiet time becomes clearly identifiable in the meetings that follow. The spirit of revelation follows the demonstration of reverence, just as President Packer has taught.

We can choose to set a similar pattern in our lives. We can arrive ten or fifteen minutes early at the chapel. We can restrict our greetings and conversations to the foyer or the hallways and then enter the chapel, find a seat, and sit quietly until the meeting begins. We can use that time to prepare our hearts for the spiritual meal that is to follow. And when it comes time for the sacrament, we can put all other things aside and use that time in the greatest reverence to renew our covenants with the One who gave His body and His blood that we might live and return to live with Him and Heavenly Father. Priesthood leaders have a special responsibility to work to improve reverence in our meetings. This doesn't just happen. It takes careful attention and constant monitoring, but the benefits are enormous.

Temple Worship

We cannot complete a discussion of things that help us draw closer to the Lord without mentioning the role of the temple in receiving personal revelation.

The power of temple ordinances lies in the process of making and keeping covenants, just as with the sacrament. The word *endowment* is not just a temple word. We speak of a university receiving an endowment from a wealthy donor. Through the centuries brides were either given a dowry or were required to give one to the husband's family. *Dowry* comes from the same root as *endowment*. An endowment is a gift, a grant of some kind or another.

So what gift are we given when we are endowed in the temple? The scriptures are perfectly clear; we are endowed "with power from on high" (D&C 38:32). That alone should give us an indication of how the temple can help us draw closer to the Lord and create a state of inner stillness. The power spoken of is spiritual power, and that is what we hope to receive.

> *In the peace of these lovely temples, sometimes we find solutions to the serious problems of life. Under the influence of the Spirit, sometimes pure knowledge flows to us there. Temples are places of personal revelation. When I have been weighed down by a problem or a difficulty, I have gone to the house of the Lord with a prayer in my heart for answers. These answers have come in clear and unmistakable ways.*
>
> EZRA TAFT BENSON,
> *TEACHINGS OF EZRA TAFT BENSON*, 251

Therefore, attending the temple worthily so that we can participate in the ordinances thereof, especially the ordinances of endowment and sealing, is a paramount step on our way to spiritual mastery.

But there is something more to be had there than the ordinances: an inner stillness that helps us hear the still, small voice. What we need is a quiet place that will help us hear that voice. This is why we go to such great lengths to maintain a reverential and hushed environment, to use only our "temple voices." We never know when someone nearby may be striving to find answers or to feel the Spirit. Temples provide a place of outer quiet so we can achieve inner stillness.

Is our desire to draw closer to the Lord? Then note this specific promise concerning temples.

> And inasmuch as my people build a house unto me in the name of the Lord, and do not suffer any unclean thing to come into it, that it be not defiled, my glory shall rest upon it;
>
> Yea, and *my presence shall be there,* for I will come into it (D&C 97:15–16).

What better place to draw closer to Him than in His own house?

CHAPTER 29

INCREASING MY ABILITY TO RECEIVE AND RECOGNIZE REVELATION
III. CONCENTRATE AND FOCUS

"They who have sought me early shall find rest to their souls" (D&C 54:10).

The third and final lesson we can draw from our analogy has to do with making a special effort to sharpen our spiritual senses by concentrating and focusing our attention on spiritual things in order to screen out unwanted or distracting noise

In many ways, this is very similar to the idea of "drawing closer." But there are several aspects of this practice which may especially intensify our search for revelation or help us better recognize it when it comes. We shall discuss three:

- Fasting
- Simplifying our lives
- Pondering

Fasting

We discussed at some length in chapter 26 how fasting adds focus and intensity to our search for answers or solutions to our challenges. Fasting brings added power and greater readiness of heart, and so becomes an important tool in receiving and recognizing revelation. More will not be said of that here.

Simplifying Our Lives

In the Parable of the Sower, the Lord said that sometimes the seed of the gospel will not survive. This is not because the soil itself isn't good. It is because the seed gets choked out by the thick tangle of thorns (see Matthew 13). He likened that to the "cares of the world." We spent some time earlier talking about the challenge we have in modern times with the sheer complexity and busyness of our lives. In addition to the frustration and exhaustion this brings, it also becomes a source of inner noise. We can become so engrossed in doing things—even good and important things—that we miss quiet spiritual promptings. Elder Harold B. Lee told of a lesson he learned while a member of the Quorum of the Twelve:

> A few weeks ago, President [David O.] McKay related to the Twelve an interesting experience, and I asked him yesterday if I might repeat it to you this morning.
>
> He said it is a great thing to be responsive to the whisperings of the Spirit, and we know that when these whisperings come it is a gift and our privilege to have them. They come when we are relaxed and not under pressure of appointments. (I want you to mark that.) The President then took occasion to relate an experience in the life of Bishop John Wells, former member of the Presiding Bishopric.
>
> A son of Bishop Wells was killed in Emigration Canyon on a railroad track. Brother John Wells was a great detail man and prepared many of the reports we are following up now. His boy was run over by a freight train. Sister Wells was inconsolable. She mourned during the three days prior to the funeral, received no comfort at the funeral, and was in a rather serious state of mind.

One day soon after the funeral services while she was lying on her bed relaxed, still mourning, she said her son appeared to her and said, "Mother, do not mourn, do not cry. I am all right." He told her that she did not understand how the accident happened and explained that he had given the signal to the engineer to move on, and then made the usual effort to catch the railing on the freight train; but as he attempted to do so his foot caught on a root and he failed to catch the handrail, and his body fell under the train. It was clearly an accident.

Now, listen. He said that as soon as he realized that he was in another environment he tried to see his father, *but couldn't reach him. His father was so busy with the duties in his office he could not respond to his call.* Therefore he had come to his mother. He said to her, "You tell Father that all is well with me, and I want you not to mourn anymore."[1]

How much do you pray, my friends? How often? How earnestly? If you have errors in your life, have you really wrestled before the Lord? Have you yet found your deep forest of solitude? How much has your soul hungered? How deeply have your needs impressed your heart? When did you kneel before your Maker in total quiet? For what did you pray—your own soul? How long did you thus plead for recognition—all day long? And when the shadows fell, did you still raise your voice in mighty prayer, or did you satisfy yourself with some hackneyed word and phrase?

SPENCER W. KIMBALL,
FAITH PRECEDES THE MIRACLE, 211

One can only imagine the sorrow this father must have felt when he learned that he had missed out on such a sacred opportunity. What was he doing that had him so preoccupied? Was he striving to become a business tycoon? Was he out playing golf? Pursuing a college degree? None of these. It was not some frivolous endeavor he was engaged in. He was in the Presiding Bishopric. He was a

General Authority. He was busy at the office, all right, but he was busy doing the work of the Lord!

There is a great lesson in that for each of us, especially for those who carry the extra demands of priesthood leadership or other forms of Church service. Take the pressures on a bishop, for example. He must administer the ward, watch over the youth, act as a common judge, do dozens of interviews monthly, hold disciplinary councils, and keep a dozen other balls all juggling in the air at the same time that he is working full time (or more) to earn a living and trying to be a good husband and father at home.

If he is not careful, he can become so busy that inspiration and revelation are almost drowned out by the "noise" this relentless pressure creates. Unfortunately, the time set aside for personal scripture study and prayer is one of the few parts of his schedule that he completely controls, and so too often they are pushed aside or neglected entirely.

If Satan can't override the voice of the Lord by tempting us to sin, then perhaps he can get us so involved we don't have the time to do what we need to do to maintain inner quiet. Either way, he reduces our effectiveness.

It is not just in Church service we have to watch the "sound effects" of being too busy. Mothers with small children have very little discretionary time when they can "be still and know that I am God." With the rapidly changing demands of technological advancement, more and more corporations demand more and more of their employees, especially management level employees. Crash projects, urgent deadlines, or required travel away from home can take a tremendous toll on our time and thus on our spirituality.

In other cases we bring this busyness on ourselves. We over-program ourselves and our children. We sign up for too many activities, accept too many projects, seek too many opportunities, play too many games, go to too many places, try to maintain too many associations, or commit ourselves to too many obligations.

We see this tendency often in the Church as we strive to be faithful in fulfilling our callings. Elder M. Russell Ballard made this observation in a recent conference:

Occasionally we find some who become so energetic in their Church service that their lives become unbalanced. They start believing that the programs they administer are more important than the people they serve. *They complicate their service with needless frills and embellishments that occupy too much time, cost too much money, and sap too much energy.* They refuse to delegate or to allow others to grow in their respective responsibilities.[2]

The answer is, of course, to simplify, to prioritize, and in some cases, to use a well-known phrase, "Just say no!" But actually doing it may prove to be one of the real challenges in our complicated, overheated lives.

Pondering

One thing that can help us combat the noise created by very busy lives is found in several places throughout the scriptures, but it is often overlooked as a key behavior in drawing closer to the Lord. Rather than try to explain it, I would like the reader to have the same discovery experience I had some years ago as I began to notice one particular pattern in the scriptures that had to do with three words: *ponder, meditate,* and *reflect.*

In order for you to discover this principle on your own, (that is, to have your own "Aha!" experience) I would urge you to create a table on a blank sheet of paper similar to the one you see below, only allow more room to write than is shown here. (A fully completed table follows on page 347.) Then carefully study the scriptural references in the left column. For each reference try to answer four questions:

1. Who is speaking in this reference?
2. What did he say he was doing at the time? (We're looking for verbs here.)
3. What was he doing these things about? (Think of the question in this way: "They were *[insert the verb]* about what?" It will make more sense once you find the verbs.)
4. What resulted from this action?

346

Reference	Who is speaking?	What was he doing?	About what?	Result
1 Nephi 11:1				
D&C 76:15–19				
D&C 138:1–11				
JS–H 1:11–12				

From these four references we learn a marvelous thing about how to intensify and concentrate our search for more revelation. Here is what the table looks like fully completed:

Reference	Who is speaking?	What was he doing?	About what?	Result
1 Nephi 11:1	Nephi	Pondering	The words of Lehi	He was "caught away in the Spirit" and had a marvelous vision.
D&C 76:15–19	Joseph Smith, Sidney Rigdon	Meditating	The words of John	"The Lord touched the eyes of our understandings" and a marvelous revelation followed.
D&C 138:1–11	Joseph F. Smith	Pondering, reflecting	The words of Peter	"The eyes of my understanding were opened, and the Spirit of the Lord rested upon me," and he had a vision of the spirit world.
JS–H 1:11–12	Joseph Smith	Reflecting again and again	The words of James	The First Vision

We can summarize that pattern in this simple statement: *By pondering, meditating, and reflecting upon the words of the prophets* (whether as found in the scriptures or from living prophets), *we will increase our ability to receive revelation.**

To make that application to our personal lives fully clear, we need to add one additional row to our chart as follows:

Reference	Who is speaking?	What was he doing?	About what?	Result
Moroni 10:3–5[3]	Us	Pondering, meditating, reflecting	On the words of God's prophets	The eyes of our understanding will be opened and we can have the Spirit of the Lord rest upon us.

LEARNING TO HEAR

Many years ago, I had two experiences within a few months of each other that changed my perspective on hearing and taught me some lessons that apply to the receiving of revelation.

Experience #1. I had a good friend who owned his own trucking company. We had a dinner date one evening and met him down at the trucking yard. He was just finishing up as I got out and we shook hands. Then one of his employees came over. He was working on one of the big diesel tractors a few yards away. "Hey, Bill," he said. "Come listen to this engine for a minute. Something is wrong but I can't tell what."

---

* We need to point out that in three of these four cases (with the exception of Sidney Rigdon), the men involved were prophets at the time. Thus the revelations that were given to them were not personal revelations as we normally think of them. They were all destined to become scripture and influence many generations. We have already noted that in individual cases, revelation generally comes in less direct forms—inspiration, promptings, premonitions, enlightenment, and so on. Other than that distinction, however, the principle applies to us today.

Bill walked over with him and, curious, I followed. Bill leaned over the idling engine and cocked his head, listening intently. I leaned closer too. All I heard was an idling diesel engine, but Bill straightened. "It's the . . ." he said, naming a specific part. "You're going to have to replace it." I just stared at him. I had listened to the same exact sounds, but he "heard" something that missed me entirely. I learned a lesson that evening. *Even with his training, Bill had to concentrate and closely focus his attention to hear what others could not hear.*

Experience #2. I was teaching a lesson on listening to the Lord in my institute class. I decided to let the students actually practice different listening experiences. I had them close their eyes, and I took out various objects I had brought, put them up to the microphone, and used them to make different sounds. I operated a stapler, rattled a set of keys, shook a small package of pencil leads, clicked a ball-point pen, and thumped a Ping-Pong ball softly with my finger. When I asked them to identify the various sounds, they quickly recognized the sounds with which they were most familiar—the stapler, the keys, the pen. Few recognized the pencil leads and the Ping-Pong ball because they didn't hear them all the time. *The students recognized that the more we hear certain sounds, the easier it becomes to recognize them.*

Next I asked them to close their eyes, hold perfectly still, and listen to the silence. They were to identify sounds they had not noticed before. It was surprising how much sound there was in the room that had always been there, but had not been heard—the hum of the florescent lights, traffic outside the window, someone shutting a door down the hall, the rustle of clothing when someone moved. *It became obvious that when we are quiet, we hear things we haven't heard before.*

Finally, I played them about two minutes of classical music, asking them to listen carefully, then tell me everything they could about it. The first student said, "It's got some scratches in the record." Another said, "It's classical music." A boy said, "I think it's a piece by Beethoven," upon which his girlfriend, who was a music major, said, "Yes, it's the second movement from the Eroica Symphony." This illustrated perfectly an important principle: *The more we know and understand about revelation, the more we will be able to recognize it when it comes.*

Every experience with revelation, or counterfeit revelation, can teach us something if we really desire to learn. Like Bill or the music major, the more experience we have, the more our spiritual ears are sensitized to the voice of the Lord. Extended experience is how we grow in wisdom and spiritual maturity to receive and recognize revelation. As the Lord said: "They who have sought me early shall find rest to their souls" (D&C 54:10).

CHAPTER 30

WE CANNOT LIVE ON
BORROWED LIGHT

"They that are wise . . . have taken the Holy Spirit for their guide"
(D&C 45:57).

WHY IT MATTERS

We began this study by citing a statement found in the opening lines of the Doctrine and Covenants: "For verily the voice of the Lord is unto all men" (D&C 1:2). That has been the theme that has run through each chapter of this book. It is a remarkable statement. *God speaks to men!*

We noted, however, that because of the many voices of the world, learning to discern the principles and patterns of personal revelation is one of life's most important and rewarding challenges.

Why are these principles and patterns of such critical importance to us today? We get an idea from another reference to the voice of the Lord which occurs just two verses later: "And the voice of warning shall be unto all people" (v. 4).

Warning about what? The answer is found in yet a third reference to His voice a few verses later:

> Wherefore the voice of the Lord is unto the ends of the
> earth, that all that will hear may hear:

Prepare ye, prepare ye for that which is to come, for the Lord is nigh;

And the anger of the Lord is kindled, and his sword is bathed in heaven, and *it shall fall upon the inhabitants of the earth* (D&C 1:11–13).

That leads to another question. What is to come that is of such magnitude the Lord feels the necessity of speaking from heaven to warn the world? The Lord explains:

[I] will that all men shall know that *the day speedily cometh;* the hour is not yet, but is nigh at hand, *when peace shall be taken from the earth, and the devil shall have power over his own dominion* (D&C 1:35).

I think we can safely say that that day has now come. That is the day in which we now live.

PERILOUS TIMES SHALL COME

Two thousand years ago, the Apostle Paul also described our day in these words. Know "This know also, that in the last days *perilous times shall come*" (2 Timothy 3:1).

Shortly after the terrorist attacks on September 11, 2001, President Gordon B. Hinckley made the following statements in general conference:

Wonderful as this time is, it is fraught with peril. Evil is all about us. . . .

We live in a season when fierce men do terrible and despicable things. . . .[1]

I do not know what the future holds. I do not wish to sound negative, but I wish to remind you of the warnings of scripture and the teachings of the prophets. . . . The time will come when the earth will be cleansed and there will be indescribable distress.[2]

In early 2004, President Boyd K. Packer addressed the religious educators of the Church and also spoke of the day in which we live:

> The world is spiraling downward at an ever-quickening pace. I am sorry to tell you that it will not get better. . . . These are days of great spiritual danger for our youth. . . . I know of nothing in the history of the Church or in the history of the world to compare with our present circumstances. Nothing happened in Sodom and Gomorrah which exceeds in wickedness and depravity that which surrounds us now.
>
> Words of profanity, vulgarity, and blasphemy are heard everywhere. Unspeakable wickedness and perversion were once hid in dark places; now they are in the open, even accorded legal protection.
>
> At Sodom and Gomorrah these things were localized. Now they are spread across the world, and they are among us.[3]

Nothing in the history of the world or the Church that compares to our present circumstance? Those are sobering words. No wonder the Lord felt impelled to send His voice in warning.

ANXIETY OR ANTICIPATION?

There is no question but what the future is dark, frightening, grim, and perilous—sufficient to fill any rational being with considerable anxiety. It would be a distressing perspective if that was all that lay before us. But the Lord has sent comforting promises for the righteous just as He has sent troubling warnings for the wicked.

- "And it came to pass that I, Nephi, beheld *the power of the Lamb of God, that it descended upon the saints* of the church of the Lamb, and upon the covenant people of the Lord, who were scattered upon all the face of the earth; and *they were armed with righteousness and with the power of God* in great glory" (1 Nephi 14:14).

- "For the time soon cometh that the fulness of the wrath of God shall be poured out upon all the children of men; for *he will not suffer that the wicked shall destroy the righteous.* Wherefore, *he will preserve the righteous by his power.* . . . Wherefore, *the righteous need not fear*" (1 Nephi 22:16–17).
- "The *Lord shall have power over his saints,* and shall reign in their midst" (D&C 1:36). (Note that this verse immediately follows the one that says that Satan shall have power over his dominion. Happily, so shall the Lord.)
- "And it shall be called the New Jerusalem, a land of *peace,* a city of *refuge,* a place of *safety* for the saints of the Most High God; And the glory of the Lord shall be there, and the terror of the Lord also shall be there, insomuch that *the wicked will not come unto it*" (D&C 45:66–67).
- "The gathering together upon the land of Zion, and upon her stakes, [will] be for a *defense,* and for a *refuge from the storm, and from wrath* when it shall be poured out without mixture upon the whole earth" (D&C 115:6).

Here is another set of promises—wonderful, comforting promises. The Lord will not abandon His people. The righteous shall be preserved. The power of God shall be sent down in their behalf. Jesus will reign in our midst. There will be peace, safety, defense, and refuge.

The contrast between these two scenarios is dramatic. To use a rather inadequate metaphor, it is as though we have two theaters before us. In the first is playing "War, Blood, Disaster, Wickedness, and Terror." In the second we are invited to see "Peace, Safety, Defense, and Refuge." That being the case, it is only natural that we should ask: *How do we get tickets for Theater II?*

It should not surprise us to know that the Father and the Son have given us a clear answer. Nor should it surprise us that the answer has much to do with personal revelation.

354

A MIDDLE-EASTERN WEDDING SUPPER

From the pen of the same man who gave us the beautiful description of shepherds in the Holy Land (see Chapter 1), comes the following description of a typical wedding of earlier times:

> Oriental [i.e., Middle Eastern] marriages usually take place in the evening. . . .
>
> During the day the bride is conducted to the house of her future husband, and she is there assisted by her attendants in putting on the marriage robes and jewelry. During the evening, the women who have been invited congregate in the room where the bride sits in silence, and spend the time commenting on her appearance, complimenting the relatives, discussing various family matters, and partaking of sweetmeats and similar refreshments.
>
> As the hours drag on their topics of conversation become exhausted, and some of them grow tired and fall asleep. There is nothing more to be done, and everything is in readiness for the reception of the bridegroom. . . .
>
> The bridegroom meanwhile is absent spending the day at the house of one of his relatives. There, soon after sunset, . . . his male friends begin to assemble, . . . to spend the evening with the bridegroom and then escort him home. The time is occupied with light refreshments, general conversation and the recitation of poetry in praise of the two families chiefly concerned and of the bridegroom in particular. After all have been courteously welcomed and their congratulations received, the bridegroom, about eleven o'clock, intimates his wish to set out. Flaming torches are then held aloft by special bearers, lit candles [or small hand lamps] are handed at the door to each visitor as he goes out, and the procession sweeps slowly along towards the house where the bride and her female attendants are waiting.

355

A great crowd has meanwhile assembled on the balconies, garden-walls, and flat roofs of the houses on each side of the road. . . . The bridegroom is the centre of interest. Voices are heard whispering, "There he is! There he is!" From time to time women raise their voices in the peculiar shrill, wavering shriek by which joy is expressed at marriages and other times of family and public rejoicing. The sound is heard at a great distance, and is repeated by other voices in advance of the procession, and thus intimation is given of the approach half an hour or more before the marriage escort arrives. . . . As the house is approached the excitement increases, the bridegroom's pace is quickened, and the alarm is raised in louder tones and more repeatedly, *"He is coming! He is coming!"*

Before he arrives, the maidens in waiting come forth with lamps and candles a short distance to light up the entrance, and do honour to the bridegroom and the group of relatives and intimate friends around him. These pass into the final rejoicing and the marriage supper; the others who have discharged their duty in accompanying him to the door, immediately disperse, and the door is shut.[4]

FIVE WHO WERE WISE

This lovely and vivid imagery adds great meaning and significance to the parable of the ten virgins found in Matthew 25. Before looking at the parable itself, however, we should take note of what circumstances drew this parable forth from the Master.

Just days before His crucifixion, Jesus was on the Temple Mount in Jerusalem with His disciples. As they passed along, some of them commented on the magnificent beauty of the edifice. In what must have come as a stunning announcement, Jesus declared that the day would come when "there shall not be left here one stone upon another" (Matthew 24:2). They left the city and climbed the Mount of Olives, which stands on the east of the Temple Mount. As they sat down to rest for a while, the disciples, clearly troubled, asked: "Tell us, when shall these things be? and what shall be the sign of thy coming, and of the end of the world?" (v. 3; see also JS–M 1:3–4).

What followed has become known as the Olivet Discourse wherein Jesus gave in great detail the answer to their question. It was at the end of that prophetic perspective that he said: "And then, at that day, *before the Son of Man comes,* the kingdom of heaven shall be likened unto ten virgins" (JST–Matthew 25:1).

The imagery shared by Mackie above adds much to our understanding of this parable in Matthew 25. It is well known, so only the key elements will be noted here.

- There were ten virgins who took their lamps and went forth to meet the bridegroom, who is Jesus (v. 1).*
- Five of these were wise, and five were foolish (v. 2). Since all had lamps and all had some oil, the distinction between the wise and foolish was that the wise had bought an additional supply of oil. The foolishness of the five lay in the fact that the small hand lamps typically used by the people on such occasions held only a small amount of olive oil, enough to burn for not more than an hour or so. In light of the marriage customs, and knowing that often the arrival of the bridegroom could be delayed until nearly midnight, it was foolish for the five to have brought nothing extra.
- At midnight, when the cry went up that the bridegroom was coming, all ten arose and trimmed their lamps (v. 7). "Trimming" consisted of making sure the wick was laid properly in the oil and that there was sufficient oil in the lamp itself.
- It was then that the five foolish saw that their lamps had "gone out" and asked the others to share their oil with them (v. 8). The

---

* President Spencer W. Kimball said that the ten virgins represented members of the Church (see *Teachings of Spencer W. Kimball,* 183).

wise said that if they did that, there wouldn't be enough for their own lamps (v. 9).

- While the five foolish were gone to try to buy oil, the bridegroom came, "and *they that were ready* went in with him to the marriage: and the door was shut" (v. 10).

- When the five others finally returned, they begged to have the door opened so they could enter, but the bridegroom said, "I know you not," and they were excluded from the marriage supper (vv. 11–13).*

THE OIL OF THE SPIRIT

A little reflection shows that the key element in the parable is the oil. The five wise had extra oil, the five foolish did not. So what does the oil represent? All ten of the virgins had lamps; all ten had oil, but only half had the foresight to bring extra. What are we to learn from this? The answer is given in modern revelation.

> At that day, when I shall come in my glory, shall the parable be fulfilled which I spake concerning the ten virgins.
>
> For they that are wise and *have received the truth, and have taken the Holy Spirit for their guide,* and have not been deceived—verily I say unto you, they shall not be hewn down and cast into the fire, but shall abide the day (D&C 45:56–57).

There it is, clearly defined. The oil represents the Holy Spirit and the truth that He brings. It is an appropriate symbol, for the oil in the lamps provided light. The Holy Ghost brings us light and truth.

Some commentators, not understanding this deeper meaning, have suggested the five wise virgins were not very "Christian" because of their unwillingness to share what they had. But President Kimball explains why this could not be.

---

* We learn from other scriptures that the "marriage supper" represents the Second Coming of Christ and the establishment of the Kingdom of God upon the earth (see for example Revelation 19:7–16; D&C 58:11; 88:92–94).

The foolish asked the others to share their oil, but *spiritual preparedness* cannot be shared in an instant. . . . This was not selfishness or unkindness. The kind of oil that is needed to illuminate the way and light up the darkness is not shareable. How can one share obedience to the principle of tithing; a mind at peace from righteous living; an accumulation of knowledge? How can one share faith or testimony? How can one share attitudes or chastity, or the experience of a mission? How can one share temple privileges? Each must obtain that kind of oil for himself.

The foolish virgins were not averse to buying oil. They knew they should have oil. They merely procrastinated, not knowing when the bridegroom would come.[5]

Note the two emphasized words in the first line. President Kimball compares the oil to spiritual preparedness. That is our answer. How does the Lord prepare us for the perilous times in which we live? How do we get tickets for Theater II? In one word, it comes down to *revelation.*

President Kimball further explored the implications and applications of the parable for us today:

In the parable, oil can be purchased at the market. In our lives the oil of preparedness is accumulated drop by drop in righteous living. Attendance at sacrament meetings adds oil to our lamps, drop by drop over the years. Fasting, family prayer, home teaching, control of bodily appetites, preaching the gospel, studying the scriptures—each act of dedication and obedience is a drop added to our store. Deeds of kindness, payment of offerings and tithes, chaste thoughts and actions, marriage in the covenant for eternity—these, too, contribute importantly to the oil with which we can at midnight refuel our exhausted lamps.

Midnight is so late for those who have procrastinated.[6]

BORROWED LIGHT IS NOT ENOUGH

I can think of no better way to emphasize the importance of personal revelation in our lives in the hour and day of the world in which we live, than to cite some counsel from Elder Harold B. Lee.

> Years ago when I served as a missionary, we had a visit from Dr. James E. Talmage of the Council of the Twelve. . . .
>
> On one occasion he said to us, "I want to tell you missionaries something. The day of sacrifice is not past! The time will come, yet, when many Saints and even Apostles will yet lose their lives in defense of the truth!"
>
> I've had occasion many times since that remark was made to remember those words, and I've come to see the reality of it. There's a testing for every human soul. And there's a test every year, every month in the year, for the Saints of the Most High God. And their blessing and progress will depend only upon whether or not they pass the test.
>
> President Heber C. Kimball, speaking about this matter, said this:
>
> "We think we are secure here in the chambers of the everlasting hills, where we can close those few doors of the canyons against mobs and persecutors, the wicked and the vile, who have always beset us with violence and robbery, but I want to say to you, my brethren, the time is coming when we will be mixed up in these now peaceful valleys to that extent that it will be difficult to tell the face of a Saint from the face of an enemy to the people of God. [Mark well that statement!] Then, brethren, look out for the great sieve, for there will be a great sifting time, and many will fall; for I say unto you there is a *test*, a TEST, a TEST coming, and who will be able to stand? . . .
>
> "Let me say to you, that many of you will see the time

when you will have all the trouble, trial and persecution that
you can stand, and plenty of opportunities to show that you
are true to God and his work. This Church has before it
many close places through which it will have to pass before
the work of God is crowned with victory. To meet the difficulties that are coming, *it will be necessary for you to have a
knowledge of the truth of the work for yourselves. The difficulties
will be of such a character that the man or woman who does not
possess this personal knowledge or witness will fall.* If you have
not got the testimony, live right and call upon the Lord and
cease not till you obtain it. If you do not you will not stand.
Remember these sayings, for many of you will live to see
them fulfilled. *The time will come when no man nor woman
will be able to endure on borrowed light.* Each will have to be
guided by the light within himself."[7]

The reference to borrowed light is, of course, a reference to the
parable of the ten virgins. Elder Lee went on:

*This is the time of which President Kimball spoke, when
each will have to stand on his own feet, and no man will be able
to exist and stand on borrowed light. Each, for himself, must
have an unshakable testimony of the divinity of this work if he
is to stand in this day!*[8]

This reason alone is reason enough to make a study of revelation
relevant to every person on earth. No wonder His voice is unto all men.
There is some urgency, then, in learning to (1) hear the voice of the
Lord; (2) recognize it for what it is; and (3) respond appropriately to it.

God has solemnly warned us of coming judgments and we should
take careful heed of such warnings. But we know Him as our Heavenly
Father. He loves us. He cares for us. He wants to bless us with all the
richness that lies at His command. Here, in His own words, is the Lord's
promise to the faithful:

For thus saith the Lord—I, the Lord, am merciful and gracious unto those who fear me, and *delight* to honor those who serve me in righteousness and in truth unto the end.

Great shall be their reward and eternal shall be their glory.

And *to them will I reveal* all mysteries, yea, all the hidden mysteries of my kingdom from days of old, and for ages to come, will I make known unto them the good pleasure of my will concerning all things pertaining to my kingdom.

Yea, even the wonders of eternity shall they know, and things to come will I show them, even the things of many generations. . . .

For by my Spirit will I enlighten them, and by my power will I make known unto them the secrets of my will—yea, even those things which eye has not seen, nor ear heard, nor yet entered into the heart of man (D&C 76:5–8, 10).

NOTES

Note: All emphasis in scriptures in this work has been added by the author.

CHAPTER 1

THE VOICE OF THE LORD

    1. George M. Mackie, *Bible Manners and Customs*, 33–34.

    2. James E. Faust, "The Voice of the Spirit," 1–2.

    3. Boyd K. Packer, "'And They Knew It Not,'" 5; emphasis added.

    4. Brigham Young, *Discourses of Brigham Young*, 32.

    5. Packer, "'And They Knew It Not,'" 5.

CHAPTER 2

WHAT IS REVELATION AND WHY IS IT SO IMPORTANT?

    1. *Random House Dictionary*, s.v., *re-* and *veil*.

    2. James E. Talmage, *Articles of Faith*, 268.

    3. Joseph Smith, *Teachings of the Prophet Joseph Smith*, 292; emphasis added.

    4. Ibid., 160.

    5. Ibid., 191.

6. Bruce R. McConkie, *The Promised Messiah*, 14.

7. Spencer W. Kimball, *Teachings of Spencer W. Kimball*, 443.

8. Joseph F. Smith, *Gospel Doctrine*, 104–5.

CHAPTER 3

What Makes Revelation Possible?

1. Joseph Smith, *History of the Church*, 4:42; emphasis added.

2. Parley P. Pratt, *Key to the Science of Theology*, 61.

CHAPTER 4

How Does Revelation Come?

1. Boyd K. Packer, *The Holy Temple*, 107.

2. Packer, *Memorable Stories and Parables by Boyd K. Packer*, 57–59; emphasis in original.

CHAPTER 5

What Form Does Revelation Take?

The More Direct Forms

1. Neal A. Maxwell, *Wherefore, Ye Must Press Forward*, 120.

2. Dallin H. Oaks, *The Lord's Way*, 22–23; emphasis in original.

3. LDS Bible Dictionary, "Light of Christ," 725; emphasis added.

4. Brigham Young, *Discourses of Brigham Young*, 10.

5. Joseph Fielding Smith, *Doctrines of Salvation*, 1:180.

6. Wilford Woodruff, *The Discourses of Wilford Woodruff*, 287.

7. Oaks, "The Aaronic Priesthood and the Sacrament," 39.

8. Harold B. Lee, *Stand Ye in Holy Places*, 139.

9. Oaks, *The Lord's Way*, 31.

CHAPTER 6

How Does the Lord Speak to Us?

I. The Still Small Voice

1. Boyd K. Packer, "The Candle of the Lord," 53.

2. Packer, "Personal Revelation: The Gift, the Test, and the Promise," 60; emphasis in original.

CHAPTER 8

How Does Revelation Typically Come?

I. As Thoughts

1. Thomas S. Monson, *Live the Good Life*, 61–62; emphasis added.
2. Harold B. Lee, "Admonitions for the Priesthood of God," 104.
3. Truman G. Madsen, *Defender of the Faith: The B.H. Roberts Story*, 311–12; emphasis added.
4. Lee, *Stand Ye in Holy Places*, 142, 143.
5. Orson F. Whitney, *Life of Heber C. Kimball*, 124.
6. María Rósinkarsdóttir and DeAnne Walker, "My Dream Came True," 40.
7. *Church News*, December 18, 2004, Z10.
8. Lee, *Teachings of Harold B. Lee*, 417.

CHAPTER 9

How Does Revelation Typically Come?

II. As Enlightenment

1. Topical Guide, "Jesus Christ: Light of the World," 249.
2. Joseph Smith, *Teachings of the Prophet Joseph Smith*, 151; emphasis added.
3. Stephen L Richards, in Conference Report, April 1950, 162.
4. Dallin H. Oaks, *With Full Purpose of Heart*, 37–38; emphasis in original.
5. Again, this is only one of many references on this subject. See Topical Guide, "Holy Ghost," "Source of Testimony."
6. Neal A. Maxwell, *Not My Will, but Thine*, 124.

CHAPTER 10

How Does Revelation Typically Come?

III. As Feelings

1. Boyd K. Packer, "Personal Revelation: The Gift, the Test, and the Promise," 61.
2. Packer, "The Candle of the Lord," 56.
3. *Church History in the Fulness of Times*, 53.
4. Packer, "Personal Revelation: The Gift, the Test, and the Promise," 77.

5. Dallin H. Oaks, "Teaching and Learning by the Spirit," 13.

6. *Random House Dictionary,* s.v., forget.

7. In Stewart E. Glazier and Robert S. Clark, *Journal of the Trail,* 62.

8. Ibid.; emphasis added.

CHAPTER 11

How Does Revelation Typically Come?

IV. As Warnings

1. Wilford Woodruff, *Discourses of Wilford Woodruff,* 295–96.

2. Terry J. Moyer, "A Voice in the Fog," 12–15.

3. Milton R. Hunter, "Directed by the Holy Spirit," 4–5.

4. Dallin H. Oaks, "Where Will It Lead?" 3–4.

CHAPTER 12

How Does Revelation Typically Come?

V. As Divine Intervention

1. Joseph F. Smith, *Gospel Doctrine,* 52; emphasis added.

2. Parley P. Pratt, *Autobiography of Parley P. Pratt,* 134–35.

3. In Theda Bassett, *Grandpa Neibaur Was a Pioneer,* and additional oral family history sources.

4. Kathy Truman, "The Power of Two Testimonies," in *Liahona,* February 2008.

5. Wallace D. Montague, "I Was a Political Prisoner of Hitler," 90–91.

6. Joseph Fielding Smith, *Life of Joseph F. Smith,* 154–55.

7. "How Gentle God's Commands," *Hymns,* no. 125; emphasis added.

8. Smith, *Gospel Doctrine,* 52.

CHAPTER 13

First Principle:

God Determines All Aspects of Revelation

1. As cited in *Millennial Star* 40:772-73; also in Andrew Jenson, *Historical Record 7* (October 1888): 621.

2. Boyd K. Packer, "The Quest for Spiritual Knowledge," 4.

3. Packer, "The Candle of the Lord," 53.

CHAPTER 14

SECOND PRINCIPLE:

WE MUST ACTIVELY SEEK REVELATION

1. "Know This, That Every Soul Is Free," *Hymns,* no. 240.
2. LDS Bible Dictionary, "Faith," 670.
3. David O. McKay, *Man May Know for Himself,* 231.
4. Boyd K. Packer, *Eternal Love,* 11; emphasis added.

CHAPTER 15

THIRD PRINCIPLE:

MOST REVELATION COMES INCREMENTALLY

1. David A. Bednar, "Line upon Line, Precept upon Precept," 2–3.
2. Joseph Fielding Smith, *Take Heed to Yourselves,* 89; emphasis added.
3. Neal A. Maxwell, *The Promise of Discipleship,* 88–89; emphasis in original.
4. Maxwell, *The Promise of Discipleship,* 99–100; emphasis added.
5. "Lead, Kindly Light," *Hymns,* no. 97.
6. Joseph F. Smith, *Gospel Doctrine,* 68.

CHAPTER 16

DIVINE TUTORIALS

1. Neal A. Maxwell, *Even As I Am,* 42; emphasis added.
2. The story of Joseph is found in Genesis 37, 39–50.
3. Joseph Smith, *Teachings of the Prophet Joseph Smith,* 304.
4. Each of these examples is briefly discussed in *Church History in the Fulness of Times,* 113–14.
5. *Church History in the Fulness of Times,* 99.
6. *Church History in the Fulness of Times,* 199; Leonard J. Arrington, *Brigham Young,* 65; Arnold K. Garr and Clark V. Johnson, eds., *Regional Studies in Latter-day Saint History: Missouri,* 17.
7. C. S. Lewis, *Mere Christianity,* in Neal A. Maxwell, *If Thou Endure It Well,* 48.

CHAPTER 17

FOURTH PRINCIPLE:

WE ARE TO DEVELOP SPIRITUAL SELF-RELIANCE

1. James E. Faust, in James P. Bell and James E. Faust, *In the Strength of the Lord,* 407.

2. Ibid., 333–34, 401.

3. Harold B. Lee, in Conference Report, April 1970, 55.

4. See heading to Doctrine and Covenants 60.

5. Bruce R. McConkie, "Agency or Inspiration—Which?" 108-9.

6. Boyd K. Packer, "Revelation in a Changing World," 14.

7. Dallin H. Oaks, *The Lord's Way,* 37–38.

8. William E. Berrett, as quoted in Joseph Fielding McConkie and Robert L. Millet, *The Holy Ghost,* 29–31; cited by Oaks, "Teaching and Learning by the Spirit," 14.

9. Joseph Smith, *Teachings of the Prophet Joseph Smith,* 22.

10. Oaks, "Scripture Reading and Revelation," 8.

11. McConkie, *Doctrines of the Restoration,* 243.

12. Packer, "Solving Emotional Problems in the Lord's Own Way," 91; emphasis in original.

13. Henry B. Eyring, "Gifts of the Spirit for Hard Times," 23–24.

CHAPTER 18

FIFTH PRINCIPLE:

GOD'S HOUSE IS A HOUSE OF ORDER

1. Joseph F. Smith, *Gospel Doctrine,* 149.

2. Harold B. Lee, in Conference Report, April 1970, 55–56.

3. M. Russell Ballard, "Strength in Counsel," 76; emphasis added.

4. Gordon B. Hinckley, "God Is at the Helm," 53.

5. Joseph Fielding Smith, *Doctrines of Salvation,* 1:287.

6. See LDS Bible Dictionary, "Ark of the Covenant," 613–14.

7. David O. McKay, *Pathways to Happiness,* 86.

8. Boyd K. Packer, "What Every Elder Should Know—and Every Sister as Well," 8.

9. Dallin H. Oaks, *The Lord's Way,* 67–69; emphasis in original.

CHAPTER 19

SIXTH PRINCIPLE:

TRUE REVELATION ALWAYS EDIFIES

1. *Random House Dictionary,* s.v., edify, edifice, edification.

2. Joseph Smith, "Try the Spirits," an editorial written for the *Times and Seasons,* April 1, 1842, in Smith, *History of the Church,* 4:580; emphasis added.

3. Smith, *History of the Church,* 4:576; emphasis added.

4. *Random House Dictionary,* s.v., decorum.

5. Smith, *History of the Church,* 4:572; emphasis added.

6. Spencer W. Kimball, *Teachings of Spencer W. Kimball,* 458.

CHAPTER 20

ADDITIONAL PRINCIPLES THAT GOVERN THE

GIVING AND RECEIVING OF REVELATION

1. Spencer W. Kimball, *Teachings of Spencer W. Kimball,* 458; emphasis in original.

2. C. S. Lewis, "The Screwtape Letters," in *The Best of C. S. Lewis,* 54; emphasis added.

3. Kimball, *Faith Precedes the Miracle,* 242–43; emphasis added.

4. Dallin H. Oaks, "Teaching and Learning by the Spirit," 14.

5. M. Russell Ballard, "Respond to the Prompting of the Spirit," 2–3.

6. Thomas S. Monson, *Inspiring Experiences That Build Faith,* 18; emphasis in original.

CHAPTER 21

ARE THERE COUNTERFEIT FORMS OF REVELATION?

1. Boyd K. Packer, "Reverence Invites Revelation," 21.

2. Joseph Smith, *History of the Church,* 1:105.

3. Ibid., 1:109–10; emphasis added.

4. Parley P. Pratt, *Autobiography of Parley P. Pratt,* 61–62.

5. Smith, *History of the Church,* 4:571.

6. *Random House Dictionary,* s.v., counter, counterfeit.

7. Packer, "Personal Revelation: The Gift, the Test, and the Promise," 61.

8. Carlfred Broderick, *One Flesh, One Heart,* 21.

9. Ibid.; emphasis in original.

10. Harold B. Lee, "Admonitions for the Priesthood of God," 105.

11. Smith, *History of the Church,* 4:540.

12. James E. Faust, "The Forces That Will Save Us," 6.

CHAPTER 22

HOW CAN WE TELL THE DIFFERENCE BETWEEN TRUE AND COUNTERFEIT FORMS OF REVELATION?

1. Joseph Smith, *History of the Church,* 4:573–74.

CHAPTER 23

WHAT IS THE ROLE OF FAITH IN LEARNING TO RECEIVE AND RECOGNIZE REVELATION?

1. David A. Bednar, "Seek Learning by Faith," 61; emphasis added.

2. Ibid.; emphasis in original.

3. James Hasting, *Dictionary of the Bible,* revised ed., s.v., "heart," 369.

4. M. Russell Ballard, *Our Search for Happiness,* 71–72.

5. Bednar, "Seek Learning by Faith," 61; emphasis added.

6. Bednar, "Seek Learning by Faith," 64; emphasis added.

7. LDS Bible Dictionary, "Faith," 670.

8. Joseph Smith, *Teachings of the Prophet Joseph Smith,* 148.

9. Smith, *History of the Church,* 3:379.

10. Bednar, "Seek Learning by Faith," 3.

11. Boyd K. Packer, "Personal Revelation: The Gift, the Test, and the Promise," 59; emphasis added.

CHAPTER 24

WHAT ARE THE KEY STEPS IN LEARNING BY FAITH AND INCREASING OUR ABILITY TO RECEIVE REVELATION?

1. David A. Bednar, "Seek Learning by Faith," 6.

CHAPTER 25

HOW DO I IMPLEMENT THE KEY STEPS IN MY LIFE?

1. Erastus Snow, in Neal A. Maxwell, *That Ye May Believe,* 137.

2. Joseph Smith, *Lectures on Faith,* 3:2–5; emphasis in original.

CHAPTER 26
WHY ISN'T GOD ANSWERING ME?

1. Dallin H. Oaks, *The Lord's Way*, 36.
2. Richard G. Scott, "Using the Supernal Gift of Prayer," 10.
3. Boyd K. Packer, "Solving Emotional Problems in the Lord's Own Way," 91–92.
4. "How Firm a Foundation," *Hymns*, no. 85.
5. *Random House Dictionary*, s.v., "importune."
6. Spencer W. Kimball, *Teachings of Spencer W. Kimball*, 123–24.

CHAPTER 27
INCREASING MY ABILITY TO RECEIVE AND RECOGNIZE REVELATION
I. SOURCES OF INNER NOISE

1. Adam Clarke, *Clarke's Commentary*, 1:369.
2. Ezra Taft Benson, *The Teachings of Ezra Taft Benson*, 435.
3. Ibid.
4. B. H. Roberts, *Defense of the Faith and the Saints*, 1:167.
5. Boyd K. Packer, *The Things of the Soul*, 91.
6. Packer, "The Quest for Spiritual Knowledge," 4; emphasis added.
7. Packer, "Reverence Invites Revelation," 21.
8. Ibid., 22; emphasis in original.

CHAPTER 28
INCREASING MY ABILITY TO RECEIVE AND RECOGNIZE REVELATION
II. REDUCE THE INNER NOISE AND DRAW CLOSER

1. George Q. Cannon, *Millennial Star*, April 1894, 260–61.
2. Bruce R. McConkie, *Church News*, January 24, 1976, 4.
3. *Random House Dictionary*, s.v. damn, 504.
4. Bryant S. Hinckley, *Sermons and Missionary Services of Melvin J. Ballard*, 150–51; emphasis added.

CHAPTER 29
INCREASING MY ABILITY TO RECEIVE AND RECOGNIZE REVELATION
III. CONCENTRATE AND FOCUS

1. Harold B. Lee, *Teachings of Harold B. Lee*, 414–15; emphasis in original.

2. M. Russell Ballard, "O Be Wise," 18; emphasis added.

3. Actually we could put any one of dozens of references here. Here are a few: 3 Nephi 17:3; 2 Nephi 32:3; D&C 88:62–63.

CHAPTER 30
WE CANNOT LIVE ON BORROWED LIGHT

1. Gordon B. Hinckley, "Living in the Fulness of Times," 5, 6.

2. Hinckley, "The Times in Which We Live," 73–74.

3. Boyd K. Packer, "The One Pure Defense," 4.

4. George M. Mackie, *Bible Manners and Customs,* 123–26.

5. Spencer W. Kimball, *Faith Precedes the Miracle,* 255–56; emphasis added.

6. Ibid., 256.

7. Harold B. Lee, *Teachings of Harold B. Lee,* 143–44; emphasis added.

8. Ibid., 144; emphasis added.

BIBLIOGRAPHY

Arrington, Leonard J. *Brigham Young: American Moses.* New York: Knopf, 1985.

Ballard, M. Russell. "O Be Wise." *Ensign,* November 2006, 17–20.

———. *Our Search for Happiness.* Salt Lake City: Deseret Book, 1993.

———. "Restored Truth." *Ensign,* November 1994, 65–68.

———. "Respond to the Prompting of the Spirit." CES Evening with a General Authority, January 8, 1988.

———. "Strength in Counsel." *Ensign,* November 1993, 76–78.

———. *When Thou Art Converted: Continuing Our Search for Happiness.* Salt Lake City: Deseret Book, 2001.

Bassett, Theda. *Grandpa Neibaur Was a Pioneer.* Salt Lake City: Artistic Printing Co., 1988.

Bednar, David A. Address to Religious Educators. February 3, 2006.

———. "Line upon Line, Precept upon Precept." Ricks College Devotional Address, September 11, 2001.

———. "Seek Learning by Faith." *Ensign,* September 2007, 60–68.

———. Worldwide Leadership Training Meeting. February 11, 2006.

Bell, James P., and James E. Faust. *In the Strength of the Lord.* Salt Lake City: Deseret Book, 1999.

Benson, Ezra Taft. *Come unto Christ.* Salt Lake City: Deseret Book, 1983.

———. *God, Family, Country: Our Three Great Loyalties.* Salt Lake City: Deseret Book, 1974.

———. "Pray Always." *Ensign,* February 1990, 2–5.

———. *The Teachings of Ezra Taft Benson.* Salt Lake City: Bookcraft, 1988.

Broderick, Carlfred. *One Flesh, One Heart.* Salt Lake City: Deseret Book, 1986.

Brown, Hugh B. "An Eternal Quest: Freedom of the Mind." In *Dialogue: A Journal of Mormon Thought* 17 (Spring 1984): 76–83.

Cannon, George Q. "Discourse." *Millennial Star,* April 1894, 241–45, 257–61.

Church History in the Fulness of Times: The History of The Church of Jesus Christ of Latter-day Saints. 2d ed. Salt Lake City: The Church of Jesus Christ of Latter-day Saints, 2003.

Church News. Salt Lake City: Deseret News, 1931–.

Clark, J. Reuben. *Behold the Lamb of God: Selections from the Sermons and Writings, Published and Unpublished, of J. Reuben Clark, Jr., on the Life of the Savior.* Salt Lake City: Deseret Book, 1962.

Clark, James R, comp. *Messages of the First Presidency of The Church of Jesus Christ of Latter-day Saints, 1833–1964.* Salt Lake City: Bookcraft, 1965–75.

Clarke, Adam. *The Holy Bible Containing the Old and New Testaments with a Commentary and Critical Notes.* 6 vols. Nashville: Abingdon Press, n.d.

Eyring, Henry B. "As a Child." *Ensign,* May 2006. 14–17.

———. "Gifts of the Spirit for Hard Times." *Ensign,* June 2007, 18–24.

———. "A Life Founded in Light and Truth." BYU Devotional, August 15, 2000.

———. "Remembrance and Gratitude." *Ensign,* November 1989, 11–13.

Farrar, Frederic W. *The Life and Work of St. Paul.* 2 vols. London: Cassell, Petter, Galphin, and Co., 1879–80.

Faust, James E. "Communion with the Holy Spirit." *Ensign,* March 2002, 3–7.

———. *Finding Light in a Dark World.* Salt Lake City: Deseret Book, 1995.

———. "The Forces That Will Save Us." *Ensign,* January 2007, 4–9.

———. "The Great Imitator." *Ensign,* November 1987, 33–36

———. "The Voice of the Spirit." CES Fireside, September 5, 1993.

First Presidency, "A Warning Voice." *Improvement Era,* September 1913, 1148–49.

Garr, Arnold K., and Clark V. Johnson, eds. *Regional Studies in Latter-day Saint History: Missouri.* Provo, Utah: Department of Church History and Doctrine, 1994.

Glazier, Stewart E., and Robert S. Clark. *Journal of the Trail.* Salt Lake City: N.p., 1996.

Grant, Heber J. *Gospel Standards: Selections from the Sermons and Writings of Heber J. Grant.* Salt Lake City: Improvement Era, 1941.

Haight, David B. *A Light unto the World.* Salt Lake City: Deseret Book, 1997.

Hasting, James. *Dictionary of the Bible.* Rev. ed. New York: Charles Scribner's Sons, 1963.

Hinckley, Bryant S. *Sermons and Missionary Services of Melvin J. Ballard.* Salt Lake City: Deseret Book, 1949.

Hinckley, Gordon B. "God Is at the Helm." *Ensign,* May 1994, 53–54, 59–60.

———. "Living in the Fulness of Times." *Ensign,* November 2001, 4–6.

———. *The Teachings of Gordon B. Hinckley.* Salt Lake City: Deseret Book, 1997.

———. "The Times in Which We Live." *Ensign,* November 2001, 72–74.

———. *Way to Be! 9 Ways to Be Happy and Make Something of Your Life.* New York: Simon & Schuster, 2002.

Holland, Jeffrey R. "'Cast Not Away Therefore Your Confidence.'" *Ensign,* March 2000, 7–11.

Hunter, Howard W. *The Teachings of Howard W. Hunter.* Salt Lake City: Bookcraft, 1997.

Hunter, Milton R. "Directed by the Holy Spirit." *New Era,* September 1973, 4–5.

Hymns of The Church of Jesus Christ of Latter-day Saints. Salt Lake City: The Church of Jesus Christ of Latter-day Saints, 1985.

Ivins, Anthony W. In Conference Report, April 1934, 95–102.

Jenson, Andrew, comp. *Historical Record.* 9 vols. Salt Lake City: Andrew Jenson, 1892–90.

Kimball, Spencer W. In Conference Report, October 1966, 21–26.

———. *Faith Precedes the Miracle.* Salt Lake City: Deseret Book, 1972.

———. Munich Germany Area Conference. 1973.

————. "Revelation: The Word of the Lord to His Prophets." *Ensign,* May 1977, 76–78.

————. *The Teachings of Spencer W. Kimball.* Edited by Edward L. Kimball. Salt Lake City: Deseret Book, 1982.

LDS Bible Dictionary. Salt Lake City: The Church of Jesus Christ of Latter-day Saints, 1979.

Lee, Harold B. "Admonitions for the Priesthood of God." *Ensign,* January 1973, 104–8.

————. In Conference Report, April 1970, 54–57.

————. *Stand Ye in Holy Places.* Salt Lake City: Deseret Book, 1976.

————. "Teach the Gospel of Salvation." *Ensign,* January 1973, 60–63.

————. *The Teachings of Harold B. Lee.* Edited by Clyde J. Williams. Salt Lake City: Bookcraft, 1996.

————. *Ye Are the Light of the World.* Salt Lake City: Deseret Book, 1974.

Lewis, C. S. *The Great Divorce.* San Francisco: HarperSanFrancisco, 2001.

————. *Mere Christianity.* New York: Macmillan Company, 1960. Quoted in Neal A. Maxwell, *If Thou Endure It Well,* 48.

————. *The Problem of Pain.* San Francisco: HarperSanFrancisco, 2001.

————. "The Screwtape Letters." In *The Best of C. S. Lewis.* Washington, D.C.: Canon Press, 1969.

Ludlow, Daniel H. *Latter-day Prophets Speak: Selections from the Sermons and Writings of the Presidents of The Church of Jesus Christ of Latter-day Saints.* Salt Lake City: Bookcraft, 1948.

Mackie, George M. *Bible Manners and Customs.* New York: Fleming H. Revell Company, 1984.

Madsen, Truman G. *Defender of the Faith: The B. H. Roberts Story.* Salt Lake City: Bookcraft, 1980.

Maxwell, Neal A. CES Symposium. 1991.

————. *Even As I Am.* Salt Lake City: Deseret Book, 1982.

————. *If Thou Endure It Well.* Salt Lake City: Bookcraft, 1996.

————. "'Lest Ye Be Wearied and Faint in Your Minds.'" *Ensign,* May 1991, 88–91.

————. *Meek and Lowly.* Salt Lake City: Deseret Book, 1987.

————. *The Neal A. Maxwell Quote Book.* Edited by Cory H. Maxwell. Salt Lake City: Bookcraft, 1997.

————. *Not My Will, but Thine.* Salt Lake City: Bookcraft, 1988.

————. "Patience." *Ensign,* October 1980, 28–31.

———. *The Promise of Discipleship.* Salt Lake City: Deseret Book, 2001.

———. *That Ye May Believe.* Salt Lake City: Bookcraft, 1992.

———. *Wherefore, Ye Must Press Forward.* Salt Lake City: Deseret Book, 1977.

McConkie, Bruce R. "Agency or Inspiration—Which?" In *BYU Speeches of the Year, 1972–1973,* 107–18. Provo, Utah: Brigham Young University Press, 1973.

———. In Conference Report, October 1947, 59–62.

———. *Doctrinal New Testament Commentary.* 3 vols. Salt Lake City, Bookcraft, 1965–73.

———. *Doctrines of the Restoration.* Edited by Mark L. McConkie. Salt Lake City: Bookcraft, 1989.

———. *Mormon Doctrine.* 2d ed. Salt Lake City: Bookcraft, 1966.

———. *The Promised Messiah: The First Coming of Christ.* Salt Lake City: Deseret Book, 1981.

McConkie, Joseph Fielding, and Robert L. Millet. *The Holy Ghost.* Salt Lake City: Bookcraft, 1989.

McKay, David O. *Cherished Experiences from the Writings of President David O. McKay.* Compiled by Clare Middlemiss. Salt Lake City, Deseret Book, 1955.

———. In Conference Report, April 1969, 150–53.

———. *Man May Know for Himself.* Salt Lake City: Deseret Book, 1967.

———. *Pathways to Happiness.* Salt Lake City: Bookcraft, 1957.

The Millennial Star. Manchester, Liverpool & London, England: European Mission, 1840–1970.

Monson, Thomas S. *Favorite Quotations from the Collection of Thomas S. Monson.* Salt Lake City: Deseret Book, 1985.

———. *Inspiring Experiences That Build Faith.* Salt Lake City: Deseret Book, 1994.

———. *Live the Good Life.* Salt Lake City: Deseret Book, 1988.

———. "'The Spirit Giveth Life.'" *Ensign,* May 1985, 68–70.

Montague, Wallace D. "I Was a Political Prisoner of Hitler." *The Instructor,* March 1963, 90–91.

Moyer, Terry J. "A Voice in the Fog." *New Era,* December 1989, 12–15.

Oaks, Dallin H. "The Aaronic Priesthood and the Sacrament." *Ensign,* November 1998, 37–40.

———. *The Lord's Way.* Salt Lake City: Deseret Book, 1991.

———. "Our Strengths Can Become Our Downfall." *Ensign,* October 1994, 11–19.

———. "Scripture Reading and Revelation." *Ensign,* January 1995, 7–9.

———. "Teaching and Learning by the Spirit." *Ensign,* March 1997, 6–14.

———. "Where Will It Lead?" *New Era,* August 2007, 2–5.

———. *With Full Purpose of Heart.* Salt Lake City: Deseret Book, 2002.

Packer, Boyd K. "'And They Knew It Not.'" In *Church News,* March 11, 2000, 5.

———. "The Candle of the Lord." *Ensign,* January 1983, 51–56.

———. *Eternal Love.* Brigham Young University Tri-Stake Fireside, November 3, 1963.

———. "Teach the Scriptures." CES Evening with a General Authority. October 14, 1977.

———. *The Holy Temple.* Salt Lake City: Bookcraft, 1980.

———. *Memorable Stories and Parables by Boyd K. Packer.* Salt Lake City: Bookcraft, 1997.

———. "The One Pure Defense." CES Evening with a General Authority, February 6, 2004.

———. "Personal Revelation: The Gift, the Test, and the Promise." *Ensign,* November 1994, 59–62.

———. "Prayers and Answers." *Ensign,* November 1979, 19–21.

———. "The Quest for Spiritual Knowledge." *New Era,* January 2007, 2–5.

———. "Revelation in a Changing World." *Ensign,* November 1989, 14–16.

———. "Reverence Invites Revelation." *Ensign,* November 1991, 21–23.

———. "Solving Emotional Problems in the Lord's Own Way." *Ensign,* May 1978, 91–93.

———. *Teach Ye Diligently.* Salt Lake City, Deseret Book, 1975.

———. *That All May Be Edified: Talks, Sermons and Commentary.* Salt Lake City: Bookcraft, 1992.

———. *The Things of the Soul.* Salt Lake City: Bookcraft, 1996.

———. "What Every Elder Should Know—and Every Sister as Well: A Primer on the Principles of Priesthood Government." *Ensign,* February 1993, 7–13.

Penrose, Charles W. In Conference Report, April 1912, 14–22.

Petersen, Mark E. Address to Teachers of Religion, August 24, 1954.

Pratt, Parley P. *Autobiography of Parley P. Pratt.* Edited by Parley P. Pratt Jr. 3d ed. Salt Lake City: Deseret Book, 1938.

———. *Key to the Science of Theology.* Classics in Mormon Literature edition. Salt Lake City: Deseret Book, 1978.

The Random House Dictionary of the English Language. Edited by Jess Stein. New York: Random House, 1983.

Rasmussen, Ellis T., and John Robert Kest. "Border Incident." *Improvement Era,* December 1943, 752–53, 793–97.

Richards, Stephen L. In Conference Report, April 1950, 161–66.

Roberts, B. H. *Defense of the Faith and the Saints.* 2 vols. Provo, Utah: Maasai Publishing, 2002.

Romney, Marion G. In Conference Report, October 1962, 92–96.

———. In Conference Report, April 1964, 122–26.

———. *Learning for the Eternities.* Salt Lake City: Deseret Book, 1977.

Rósinkarsdóttir, María, and DeAnne Walker. "My Dream Came True." *Liahona,* June 1997, 40–41.

Scott, Richard G. "Helping Others to Be Spiritually Led." CES Symposium, August 11, 1998.

———. "Using the Supernal Gift of Prayer." *Ensign,* May 2007, 8–11.

Smith, Joseph. *History of The Church of Jesus Christ of Latter-day Saints.* 7 vols. Salt Lake City: Deseret Book, 1976.

———, comp. *Lectures on Faith.* Salt Lake City: Deseret Book, 1985.

———. *Teachings of the Prophet Joseph Smith.* Selected by Joseph Fielding Smith. Salt Lake City: Deseret Book, 1976.

Smith, Joseph F. *Gospel Doctrine.* Salt Lake City: Deseret Book, 1919.

Smith, Joseph Fielding. *Doctrines of Salvation.* Edited by Bruce R. McConkie. 3 vols. Salt Lake City: Bookcraft, 1954–56.

———. "Eternal Keys and the Right to Preside." *Ensign,* July 1972, 87–88.

———. *Life of Joseph F. Smith.* Salt Lake City: Deseret News Press, 1938.

———. *Man, His Origin and Destiny.* Salt Lake City: Deseret Book, 1954.

———. *Take Heed to Yourselves.* Salt Lake City: Deseret Book, 1966.

Talmage, James E. *Articles of Faith.* 12th ed. Salt Lake City: Deseret Book, 1924.

Taylor, John. *The Gospel Kingdom.* Salt Lake City: Bookcraft, 1943.

Topical Guide. Salt Lake City: The Church of Jesus Christ of Latter-day Saints, 1979.

Truman, Kathy. "The Power of Two Testimonies." *Liahona,* February 2008.

Vincent, Marvin R. *Word Studies in the New Testament.* 4 vols. New York: C. Scribner's Sons, 1887–1900.

Whitney, Orson F. In Conference Report, April 1930, 133–35.

———. *Life of Heber C. Kimball.* Salt Lake City: The Kimball Family, 1888.

———. *Saturday Night Thoughts: A Series of Dissertations on Spiritual, Historical and Philosophic Themes.* Salt Lake City: Deseret News, 1921.

Wilson, William. *Old Testament Word Studies.* Grand Rapids, Mich.: Kregel Publications, 1978.

Wirthlin, Joseph B. *Finding Peace in Our Lives.* Salt Lake City: Deseret Book, 1995.

———. "The Unspeakable Gift." *Ensign,* May 2003, 26–29.

Woodruff, Wilford. *The Discourses of Wilford Woodruff.* Selected by G. Homer Durham. Salt Lake City: Bookcraft, 1946.

Young, Brigham. *Discourses of Brigham Young.* Selected by John A. Widtsoe. Salt Lake City: Deseret Book, 1954.

———. In *Journal of Discourses.* 26 vols. London: Latter-day Saints' Book Depot, 1854–86.

———. *Manuscript History of Brigham Young, 1847–1850.* February 23, 1847. Edited by William S. Harwell. Salt Lake City: Collier's, 1997.

INDEX

learning by faith, 264, 269, 273, 280
Belief, as key to learning by faith, 287–93
Benson, Ezra Taft: on being worthy for revelation, 83; on receiving revelation through feelings, 93; on having peace through trials, 95; on balancing self-reliance and spiritual guidance, 193; on pride, 320; on finding inspiration in the temple, 340
Berrett, William E., on demanding constant spiritual guidance, 193–94
Bike, 104–5
Bishops: conferring authority to, 209–10; busyness and, 344–45
Blessing. See Priesthood blessing
Blizzard, 99–102
Boggs, Lilburn W., 297
Book of Mormon, woman finds father's testimony in, 118–19
Booth, Ezra, 177–78
Bountiful, 49–50
Broderick, Carlfred, 245
Brother of Jared, 190–91
Brough, Monte J., announces mission in Mongolia, 76–77
Brown, Hugh B., on divine intervention, 119
Burning in the bosom, 95–97
Busyness, 322–23, 344–46

Callings, busyness and, 344–46
Cannon, George Q., on praying for gifts of the Spirit, 332
Car accident, soldier survives, 109
Cares of the world, 325–26
Carriage, 108–9
Children, revelation given to women with difficulties having, 69–70
Church of Jesus Christ of Latter-day Saints, The: revelation and, 15;

order in, 199–205; Harold B. Lee on upcoming hardship for, 360–61
Clark, J. Reuben, on materialism, 301
Clarke, Adam, on Moses' revelation, 318
Cluff, Harvey, 99–101
Coincidence, versus revelation, 124–26
College, author counsels young man to go to, 305
Concentration, 342–50
Confirmation: for revelation, 57–59, 76–77; Marion G. Romney on praying for, 97; comes after moving forward in faith, 164–68, 273; accompanies true spiritual experiences, 256–57
Consequence, agency and, 268
Contention, 321–22
Continuum, 31–32, 41, 126
Conversion, testimony and true, 86–87
Counsel, following, 305
Counterfeit revelation, 242–46. See also False revelation
Courtship, 149–52, 244–45
Covenants, 334–35
Cowdery, Oliver: revelation given to, 52–53, 95–96; receives peace to his mind, 94; commanded to ask, 146–47; receives false revelation, 239–40; as example of gaining revelation through faith, 278–79
Croup, 294–95

Desire: as key to learning by faith, 281–84; as inner noise, 326
Directive feelings, 104–6
Discernment, 84–86
Discipleship, membership versus, 83–84